MW00427494

# In Pursuit of Liberalism

# In Pursuit of Liberalism

*International Institutions in Postcommunist Europe*

RACHEL A. EPSTEIN

The Johns Hopkins University Press
*Baltimore*

© 2008 The Johns Hopkins University Press
All rights reserved. Published 2008
Printed in the United States of America on acid-free paper
2  4  6  8  9  7  5  3  1

The Johns Hopkins University Press
2715 North Charles Street
Baltimore, Maryland 21218-4363
www.press.jhu.edu

*Library of Congress Cataloging-in-Publication Data*
Epstein, Rachel A., 1970–
In pursuit of liberalism : international institutions in
postcommunist Europe / Rachel A. Epstein.
p. cm.
Includes bibliographical references and index.
ISBN-13: 978-0-8018-8977-6 (hardcover : alk. paper)
ISBN-10: 0-8018-8977-4 (hardcover : alk. paper)
1. Europe, Eastern—Politics and government—1989–  2. Europe,
Eastern—Economic policy—1989–  3. Liberalism—Europe, Eastern.
4. International agencies—Europe, Eastern. I. Title.
JN96.A58E67 2008
320.947—dc22       2007052865

A catalog record for this book is available from the British Library.

*Special discounts are available for bulk purchases of this book. For more
information, please contact Special Sales at 410-516-6936 or
specialsales@press.jhu.edu.*

The Johns Hopkins University Press uses environmentally friendly book
materials, including recycled text paper that is composed of at
least 30 percent post-consumer waste, whenever possible.
All of our book papers are acid-free, and our jackets
and covers are printed on paper with recycled content.

*To my parents*

# Contents

# Tables

# Acronyms and Abbreviations

AWS          Solidarity Electoral Action (Poland)
BCR          Commercial Bank of Romania
BPH          Bank Przemysłowo-Handlowy of Krakow (Poland)
BRD          Romanian Bank for Development
CBI          central bank independence
CDR          Democratic Convention of Romania
CEE          central and eastern Europe
CIS          Commonwealth of Independent States
CPU          Communist Party of Ukraine
CRS          Congressional Research Service
EBRD         European Bank for Reconstruction and Development
EC           European Commission
ECB          European Central Bank
EMU          European Monetary Union
ESCB         European System of Central Banks
FDSN         Democratic National Salvation Front (Romania)
FIDESZ       Federation of Young Democrats (Hungary, from 1988)
Fidesz-MPP   Fidesz–Hungarian Civic Party (Hungary, from 1995)
FSN          National Salvation Front (Romania)
GDP          gross domestic product
IFC          International Finance Corporation
IFI          international financial institution
IFOR         Implementation Force (NATO-led international force in Kosovo)
IMF          International Monetary Fund
MDF          Hungarian Democratic Forum
MHB          Hungarian Credit Bank
MKB          Hungarian Foreign Trade Bank
MNB          National Bank of Hungary

| | |
|---|---|
| MoD | Ministry of Defense |
| MoF | Ministry of Finance |
| MSzMP | Hungarian Socialist Workers' Party |
| MSzP | Hungarian Socialist Party |
| NATO | North Atlantic Treaty Organization |
| NBP | National Bank of Poland |
| NBR | National Bank of Romania |
| NBU | National Bank of Ukraine |
| NGO | nongovernmental organization |
| OECD | Organisation for Economic Co-operation and Development |
| OT | Obronna Terytorialna (Poland) |
| OTP | National Savings and Commercial Bank Limited (Hungary) |
| PDSR | Party of Social Democracy of Romania |
| PfP | Partnership for Peace |
| PiS | Law and Justice Party (Poland) |
| PRM | Greater Romania Party |
| PSD | Social Democratic Party (Romania) |
| PSL | Polish Peasant Party |
| PSM | Socialist Party of Labor (Romania) |
| PUNR | Romanian National Unity Party |
| PUWP | Polish United Workers' Party |
| SFOR | Stabilization Force (NATO-led mission in Bosnia) |
| SLD | Democratic Left Alliance (Poland) |
| SzDSz | Alliance of Free Democrats (Hungary) |
| UDMR | Democratic Alliance of Hungarians in Romanian |
| UN | United Nations |
| USAID | United States Agency for International Development |
| USD | Social Democratic Union (Romania) |
| UW | Freedom Union (Poland) |

# Acknowledgments

The topics in this book have commanded my interest for a very long time. And, as every author knows, turning interests into coherent arguments requires the help of many people and institutions along the way. I would first like to thank the members of my committee at Cornell University, whose counsel, they may be surprised to learn, I still think of and use every day—in the classroom, advising students, and conducting my research. Peter Katzenstein, Valerie Bunce, Matthew Evangelista, and Jonathan Kirshner were discerning and generous in their advice and, in Jonathan's case, delightfully if dryly funny. I also had a great cohort at Cornell, all of whom not only became part of this project but, in that formative time, shaped my very character. They are Rawi Abdelal, Clem Fatovic, Alexandra Gheciu, Kate Gordy, Derek Hall, Juliet Hooker, Peggy Kohn, Matthew Rudolph, David Rueda, Lisa Sansouci, and Megan Thomas. Mary Katzenstein, Judith Reppy, and Chris Way were also enormously helpful to me, in ways too diverse to enumerate here.

I owe a big debt of gratitude to the European University Institute in Florence, which both provided me with the time and space to write and introduced me to some wonderful colleagues and friends, including Abby Innes, Gallya Lahav, Mark Pollack, Gwen Sasse, Frank Schimmelfennig, and Uli Sedelmeier. They were a pleasure to work with and have given me invaluable feedback ever since. Last but certainly not least, it was at EUI that I met my husband, Martin Rhodes, whose unparalleled skills as writer, editor, and scholar undoubtedly made this book better and more accessible than it otherwise would have been.

The Graduate School of International Studies at the University of Denver, where I have worked since 2002, also deserves a huge thanks. Without the supportive atmosphere there and the numerous grants for research and writing, this book would not have the scope that it currently does. GSIS has also provided me with some top-rate students over the years, not to mention a bevy of outstanding research assistants. I am especially grateful to Olexia Basaraba, Figaro Joseph, Dana Morris, Zhanna Soushko, and Kerry West for help on this project.

This book would not have been possible without the generosity of the many people I interviewed for the project in Warsaw, Washington, Brussels, Berlin, Kyiv, and Bucharest. I was assisted in my research especially by Don Abenheim, Catherine Kelleher, and Jorgen Dragsdahl—the last of whom was essential in scoping out the issues of military reform presented in this study. Additional help came from people who gave me insightful feedback along the way, on parts or all of the manuscript: Jeffrey Checkel, Wade Jacoby, Juliet Johnson, Jeffrey Kopstein, Diana Panke, Roger Schoenman, and Milada Anna Vachudova. An anonymous reviewer at the Johns Hopkins University Press provided very helpful comments, all of which found their way into the final version of the manuscript. Financial support was provided by the US Department of Education, Foreign Language and Area Studies fellowships, for the study of Polish; the Center for European Studies at Cornell University, for field research; the Department of Government at Cornell University, for a dissertation completion fellowship; the Robert Schuman Centre for Advanced Studies at the European University Institute, for postdoctoral support; and the University of Denver, for additional field research and write-up support. Having thanked these many institutions and individuals for their help, I should point out that any remaining errors are mine alone.

On a more personal note, I would like to express my gratitude to my family. Their love and support through the duration of this project was a solid source of inspiration. To Martin, first of all, who has had to live with the book day-in and day-out ever since he's known me. His intense interest in the book, not to mention his patience through all of the ups and downs, kept me afloat. To my sister, Lisa Epstein, who has been constantly encouraging. And to my parents, Edward and Marilyn Epstein, who, with great generosity and love, expanded my horizons early.

# In Pursuit of Liberalism

# Introduction

Why do states adopt liberalizing reforms when doing so contradicts their domestic preferences and threatens to undermine their policy autonomy and national tradition? Even with the end of the Cold War and the collapse of communism, the appeal of political pluralism and free market enterprise was far from universal. For although countries in central and eastern Europe (CEE) converged on liberal political and economic models, most other states from across the former Soviet space maintained degrees of authoritarianism or central planning or both.

Exceptionalism in CEE with regard to liberalization might seem easy to explain, given the active role of international institutions in that region. After all, the European Union and the North Atlantic Treaty Organization (NATO), both guardians of the liberal order, were poised at the outset of the transition to provide advice, assistance, and, ultimately, membership. Thus the CEE countries—the only credible future members of NATO at that point—were particularly susceptible to liberalization. Moreover, to win admission, they had to implement core parts of a liberalizing agenda, including the convincing consolidation of democracy and capitalism.

Accordingly, there often was a correlation between external incentives and eventual liberalization in CEE. But this book's major finding is that despite the enormous material leverage of international institutions vis-à-vis target countries, financial or membership incentives on their own explain very little about the extent to which states embrace liberalizing policies and why. This may seem paradoxical, given that NATO, the European Union, the International Monetary Fund (IMF), and the World Bank generally predicate financial assistance or membership on the fulfillment of specific criteria—conditionality—in which compliance is supposedly won by the promise of particular rewards. In truth, however, although some studies do show that credible conditionality sometimes elicits its intended effect if the domestic opposition is low (Stone 2002; Kelley 2004a, 2004b; Schimmelfennig and Sedelmeier 2005; Vachudova 2005), other research highlights the puzzling extent to which conditionality has perverse, limited, or no effects on domestic outcomes (Killick 1996; Collier 1997; Hunter and Brown 2000; Grabbe 2002; Barnett and Finnemore 2004; Hughes, Sasse, and Gordon 2004; Epstein 2005a, 2006a; Sasse 2005; Weyland 2005; Sissenich 2007).

If in some cases conditionality yields no results, in others it may not even be required to encourage compliance. To explain this puzzle I make the following argument: that pushing transition states toward a liberalizing agenda—for both state institutions and markets—depends on a social context in which compliance becomes desirable by virtue of the status it secures and the relationships it cements. Indeed, as this book shows, the power of international institutions is largely misunderstood. What drives compliance is not how much money or military power is on offer, but rather the extent to which such money or military power reinforces a state's perceived international orientation. And that orientation depends, in turn, on where a society and its leaders believe authority appropriately lies.

The central dilemma for postcommunist states in determining the appropriate location of authority lay in balancing the demands of globalization and interdependence—two features of a liberal world order—against the protection of national autonomy and tradition. Thus, when it came to reorganizing defense or restructuring banks, the central question reformers faced was whether to locate authority in international institutions, which were pushing internationalization and liberalization, or to use national tradition and autonomy as guides instead. The dilemma proved particularly vexing for states that had only recently won their independence. Maximizing power was certainly their aim. But the question remained, How was power best maximized? In finance, would more power accrue to states that kept control of their banking sectors through domestic ownership, as many industrialized democracies had done in the past? Or would they gain more power by yielding to international financial institutions (IFIs) and allowing foreign domination of the sector? In defense, was security best achieved by preparing for enduring regional threats through robust territorial defense plans? Or would countries become more secure by currying favor with a powerful military alliance and agreeing to dedicate the bulk of their defense resources to far-flung multilateral missions?

How postcommunist countries weighed the options and reached their conclusions is the central subject of this book. Whereas the CEE instinct was usually to

protect autonomy, international institutions were more likely to demand conformity with a liberalizing agenda. I argue that given competing claims between
autonomy and conformity, international institutional definitions of power maximization were more likely to prevail when countries and sectors experienced
exceptional uncertainty in the transition and when the international institutions
were consistent in their reform advice. *National* definitions of power maximization were likely to prevail, by contrast, when countries and sectors had strong
institutional legacies and their own views of what an optimal policy course en-
tailed, and when the prescriptions of international institutions were inconsistent.
The critical starting point for predicting the potential power of international
institutions' incentives to win compliance is in knowing whether it is their expectations or national experience that informs states' beliefs about what constitutes
power.

If there are competing notions of what constitutes power, then it follows that
incentives, including money and membership, have a subjective quality. In arguing for the subjective quality of incentives, I am making an additional claim,
rooted in a social constructivist tradition, about the nature of the social world.
Many studies conceptualize actors as *autonomous* maximizers responding to incentives (e.g., Friedman 1953; Becker 1976; Olson 1982; Frieden 1991), but I take a
different view. If incentives are subject to interpretation, then it necessarily follows
that actors are not autonomous—otherwise, similarly positioned actors would
respond uniformly to the same incentives, which, as this study highlights, is not
the case. Furthermore, actors' behavior is not triggered exclusively by external
stimuli but is continuously informed by history, institutions, and social interaction
—the very forces that make actors who they are. I do not take issue with the idea
that actors engage in "maximizing," but I do question what they are maximizing
and why. And, most important for this study, I investigate who decided that the
specified goals were the correct ones. As the many case studies in this book show,
where domestic politics were highly fluid and international institutions were
consistent, external actors, as opposed to national tradition, were more likely to
shape states' goals.

The conditions for liberalization in CEE were generally propitious from international institutions' point of view. And the consequences of international institutional engagement with postcommunist Europe—through assistance, advising,
and in some instances accession processes—have been path-breaking for a number of countries. Nevertheless, when it came to institutionalizing the Western
conception of a liberal order—including, for example, central bank independence and democratic civil-military relations—there was heated political contro-

versy and plenty of variation in compliance, over time and across countries. It is by studying that variation that this book assesses the power of social context in facilitating states' acceptance of international institutions' demands.

_⌒ ⌒_

Throughout the theoretical and empirical chapters, I return repeatedly to the themes discussed above. The role of international institutions in central and eastern Europe has been fundamental for those states and for the organizations they have joined. However, what constitutes international institutional power is often misunderstood. And while states' international orientations and underlying goals are malleable, such is the case only under narrow conditions.

Chapter 1 outlines a theory of institutional influence, specifying the conditions under which international institutions are able to manipulate the perceived costs and benefits of complying with their incentives. I argue that the presence or absence of those conditions, which include the *uncertainty* of domestic actors, their perceived *status* vis-à-vis international institutions, and the *credibility* of the latter's policies, creates a social context that will help or impede international institutions in endowing incentives with particular meanings. For domestic actors, the meanings attached to incentives make them worthy of compliance or not. I map these conditions onto the postcommunist world in measurable ways to test the validity of the theory throughout the study. The first chapter also explains why I have chosen the following four areas of postcommunist reform: the institutionalization of central bank independence, the internationalization of bank ownership, the democratization of civil-military relations, and the denationalization of foreign policy and defense planning. Outcomes in these areas vary across the four countries under consideration: Poland, Hungary, Romania, and Ukraine.

In chapter 2, I investigate a key area of domestic economic reform—the institutionalization of central bank independence (CBI). At stake here was whether governments would exercise control over monetary policy and macroeconomic conditions, or would delegate that authority to central bankers charged with guarding price stability at the expense of other policy goals. For many (though not all) CEE politicians and banking bureaucrats, the idea of CBI was alien. International institutions provided incentives in order to win compliance. But variation in the timing and degree of CBI adoption corresponded more consistently with the social context than with strict conditionality. Thus, although IMF–World Bank conditionality was applied in all four countries, Poland and Hungary had already institutionalized high levels of CBI in the early 1990s, while Romania waited until a decade later. Ukraine was an outlier, diverging from some key indicators of CBI as late as 2006. Moreover, contestation over central bank authority despite EU strictures—concerning monetary policy and regulatory capacity— continued everywhere into the mid-2000s.

Chapter 3 explains why levels of foreign ownership in CEE banking sectors are far higher than those that industrialized countries generally accept for themselves. Without exception, postcommunist states set out to protect this strategic sector from foreign control, but over time that goal shifted—from seeking to preserve domestic ownership to securing rapid modernization through the participation of foreign capital. International institutions promoted foreign ownership, but with a varying impact across countries and over time, depending on the evolving social context as specified by the theory. Hungary had the highest levels of foreign ownership by the early 2000s, at close to 80 percent. Foreign investment in Poland's banking sector was near 70 percent by the same date, but the Polish state also maintained an ownership position in the country's largest bank as of late 2005. In 2002 Romania and Ukraine had much lower levels of foreign ownership (near 40% and 10%, respectively), but by 2004 foreign investment in finance was rising sharply. In 2005, Romania's commercial banking sector was set to become one of the most internationalized in the region, with just over 80 percent of its banking assets owned by foreign interests. These discrepancies reveal the varying access of international institutions to domestic reform debates, and correspond not to conditionality but to the desire among domestic actors to preserve or rupture high-profile relationships with their external advisors.

Chapter 4 focuses on the democratization of civil-military relations. Although three of the four states under consideration had similar strategic concerns stemming from historical experience, their response to the incentive of NATO membership and the requirement of democratic civil-military relations varied considerably. In addition, in every state, regardless of either public opinion on NATO membership or historical vulnerability, the perceived "natural" balance of authority between civilians and military leaders was uniformly different from what the alliance found acceptable. Whereas every CEE state, left to its own devices, was likely to invest its General Staff with considerable autonomy and authority, membership in NATO demanded an entirely different set of power relations among groups in society. Rather than allowing military personnel to run military affairs, NATO officials were promoting a particular kind of oversight—diffused among multiple branches of government, the media, and society—that was anathema to military tradition in the region. Although all four countries made at least some concessions to the alliance's democratic principles, NATO's democratizing impact varied considerably, once again in line with the uneven influence it could exert in the different social contexts between the alliance and national actors.

Whereas chapter 4 concerns a fundamental area of internal security reform, chapter 5 covers NATO attempts to denationalize CEE states' foreign policies and defense planning. Here again, NATO encountered resistance to what its founding members, especially the United States and United Kingdom, considered the alliance's evolving strategic mission. Threat perceptions in CEE were about Russian power, regional rivalries, protection for diasporas, and irredentist claims—all of which had made NATO membership seem desirable. But not only did NATO *not* show great concern for CEE threat perceptions, it actively discouraged CEE states from engaging in forms of military planning that would have addressed such concerns. In response to the alliance's effort to convince CEE states of how best to maximize their power and influence, some of its newest members proved to be among the biggest contributors to multilateral operations in both Afghanistan and Iraq. Although CEE political and material support for these far-flung missions was particularly notable in the light of the dramatic fissure between the United States, the United Kingdom, and many of their long-time allies in NATO, what also stood out was the great degree of variation in CEE states' willingness to go global. Poland was a staunch contributor to out-of-area missions, Hungary was mostly a security consumer, while Romania and Ukraine were somewhere in between. Underlying the differences were contrasting national perceptions of the utility of military power and of NATO's shifting credibility—conditions that informed the social context between NATO and aspiring members.

In the book's conclusion I assess the strengths and weaknesses of the explanatory variables considered throughout the study—uncertainty, status, and credibility. I then compare my theory of institutional influence with other approaches that examine international institutions and domestic compliance, and gauge the explanatory power of uncertainty, status, and credibility against rival hypotheses. Finally, I consider the implications of the findings of this study for the ongoing pursuit of liberalism by international institutions, both within the postcommunist region and globally.

# CHAPTER ONE

# Cultivating Consensus

*International Institutions and a Liberal Worldview*

I present here a theory of institutional influence that locates the impetus for state-level compliance in social mechanisms, specifically in the cultivation of a common worldview. This common—liberal—worldview is anchored by a shared perception of where authority lies. For much of central and eastern Europe (CEE), the postcommunist transition has been marked by a shift from domestic sources of authority, such as historical experience and nationalist striving, to international sources of authority, such as the North Atlantic Treaty Organization (NATO), the European Union, and the Bretton Woods institutions—the World Bank and the International Monetary Fund (IMF). The policy manifestations of the liberal worldview embraced by these institutions, and to varying extents transferred to CEE states, include the institutionalization of central bank independence (CBI), the internationalization of bank ownership, the democratization of civil-military relations, and the denationalization of defense planning and foreign policy.

This chapter also introduces three hypotheses used throughout the study to assess the validity of the theory. The cultivation of a liberal worldview around specific issues depends on both domestic and international variables. On the domestic side, international institutions are more likely to gain access to reform processes, and thereby define what constitutes "optimal" policy, under conditions of interest demobilization and uncertainty in the domestic sphere and when target states seek the social recognition of external actors. On the international side, the power of institutions to cultivate support for their policy preferences is heightened when their prescriptions are normatively consistent with the practices of their member states. This combination of factors gives international institutions access to domestic reform processes and allows them to cultivate a consensus around the policy orientations of a liberal worldview. Whereas realist approaches in international relations have traditionally argued that it was the distribution of capabilities in international politics that produced particular outcomes, I contend that, rather, it is the distribution of knowledge that shapes enmities and alliances. In this book, the focus is on the distribution of knowledge that concerns where authority appropriately rests—in international institutions or in domestic claims for national autonomy and tradition.

Although I emphasize the cultivation of "knowledge" and "consensus" around shared understandings of who wields authority in the international system, my theory of institutional influence should not be construed in terms of harmonious volunteerism among actors or even in terms of socialization. Building transnational coalitions that support the denationalization of defense planning or the internationalization of bank ownership, for example, is often a politically charged process in which even formidable domestic players are shamed into embracing policies they believe to be bad ideas. Moreover, the same transnational coalitions, once constituted, are powerful agents of internationally inspired agendas. Should subsequent challenges to an initial liberal consensus emerge (and they often have), international institutions can use coalition partners to help isolate that opposition. Although cultivating consensus around who should wield authority may seem shallower than socialization or persuasion, outcomes of the consensus on authority are no less consequential for international politics.

I begin by introducing my theory of institutional influence. Since this theory is at odds with much recent constructivist literature that recognizes a clear distinction between the logic of consequences and the logic of appropriateness, I make the case for a constructivist-rationalist synthesis and locate it within the international relations literature. I then detail and operationalize the three hypotheses used throughout the study. The aim is to assess conditions under which international institutions can influence domestic reform processes and to explain variation in the timing and nature of outcomes. Finally, I set out the rationale for my case selection and consider alternative approaches.

## A THEORY OF INSTITUTIONAL INFLUENCE

Under certain, rather narrow conditions, international institutions can transform political dynamics and shape choices in societies undergoing transition. Three conditions in particular, which form the foundations of this study, boost the power of international institutions over target states. These conditions comprise a particular social context and include the *uncertainty* of domestic actors, their perceived subordinate *status* vis-à-vis international institutions, and the *credibility* of the policies in question. As the case studies show, a social context informed by uncertainty, status, and credibility, mapped onto measurable domestic and international conditions, is more important for securing liberalizing outcomes than is new information or incentives taken on their own. Uncertainty, status, and credibility allow international institutions to imbue information and incentives with particular meanings, and thus power. A radically different social context can likewise render the same information and incentives, provided by the same international institutions, meaningless.

Uncertainty among domestic actors, their perceived location in a hierarchy in relation to foreign advisors, and the credibility of international institutional policies all permit international actors to persuade their domestic interlocutors of where authority appropriately lies. Such persuasion can be based on the merits of an argument or on the affective relationship between domestic and international actors—or both. Alternatively, social influence, in which actors comply with the prescriptions of international institutions because they believe that not everyone else can be wrong, may also encourage domestic players to recognize new sources of authority. If international institutions can exert power over policymaking elites, they can influence not just proximate outcomes but the basic properties of states, where "property" refers to the balance of power among groups in society or the international orientation of states.

Although the consequences of social dynamics have more often been the concern of constructivists than rationalists, this is not a study that pits rationality against norm-governed behavior as is so often the case in constructivist research. Rather, I argue that instrumentality among actors is central to the construction of normative contexts in which only narrow manifestations of rationality are politically tenable. Thus while actors and their choices are heavily structured by social practice, I contend that outcomes, in this study and beyond, are not strictly characterized by either a consequentialist or an obligatory logic.[1]

In a social context defined by uncertainty, status, and credibility, international institutions can cultivate transnational coalitions that strengthen their domestic members—not by virtue of their authority in terms of popular support but by virtue of their internationally recognized status. To be clear, the cultivation of a domestic consensus by international institutions is not simply the empowerment of particular preexisting domestic interests. In this sense, my argument is somewhat different from those contending that policies make their way into domestic settings largely as a consequence of "goodness of fit" (e.g., Checkel 2001a, 187–89; Cowles, Caporaso, and Risse 2001). Rather, I argue that consensus evolves via a process of domestic interest mobilization through which policy "fit" takes on the appearance of being "good" in the eyes of reformers and the public alike.

International institutions, even under the most propitious conditions, are not uniformly successful in shaping domestic political choices, either within or across countries. Indeed, in postcommunist Europe, where a range of international institutions has been actively trying to direct outcomes, observers have noted a wide variation in political and economic systems (Bunce 2003; Kitschelt 2003, 49). The objective here is to provide a theoretical framework that explains this variation in compliance with international institutional policy prescriptions. I argue that both compliance and defection are possible, depending on the presence or absence of particular social contexts and the degrees of uncertainty, status, and credibility produced within them.

## Combining Constructivist and Rationalist Perspectives

There are three elements to my argument for a constructivist-rationalist synthesis. Whereas rationalists have assumed instrumentality among actors, constructivists have argued that actors are largely socially motivated—to fit in, to follow norms, to fulfill roles. Thus the first component of my constructivist-rationalist synthesis is to claim that despite instances in which agents are acting *either* instrumentally *or* according to social motivation, more often they are doing both. Acting on and identifying instrumentality depends, after all, on being able to assess and agree on costs and benefits, respectively. One example of divergent perceptions of costs and benefits that ultimately converged in CEE (albeit to varying degrees) is in the area of civil-military relations. NATO officials believed that democratizing civil-military relations was the right course for postcommunist countries. But getting them to do so depended on NATO's ability to create a social context in which the failure to democratize was embarrassing—and therefore costly. But for something to be embarrassing, actors must share social reference points—which NATO had to create because they did not yet exist. Where such reference points remain different for the several parties to an action, however, one person's instrumentality is another person's irrationality.

The second element of the constructivist-rationalist synthesis is that although actors may be "optimizing" in that they seek to achieve their preferences, this study does not assume a baseline rationality. Rather, I investigate what actors believe is rational in a given context and why what constitutes "rationality" shifts over time. Finally, although incentives are typically construed as regulative rules that direct actors' behavior but do not change who or what those actors are, I reach a different conclusion. The evidence here suggests that incentives, when embedded in a social context, can in fact be *constitutive* of actors or, in other words, can fundamentally shape their preferences.

Three theoretical goals follow from this constructivist-rationalist synthesis. The first is to engage the rationalist literature on transitions, institutions, conditionality, and compliance. I argue that the social context in which actors make choices should be at the center of any analysis that seeks to enhance our understanding of why certain outcomes prevail. The second is to avoid neoliberal and constructivist approaches that attempt to carve out a separate sphere for the role of ideas in politics, distinct from power and interests, which, as I argue, ratify an artificial divide between instrumental and obligatory (i.e., socially motivated) action. Finally, I provide a theoretical framework that specifies the conditions that favor the institutionalization of particular ideas at the domestic level.

Building a constructivist-rationalist synthesis stems from a dissatisfaction with rationalist approaches and the constructivist responses to them. In international relations, rationalist approaches that assess the influence of international institutions have tended to focus on the role of incentives—in the form of financial assistance, security, transparency, and autonomy—in eliciting particular behaviors from states (for the postcommunist states, see Wallander 2000; Moravcsik and Vachudova 2003; Kelley 2004a, 2004b; Schimmelfennig 2005; Schimmelfennig and Sedelmeier 2005; Vachudova 2005). This conceptualization of action as a utility-maximizing response to signals in the environment is consistent with neoliberal institutionalism, which is largely concerned with the constraining, regulative, and coordinating role of international institutions in the life of states (Keohane 1984; Goldstein and Keohane 1993; Haftendorn, Keohane, and Wallander 1999; Wallander 1999). Building on the assumptions of neorealism rather than radically departing from them, neoliberal institutionalists hold actors' interests, and the social contexts in which they find themselves, to be "preexisting" and "exogenous." These "rationalist" studies therefore elide some of the most important dynamics in explaining the incidence of domestic conformity with burgeoning or prevailing global trends—including, for example, the increasing use of markets as opposed to authoritative methods of allocation as a primary means of resolving political conflict.

Dissatisfaction with rationalist explanations led constructivists to demonstrate that some behavior is driven not by instrumentality, but rather by "rules." In contrast to the "logic of consequences," in which actors make a decision based on self-interest and a cost-benefit calculation, the "logic of appropriateness," which is said to underpin rule-based behavior, refers in its most pristine form to action that is "taken for granted" and consistent with an actor's identity (March and Olsen 1989, 1998).[2] Such choices are guided by a sense of what one "should" do—for moral, social, or taken-for-granted reasons—in any given situation.

The tendency, first among constructivists, to link sociological approaches in international relations to the logic of appropriateness led to a false and counter-productive divide. Because cost-benefit analysis and instrumental action were characterized as features of "rationalist" analysis, obligatory action was catego-rized as something other than, and possibly less than, rational. Constructivist scholars tried to show either that "culture" operated in some instances where "rationality" might have triumphed instead (e.g., Legro 1996) or that some kinds of political systems allowed norms to have constitutive effects while others al-lowed them to have only constraining ones (e.g., Checkel 1997).[3] Both kinds of studies conceive of consequential and obligatory actions as distinct, with actors responding to incentives in some instances and rules in others.

The methodological challenge posed by constructivism also fueled the no-tion that distinctive logics underpinned action. In an effort to distinguish be-tween material and social causal forces and to avoid overdetermination, some constructivist scholarship focused on issues in which explanations based on na-tional interests, as conceived by the dominant international relations paradigms, fail (Katzenstein 1996). Or, where policies concern questions other than wealth and power—such as human rights—realist, interest-based explanations are argu-ably not relevant.[4] But the problem with the obligatory/consequentialist dichot-omy is that the insistence on separate logics of behavior upholds the notion that power and interest have meaning and effects independent of social relations—a claim that several scholars have already convincingly dismissed (e.g., Kratochwil 1989; Onuf 1989; Wendt 1999).

An additional drawback of the obligatory/consequentialist conceptualization is that it leaves the misimpression that constructivists have little systematic to say about core issues of our field—war, capabilities, power, and interest. Rarely do we find instances of pure "sociological" phenomena in our highly instrumentalized world that do not also illustrate the centrality of deliberation and, with it, optimi-zation. But this fact should do nothing to diminish the salience of sociological approaches. Our ability to "calculate" stems precisely from our capacity as in-dividuals and collectivities to imbue events with particular meaning (Kratochwil 1989, 11; 2000b, 56; Ruggie 1998, 861).[5] Irrespective of this key insight, rational-

ists tend to suppress the social dynamics inherent in many political processes or
to understate their causal and constitutive significance (e.g., Walt 1987, 1996;
Schweller 1998; Wallander 1999, 2000; Schweller and Wohlforth 2000). This
study is an attempt to make these underlying social forces explicit and central—
with actors behaving rationally.[6]

Another problem for constructivists derives from the notion that certain norms
have constitutive effects while others are basically regulative. This suggests that
regulative rules do not affect the properties of actors and that constitutive norms
do not regulate behavior.[7] Neither claim endures under empirical scrutiny. For
example, as CEE political parties adopt the policy prescriptions of international
institutions, even if only nominally in response to incentives, they are implicitly
recognizing a new authority. In postcommunist Europe, such recognition is accompanied by more general changes in the underlying goals of states. In this
study, recognizable changes of this kind include shifts from preferring executive
authority over the armed forces and high levels of military autonomy to securing
civilian oversight; from seeking territorial integrity against historical rivals to supporting an alliance pursuing "out-of-area" (i.e., foreign) missions; and from preserving national power through control over domestic credit allocation to accepting high levels of foreign investment in banking.

I develop a theoretical framework that specifies the conditions under which
such shifts in the distribution of knowledge in the international system are likely to
occur. I argue that international institutions provide incentives attached to conditions because that is the language in which they speak, and from the highly
instrumentalized perspective in which international institutions operate, exchanging incentives for compliance seems rational to them. Indeed, international institutions apply conditionality as though it were a consistently proven method of
winning compliance, even though many studies have reached more ambiguous
conclusions (Killick 1996; Collier 1997; Hunter and Brown 2000; Grabbe 2002;
Stone 2002; Hughes, Sasse, and Gordon 2004; Jacoby 2004; Kelley 2004b; Epstein
2005a, 2006a; Sasse 2005; Weyland 2005). Incentives are only the tip of the ice-
berg, however, insofar as money or membership—or even, as previously noted,
instrumentality—are meaningless outside the context of how the parties to an
interaction constitute and interpret money, membership, or instrumentality.

In the case studies presented in this book, I trace a series of causal and constitutive episodes in which international institutions denationalized the frames
through which CEE politicians perceived their interests. This in turn affected
how politicians structured their domestic political institutions. Instrumentality

pervades the story. But so too do the social processes through which a certain kind of instrumentality—in which Western rewards were exchanged for compliance with Western norms—became the rule.

## Accounting for Variation

My three hypotheses for understanding the circumstances under which international institutions can generate domestic support for a particular idea are based on measures of uncertainty, status, and credibility that vary over time and across sectors and countries, and that help account for fluctuating levels of compliance. International institutions can maximize their influence over domestic reforms under the following conditions:[8]

1. When sectoral or regime discontinuity demobilizes interest groups and leaves domestic actors uncertain about how to make policy (the *uncertainty* hypothesis, H1).
2. When domestic actors seek the social approbation of the international institutions that are undertaking policy transfer (the *status* hypothesis, H2).
3. When purveyors of policy are normatively consistent in the ideas they promote and the policies they prescribe (the *credibility* hypothesis, H3).

The presence of these variables renders domestic actors relatively more open to adopting foreign advice and definitions. Uncertainty, status, and credibility give international institutions the power to assign positive meanings to information and incentives, making them worthy of compliance for domestic actors.

In this study, I operationalize each of these variables for postcommunist conditions. In the first hypothesis, in the course of breaking with communism, states had to create some entirely new institutions around which domestic interests had yet to coalesce (H1). I argue that when policy areas are new, domestic actors are more dependent on foreign expertise and policies become "functional" by virtue of their association with internationally respected opinion. This is especially true when domestic actors have little assurance of what the consequences of different policies will be.

I operationalize the resulting "uncertainty" (i.e., the disorientation and dislocation of interests) by assessing both sectoral and regime discontinuity. Interest demobilization, and thus uncertainty, is stronger in sectors where the statesocialist system was all-controlling. In finance, for example, price liberalization and the creation of two-tiered banking systems during the transition yielded entirely new environments. International institutions therefore had more intellectual access to processes of financial reform than, for example, to military reform early in the transition, because the functioning of the armed forces was not peculiar to the state-socialist system and uncertainty was correspondingly weaker. Regime discontinuity also varied. Poland and Hungary, for example, experienced uncertainty at the outset of transition when opposition movements came to power (in the form of leaders new to office), but this did not occur in Romania and Ukraine until later. (Case selection of these four countries is discussed below.)

In the second hypothesis, international institutions can imbue ideas with status —that is, render them desirable—if domestic actors seek social affirmation when engaged in promoting domestic reform (H2). International institutions may confer social recognition through partnership agreements, by providing public praise, or by awarding membership or money. When domestic actors solicit social affirmation, they seek association with the values and status embodied by an international institution.

The perceived status of international institutions corresponds closely to the quality of political competition.[9] When political competition is robust, the salience of international opinion is higher because the domestic desire to win international approval also increases—especially among communist successor parties. I argue that the intensified desire to win approval is a result of such parties using international opinion to rebuild their post–Cold War image. In the absence of political competition, a ruling party has thorough control over political discourse and can choose the basis on which it cultivates domestic support. When two or more blocs are competing for power, however, international institutions have the opportunity to choose sides and confer legitimacy, and by doing so gain domestic partners that can speak for the preferences of international institutions at the national level.

The quality of political competition, and thus the status of international institutions, can change over time. In Romania and Ukraine the desire for international approbation was initially low but grew as political competition intensified. By contrast, in Poland and Hungary, regular political party turnover from the outset of transition ensured the early access of international institutions to domestic reform debates: the presence of at least two oppositional blocs encouraged parties to use international opinion as a point of competition. Political parties' mimicking of one another based on the judgments of international institutions is one consequence of the elevated status of these institutions.

In the third hypothesis, assessing the credibility of policies requires measuring the extent to which international institutions take the technical correctness or political desirability of a policy for granted (H3). "Taken-for-grantedness" is high where a particular policy prescription is the outcome of a political battle already fought and settled in Western industrialized states. Central bank independence (Epstein 2006a) and democratic civil-military relations (Epstein 2005a) are two such examples. But a low level of policy contestation in Western states does not mean the distributional consequences of a particular policy are negligible. All economic arrangements produce winners and losers—even those portrayed as Pareto optimal.[10] The question is whose interests deserve protection at the expense of others.

Where there is strong international consensus behind a policy, that policy is more likely to be perceived as credible and international institutions can more easily undermine the legitimacy of the losers' claims in a target state, thus suppressing domestic political debate about the policy. But where the existing (Western) member states of international institutions behave inconsistently, space is created for target actors to question the credibility of a policy. A high level of taken-for-grantedness among promoters of a policy powerfully conveys to target actors who does and does not have legitimate claims.

The presence of the three conditions—the uncertainty of domestic actors, their perceived subordinated status relative to international institutions, and the high credibility of policies under consideration—enhances the power of international institutions to build transnational coalitions in support of their ideas and preferences.[11] By imbuing ideas with elevated status, international institutions mobilize support for particular practices. The social dimensions of policies are crucial: their origins, their uses, their supporters, and even their detractors will determine the chances of compliance or defection.

Incentives that purportedly bolster a country's wealth, security, and independence are not independent from perceptions of whether and how certain incentives make such contributions. As an example, selling the bulk of a country's banking assets in response to IMF incentives may enhance that country's long-term security by breaking up business networks and eliminating political lending. But the same policies could also be construed as diminishing long-term security by relegating authority over the availability of credit to foreigners and by potentially limiting state power. The point is that wealth, security, and independence are not objective entities. Their definitions depend on the answers to value-laden questions concerning wealth for whom, security from what, and, given that no country is literally autonomous, "independent" in what sense. In CEE states in transition, international institutions, where they had access, weighed in on precisely these value-laden questions, usually promoting the liberalizing or internationalizing perspective at the expense of national autonomy or tradition.

I use the uncertainty, status, and credibility hypotheses as reference points when evaluating alternative explanations, in the spirit of making my work more useful to others. I fully acknowledge the eclecticism of claiming that social forces are central to any explanation of political outcomes, while also adopting a positivist epistemology of hypothesis-testing to demonstrate that this is the case. The difficulty, of course, as at least two scholars have lucidly explained, is that the intersubjective nature of the concepts that populate our social world make them inextricably linked to us and thus not subject cause-effect processes.[12]

Equally, I recognize that my hypotheses, stated in their general form, are not readily falsifiable. Although my effort to identify falsifiable proxies with "concrete" measures in the real world may suggest a strong commitment to the hypothesis-testing epistemology, in fact it signals an awareness of the kind of intractable backward reasoning that is impossible to operationalize, for which some constructivist work has justifiably been criticized (Moravcsik 1999). And although I refer to the hypotheses throughout my empirical analysis—with comparisons between what a hypothesis would predict and observable outcomes—I am also telling a story in which perspectives compete for dominance, an avowedly interpretative exercise.

Dealing with such inconsistencies is daunting, but not prohibitive. Ultimately, research is a social enterprise in which deliberation among many scholars adjudicates the utility of competing approaches (see Vasquez 1997, 900). I have therefore chosen a strategy that speaks to warranted mainstream anxieties about methodology as well as to constructivist concerns about the importance of social forces for understanding politics.

## CASE SELECTION
### Sectors

I devote a chapter each to the institutionalization of CBI, the internationalization of bank ownership, the democratization of civil-military relations, and the denationalization of defense and foreign policy. The focus on financial sectors and military-security apparatuses serves several purposes. As proxies for capitalist development and democratic consolidation, outcomes in finance and defense are critical for measuring the extent of transition from central planning and authoritarian rule. Just as the erosion of state power over domestic capital allocation has become a lodestar of free market enterprise, so has the subordination of the armed forces to democratically accountable civilian officials become a cornerstone of democratic governance.

Finance and security are hard cases for constructivists. For all of the constructivist discussion about the unique human capacity to attach particular meanings to concepts and thus deliberate about them, finance and security seem to come awfully close to being features of a material base that exist independent of any meaning we might assign them (Wendt 1999). I therefore use these cases to demonstrate not only that rationalist approaches are incomplete on a case-by-case basis (Katzenstein 1996) but also that constructivist analyses can explain recurring patterns that have social and ideational sources—even in the difficult cases of money and security.

Finance and defense are also empirically important cases both in terms of domestic distribution and in terms of how the international system functions. Banking, for example, is one determinant of the state's role in the economy (Gerschenkron 1962; Zysman 1983) and may shape institutional complementarities according to which other domestic political and economic institutions develop (Hall and Soskice 2001; Hancké, Rhodes, and Thatcher 2007). Defense planning—another example—has ramifications for the military's role in society and consequent modes of governance (Ralston 1990). Both sectors also bear on the functioning of the international system insofar as they signal the willingness of states to embrace interdependence or preserve relative autonomy (Adler and Barnett 1998).

The range of sectors also provides variation on the first and third variables, concerning the uncertainty of actors and the credibility of international institutional policies. Sectoral discontinuity and consequent uncertainty during the CEE transitions gave international institutions more access to some areas of reform than others (H1). Militaries across CEE were reluctant to embrace NATO's standards of democratic civil-military relations, in large measure because their legacies and traditions endured through the transition.[13] Sectoral discontinuity and uncertainty were comparatively greater in banking, where price liberalization rendered state-socialist bankers unsure about what policies would best serve their interests.

The credibility of policies also varies across sectors, largely in keeping with the degree of international consensus underpinning a policy (H3). There was a strong (albeit new) international consensus in support of CBI and low inflation by the early 1990s, even if at the expense of national monetary flexibility. By contrast, at least at the outset of transition, there was a weaker consensus on the wisdom of selling state-owned banks mostly to foreign interests, given that the majority of OECD (Organisation for Economic Co-operation and Development) states had proved unwilling to follow a similar course themselves. The denationalization of defense planning was also problematic in states that had suffered inadequate security guarantees in World War II, because of the West's perceived lack of credibility in living up to its security commitments.

Finally, the range of sectors necessitates coverage of several international institutions. My inclusion of NATO, the European Union, the IMF, and the World Bank, among others, helps address alternative explanations predicated on the power of markets, incentives, and membership independent of any social context. Similarly situated countries respond differently to the same incentives (Killick 1996; Stone 2002; Jacoby 2004; Vachudova 2005). At the same time, international institutions may offer the same rewards for different levels of compliance (Grabbe 2002; Hughes, Sasse, and Gordon 2004; Sasse 2005; Sissenich 2007). Uneven application of and inconsistent responses to incentives highlight the extent to which social forces come into play, thus undermining a strictly rationalist interpretation of events.

## Countries

The choice of Poland, Hungary, Romania, and Ukraine as cases provides additional variation, principally in terms of sectoral or regime continuity and uncertainty (H1) and the perceived status of international institutions, measured according to the quality of political competition (H2). Because it is both representative and exceptional, Poland, the central case in the study, is particularly appropriate for examining the effects of international institutions on postcommunist domestic policymaking. It is representative in that Poland faced an array of challenges common to all states in the post-Soviet bloc—the result of decades of authoritarian rule and central planning and the economic and political crises they precipitated. From the standpoint of pursuing liberalization, however, Poland is exceptional. Episodes of democracy in Polish history have repeatedly given way to internal strife, foreign domination, and domestically generated authoritarianism. Even Solidarity, the most commonly cited of Poland's anticommunist credentials, has an ambiguous relationship with liberal economic reform, given its origins as a movement fighting for the expansion of workers' rights rather than market ideals (Powers and Cox 1997; Orenstein 2001; Ost 2005). Analysts made the most pessimistic forecasts for Poland in 1990 precisely because of its turbulent past, its nationalist proclivities, and the severity of its economic collapse. Those fears seemed to materialize in 1993 when Poland joined Lithuania as one of the first countries where communist successor parties expressing ambivalence about Western institutions returned to power.[14]

And yet within a decade of transition, liberal political and economic reforms had clearly prevailed in Poland. Despite volatile turnover in governing coalitions, the country consistently stayed the liberalizing course. Poland joined NATO and became an essential player in the first round of EU enlargement. In the same period, CBI was enshrined in the 1997 Constitution, and Polish politicians, albeit reluctantly, opened the banking sector to substantial foreign investment. In 2003, the United States chose Poland to lead the third stabilization zone in post-invasion Iraq.

Hungary, Romania, and Ukraine are to varying degrees comparable and contrasting. Hungary most resembles Poland in terms of both explanatory factors and liberalizing outcomes in the economic sphere. Hungary had for decades had a vibrant democratic opposition to communism, so international institutions had broad access to domestic reform processes in finance and, to a lesser extent, in defense. An elite political class born of that opposition identified with the values embedded in a range of Western policy prescriptions, from economic liberalization to military reform. Hungary was an obvious candidate for EU membership and ultimately—even though it was not geographically contiguous with the alliance—persuaded NATO that it should be included in the alliance's first post–Cold War enlargement. Important for all those developments was the communist successor party's eventual cooptation of Western reform ideas as it sought to create a political image more appropriate for the postcommunist era, in opposition to the more conservative center-right and nationalists.

Romania had quite different starting conditions. Owing to its highly repressive communist regime, economic backwardness, and lack of democratic opposition, and the ability of members of the communist apparatus to "manage" the revolution and govern in its aftermath—in sharp contrast to Poland, Hungary, and Czechoslovakia—those in power initially had little concern for social recognition from the West. But in a case of telescoped transformation, although international institutions initially lacked access to Romanian reform processes, by the early 2000s they had helped transform the political context such that everything from democratic civil-military relations to CBI was on the reform agenda and moving toward Western models. Whereas the potential benefits of both EU and NATO membership *failed* to elicit Romanian compliance in the first half of the 1990s, both major political groupings—including, crucially, the direct communist successors—were competing for international approval by the end of that decade.

Ukraine provides a different kind of variation because is not a member of either the European Union or NATO. The European Union and, to a lesser extent, NATO have held Ukraine at arm's length.[15] Although similar in some ways to Romania in its starting conditions, the divergence between the two countries since the embrace of Romania by NATO and the European Union illustrates the difference that international institutions can make. Despite the presence of a Ukrainian Westernizing elite, the country has only sporadically embraced those reform strategies most often associated with Western norms—democratization of civil-military relations, institutionalization of CBI, or denationalization of commercial banks through privatization with foreign capital. The European Union's reluctance to categorize Ukraine as a potential candidate for membership has no doubt diminished the salience of Western influence on Ukrainian reform. Inclusion of the Ukraine case in this study helps address the best-practice argument in which observers claim that market pressures would have forced CEE states to adopt liberalizing reforms even in the absence of international institutional influence. Market pressures evidently have not been decisive in Ukraine, so it is not clear why they should have been decisive elsewhere.

The case selection here, of both sectors and countries, is designed to address the major questions considered in the book. With variation in my explanatory factors and controlled consistency in possible alternative explanations, the study demonstrates that the predicted outcomes correspond more frequently with the presence of uncertainty, status, or credibility than with rival hypotheses. Apart from design, however, the cases are also empirically important because of the countries' strategic significance and what the issue areas reveal not only about domestic reform but also about the international orientation of states.

## ALTERNATIVE APPROACHES

Four kinds of alternative approaches serve as points of comparison for my explanation of liberalization in finance and defense in postcommunist Europe: domestic politics, neoliberal institutionalism, conditionality, and socialization. Although I borrow from each of these approaches, I depart from them in significant ways. Domestic political explanations tend to downplay the role of international institutions. Neoliberal institutionalism and conditionality take a strictly rationalist view in which the properties of agents do not change. Socialization captures an understudied cause of political change but also, in my view, too narrowly defines the scope of constructivist claims.

## Domestic Politics

Some studies understand democratic and economic outcomes in postcommunist Europe as primarily the consequence of domestic actors making decisions solely in reference to national factors (Vachudova and Snyder 1997; Fish 1998; Bunce 1999, 2003; Orenstein 2001; Reiter 2001; Grzymała-Busse 2002). I concede that domestic politics can indeed trump international forces, and point to the conditions under which this is likely to occur. I also argue, however, that an exclusively domestic approach mistakenly omits international pressures as a crucial source of reform.

An important theme in the comparative literature is the degree to which political competition facilitates the development of democratic institutions and free market enterprise. Fish (1998) argues that the first electoral outcomes of the postcommunist transition set the stage for liberalizing and privatizing trajectories thereafter. Where communist rulers were replaced with reformers, the result was more aggressive economic reform in the short run and greater sustainability of medium-term reform. In separate studies, Vachudova (2005) and Grzymała-Busse (2002) theorize that two prior conditions were essential to a victorious opposition and a subsequent high quality of political competition: the existence of a democratic resistance movement under communism and a communist party that reformed itself before the collapse of state socialism.[16] Comparativists argue that political competition ensures greater transparency in the political system,[17] and that it encourages consensus rather than polarization, equity rather than rent-seeking, and the emergence of future-oriented constituencies that trump detractors focused on the past.

I borrow from these approaches while also providing an alternative to them. As noted above, domestic conditions are central to my analysis. Indeed, I argue that at least early in the transition, the ideational appeal of Western international institutions to eastern European reformers can be mapped onto democratic opposition under communism. The presence of communist-era dissident movements and an opposition takeover during transition are powerful indicators of early postcommunist compliance with liberal norms. But a purely domestic explanation for political and economic outcomes raises two sets of issues.

First, comparative studies take the objective of liberalization for granted without exploring the political origins of the reform agenda—the uniformity of which constitutes a significant puzzle.[18] Few scholars are concerned with questions about why liberalism and why now, because they typically assume that liberal objectives amount to "best practice."[19] Given the historical context in which CEE "had mimicked fascism in the 1930s and socialism in the 1950s" (Orenstein 2001, 3), it is also not surprising that the region should once again provide a microcosm of global trends.[20] But the strong correlation between political trends external to and developments within CEE points to processes of international diffusion that in all likelihood facilitate such convergence. But these are conspicuous by their absence in comparative studies of transition.

A second weakness of cross-national comparisons that depend on country-level variables is that they have trouble explaining sector-level variation *within* countries. That cross-national studies "necessarily do violence to detail and fine distinctions" (Fish 1998, 32) is in my view an acceptable price to pay for the significant advances such generalizations bring to our understanding of macro trends. But to the extent that we can refine theories over time to reduce such "violence," we should. Moreover, although efficient, the claim that political competition alone explains initial patterns of liberalization and democratization is somewhat reductionist in suggesting that characteristics desirable from a liberal point of view—that is, democratization and cross-sectoral liberalization—will cluster together in the "good" countries and not emerge in the "bad."

The political competition thesis on its own thereby elides several important facts about the CEE region that contradict expectations. Otherwise liberal regimes could be "illiberal" when they so wished: Poland and Hungary had trouble democratizing civil-military relations; Slovenia insisted on maintaining significant state control over its banking sector; and Latvia was decidedly illiberal in matters of citizenship and linguistic rights for all of its citizens. As for "illiberal" regimes, Bulgaria and Romania ultimately institutionalized CBI, and Ukraine may yet do so. In the medium term, liberal and illiberal policies may not conform to the democratic starting conditions that initially resulted in high- or low-quality political competition. Only by addressing the international dimensions of transition and how they affect domestic politics can we explain such apparent anomalies.

## Neoliberal Institutionalism and Conditionality

Neoliberal institutionalism, which takes its assumptions and insights from contractual economics, is also relevant to understanding how international institutions affect state behavior (Keohane 1984; Haftendorn, Keohane, and Wallander 1999). According to this approach, international institutions arise out of uncertainty and insecurity and the desire of states to counter both by institutionalizing the rules, norms, and procedures that create transparency. The rationality assumption on which this approach is premised suggests that actors' interests are exogenous. This means that rules, norms, and procedures have only regulative, not constitutive, effects (Wallander 1999). Institutions can thus change how actors behave, but not who or what they are.

The rationality assumption is problematic because it understates the potential power of international institutions and leads to logical inconsistencies between theory and evidence. For example, in explaining the post–Cold War preservation and adaptability of NATO, Wallander uses a transaction costs approach to develop hypotheses about when states adapt rather than dissolve institutions in response to altered geostrategic conditions. She argues that if it is less costly to change old institutions than to create new ones, then "states will choose to sustain existing arrangements rather than abandon them" (2000, 706). She goes on to take stock of NATO's specific and general assets and the efficiency gains they produce, arguing that the cost-efficiency of the alliance's preservation was linked to the adaptability of its risk-management assets to post–Cold War security concerns (712).

Although Wallander concedes that the "objectives, beliefs, and roles" of particular states are relevant to institutional adaptation, she maintains that structural incentives and opportunities are more important.[21] The concession is noteworthy, however, for throughout her presentation of evidence, Wallander repeatedly points to political processes and motivations that fall outside the ontological assumptions of a transaction costs approach, such as the importance of NATO after World War II for bolstering public support for Germany's semi-sovereign status, for cultivating "trust" among alliance members, and for "enmeshing" Turkey and Greece in a "web of relations" (716). In the post–Cold War period, NATO did the same for the CEE states. The alliance's denationalizing, democratizing efforts most certainly had regulatory effects. But they also changed these states and their polities and policies (a constitutive effect), especially regarding the balance of power among groups in society and their international orientation. Moreover, as Wallander also points out, NATO officials often talked about the primacy of creating solidarity in this process, rather than the need to produce "efficiencies" (726–27).

Neoliberal institutionalism poses two, related problems. The first is ontological inconsistency. It is difficult to sustain the argument that transparency is the putative objective of an international institution but that transparency can be achieved only through solidarity. For while transparency may exist independent of our competing perceptions of it (and I am skeptical even on this point), solidarity certainly does not. This means that for NATO to have the effects that neoliberal institutionalists attribute to it, they must assume something different about the nature of institutions and actors than they acknowledge. Indeed, implicit in Wallander's analysis is an assumption about the centrality of intersubjective social forces that in turn contribute to outcomes—and not just on the margins.

The second problem is the language of "costs." I would not dispute the claim that states work to preserve institutions when the costs of losing them are higher than those of keeping them. But then the argument hinges on what constitutes cost—a judgment that I argue is informed by actors' interests that can readily change over time. Both problems—ontological inconsistency and the indeterminacy of costs—stem from the rationality assumption. My rejection of it does not mean that on the whole I think people are irrational. It simply means that we have to understand the terms of rationality and where they come from if discussions about costs are to have any meaning or measurability.

Research on EU conditionality also tends to view states' choices about whether to comply in terms of costs (e.g., Moravcsik and Vachudova 2003; Kelley 2004a, 2004b; Schimmelfennig 2005; Schimmelfennig and Sedelmeier 2005; Vachudova 2005). Assessing the costs of compliance is certainly a logical first step, given that all former Soviet satellites would in theory have been equally eligible to join European institutions but responded differently to that uniform incentive. But again, in the conditionality literature, "costs" are normally not well enough specified in the hypotheses to tell us in advance whether we could expect compliance or not.

Schimmelfennig argues, for example, that between 1994 and 1998, Slovakia failed to comply with EU and NATO prescriptions concerning minority rights legislation because the domestic power costs for Prime Minister Vladimir Mečiar would have been too high—that is, his nationalist coalition partners would have brought down the government (2005, 849). As it turned out, the costs of *not* complying were also high for Mečiar; his party lost power in the next elections in no small measure because Slovak opposition parties and groups were able to rally the public that strongly favored European integration (Vachudova 2005, chap. 6). The theoretical point here is that had Mečiar made the opposite calculation—to advance Slovakian compliance in the short term with an eye toward longer-term political viability—Schimmelfennig would still be right. In other words, hypotheses premised on costs are generally not falsifiable because most policies imply some cost and it is usually not obvious what course actors should prefer, except in retrospect.

More important for my purposes, however, is that conditionality arguments do not normally investigate the origins of interests. More interesting than the fact that Mečiar seemed to be trapped in a nationalist coalition that was unwilling to comply with Western minority rights prescriptions is that Mečiar's governing partners apparently perceived that the right to continue discriminating against minorities was more valuable than EU or NATO membership. Rather than dismiss this preference as irrational, my theoretical framework systematically investigates its origins—by measuring the uncertainty of actors, the perceived relative status of international institutions, and the credibility of their policies in terms of Western practice. On at the least the third of these variables my framework would anticipate such problems with compliance, based on the uneven adherence to any codified minority rights policy in western Europe (Grabbe 2005; Sasse 2005).

My aim is not to dismiss the power of conditionality or to argue that a social context informed by uncertainty, status, and credibility independent of incentives more often explains outcomes. Rather, the purpose is to specify why conditionality is compelling in some instances but apparently meaningless in others. The attention to social context is meant to shed light on exactly that question.

## Socialization

The recent attention to socialization in international relations is a welcome innovation that has expanded our understanding of what drives political and institutional change (Checkel 2001b, 2005; Johnston 2001, 2003; Kelley 2004a; Gheciu 2005a, 2005b). The variables presented here (uncertainty, status, and credibility) overlap with those used for theorizing the impact of persuasion (Checkel 2001b; Johnston 2001; Gheciu 2005a). But important points of intellectual convergence notwithstanding, there are two, related ways in which my theoretical framework departs from this literature. First, socialization is too narrow to capture the full range of outcomes this study examines; and second, as noted above, I disagree with the insistence on distinctive—instrumental and obligatory—logics of actions.

Although I refer to "consensus" in this study, I am not primarily interested in the causes of socialization in the strictest sense of that term. Nor do I make strong claims about how the political processes examined here alter privately held beliefs. The growing literature on argumentation, persuasion, and socialization rightly emphasizes that the "distribution of knowledge" in the international system bears on political outcomes. I take the position, however, that community-held norms about what constitutes an appropriate belief, as expressed in language or in action, is the more relevant measure on liberalizing outcomes in post-communist Europe. The reasons for this are twofold. First, while beliefs are not observable, language and action are. Second, since language and action can readily belie beliefs, I argue that it is language and action rather than beliefs that must have proximate effects on outcomes. This is particularly salient to my argument when one considers the power of social pressure to shape conflicts and their resolution in the political sphere.

Given my emphasis on actors' beliefs about where authority lies based on their language and actions, Checkel's analysis might seem to subsume the processes in my study under what he calls "Type I socialization" (2005, 804). Checkel defines Type I socialization as the perfunctory adoption of rules that does not require actors' reflexivity but does necessitate a shift from the logic of consequences to the logic of appropriateness. It is doubtful, however, that perfunctory adherence to rules actually constitutes socialization, since Checkel stipulates on the same page that socialization implies an internalization of new rules. More important for my argument, however, is that not only is the shift from a logic of consequences to a logic of appropriateness unobservable, but under most circumstances actors are not adhering to either one logic or the other—they are drawing on both. Rules emerge as a consequence of social interaction, to be sure. But a failure to adhere to social rules can also carry costs—a fact not lost on the generals and bankers responsible for weighing national autonomy and tradition against international pressures.

Attention to socialization in international politics narrows the scope of constructivist claims by insisting that we show there is a shift away from the logic of consequences and that actors have internalized new rules (see also Epstein 2005b). With such evidentiary requirements, social forces risk being relegated to that rare category of events in which actors are persuaded of the rightness of an idea and implement policy on that basis. Indeed, the either/or approach in which international institutions have *either* persuaded domestic actors *or* pressured them into complying has unjustifiably limited the salience of constructivist insights and social forces.

Kelley (2004a, 2004b), for example, in reference to minority protection and language policies in four postcommunist countries, argues that conditionality seems to be the most powerful mechanism in assuring legislative compliance with the policy prescriptions of the Council of Europe, the European Union, and the Organization for Security and Cooperation in Europe. She presents three propositions that, when tested against the evidence, seem to show that only in very few cases does socialization register an independent effect, and then only when domestic opposition is low. Kelley concedes that it is difficult to separate the effects of socialization from conditionality because there are few cases in which European institutions apply conditionality without also making some effort to persuade target states of the desirability of a policy (2004b, 439). She nevertheless concludes that the absence of socialization would probably not have seriously undermined the power of conditionality to encourage states to adopt liberal legislation, even where domestic opposition was high (449–53).

I have no doubt that Kelley's claims are generally correct, but her conceptualization of socialization, which is consistent with Checkel's, is too narrow to infer anything about the constructivist-rationalist debate. Normative pressure, as Kelley defines it, "occurs when an institution advises a government on the direction a policy should take, offering no reward other than the approbation of the institution" (2004a, 3). Because the definition limits the possible constructivist scope of explanation to instances in which target actors are persuaded by the power of arguments alone, it understates the degree to which social forces could be at play (Epstein 2005b). Social processes that might contribute to an explanation of why states respond variably to EU minority rights prescriptions include the degree to which western European states follow such prescriptions, the perceived value of EU membership versus national autonomy, and the prior politicization of ethnic differences. These variables roughly correspond to credibility, status, and uncertainty—the presence or absence of which, I argue, explains whether international institutions can embed liberal policies in transition states.

## CONCLUSION

Although I specify the processes through which international institutions cultivate consensus around the policy manifestations of a liberal worldview, the argument is more broadly applicable to contemporary global politics. Capitalist and democratic cultural forms increasingly animate societies' understandings of our world.[22] Technology in all its applications—transport, communication, and international economic flows—may well shape the material bases that in turn make the global spread of particular cultural forms possible. But both material bases and the technology that structures them are underdetermining insofar as neither bears on the central issue of why *these* particular cultural forms. By addressing this critical question in the context of postcommunist transition, I hope to contribute to more general debates about how knowledge is transmitted in the international system and with what political consequences.

My use of uncertainty, status, and credibility as core elements of the analysis of what makes incentives powerful distinguishes this approach from studies premised on stable interests or the rationality assumption. However, my simultaneous insistence on the role of instrumentality in assigning meanings to concepts also distinguishes my theory of institutional influence from constructivist work dedicated to specifying the conditions under which competing logics of action—consequential and obligatory—obtain. By detailing how the initial establishment and further embedding of a liberal worldview take place, I also demonstrate that incentives embedded in a social context have both regulative and constitutive effects. Where international institutions have had the power to delineate what kind of capitalism and what kind of defense, they are also defining what kind of state.

Where the social context in postcommunist Europe allowed, international institutions limited the range of policy options that politicians could pursue and circumscribed the kinds of arguments they could use to cultivate public support. The result in finance and defense has often, though not always, been denationalization, such that governments have opted for market-oriented economic policies and multilateral security strategies. Limiting policy options and discourses to denationalization transforms previously contested ideas into commonly held assumptions. Denationalization in finance and defense has distributional consequences domestically. But it also signals a state's willingness to engage in interdependence or defend relative levels of autonomy.

As the evidence will show, the distribution of knowledge in these cases is not about convergence around economic best practice or optimal strategies for security maximization. It is, rather, about convergence around what constitutes rational political action in a particular social context, a perhaps even more profound manifestation of a state's intention to signal its solidarity with a particular community. The role of international institutions in cultivating support for liberalism brings us closer to understanding processes of reconciliation or alienation between national politics and our increasingly integrated international system.

# CHAPTER TWO

# Institutionalizing Central Bank Independence

Converting socialist-era monobanks from quasi-fiscal instruments of the state into politically independent central banks is among the most important measures of how far postcommunist states have traveled on the road to Western-style market economies. By the late 1990s, many central and eastern European (CEE) central banks had already outdone even the German Bundesbank on measures of independence—at least in formal terms (Loungani and Sheets 1997; Maliszewski 2000, 7; Cukierman, Miller, and Neyapti 2002, 239, 244). Given the distribution of power and resources at stake, we might have expected a contentious and protracted trajectory around the institutionalization of central bank independence. That this outcome materialized in some postcommunist states but not in others requires explanation.

Theories of central bank independence (CBI) and the sources of inflation in OECD countries focus on either institutional arrangements or domestic factors, such as labor market organization, social transfers, or partisanship. CBI in eastern Europe evolved in the absence of the usual causes, however. Rather than its being generated primarily by domestic interests, the 1990s emphasis on price stability and financial market regulation being enforced by politically independent actors was largely the result of an organized campaign among international institutions to instill these goals in target states. I argue that varying degrees of CBI and its institutionalization at different times across postcommunist Europe are a function of how open CEE reformers were to international institutional policy prescriptions. As in other cases detailed in this volume, the uncertainty of CEE reformers, their perceived subordinate status vis-à-vis international institutions, and the Western consensus underpinning the credibility of CBI explain much of the variation in reform.

The relatively recent worldwide rush to institutionalize CBI, starting in industrialized states in the 1970s and spreading with vigor to lesser-developed countries in the 1980s and 1990s (Maxfield 1997; Polillo and Guillén 2005), seems to suggest that aiming for price stability is a key feature of economic "best practice." Comparing security and financial sectors, rationalists might acknowledge that there is some room for national discretion in the areas of civil-military relations or defense planning, because historical experience conditions states' interests differently (see chapters 4 and 5). But according to new classical economists and international financial institutions (IFIs), states in transition that are hoping to achieve growth, prosperity, and stability—in part by attracting foreign capital—have no rational alternative to putting monetary policy beyond the political fray (Loungani and Sheets 1997; Notermans 1999; Cukierman, Miller, and Neyapti 2002).

This chapter highlights the ways in which CEE reformers viewed the formulation of monetary policy and the execution of bank regulation as realms of debate and choice. Yet there was a high degree of convergence in postcommunist states around CBI before EU enlargement in 2004, and in some cases many years before. The CBI outcome is testament to the fact that international institutions, including the World Bank, the IMF, the European Union, and the US Agency for International Development (USAID), used their technical authority and elevated status to promote price stability. I discuss here what is at stake in the CBI debate, examine how uncertainty, status, and credibility explain variations in the degree of CBI, and reflect on how enduring the shift to CBI is likely to be.

## CENTRAL BANK INDEPENDENCE: THEORY AND PRACTICE

According to new classical economic theory, CBI contributes to price stability because it implies a set of institutional arrangements that solve the "time inconsistency" problem, also referred to as "dynamic inconsistency." Time inconsistency occurs when the best plans made for some future period are no longer the best plans once that future arrives. The theory assumes that discrete groups have exogenous, fixed interests rooted in their material and professional positions. With access to central bank policy, short-term electoral considerations encourage governments to pursue expansionary policies in the form of monetary easing or government spending. Such episodes of "surprise" inflation may boost employment, provide government revenue from seigniorage, or adjust the balance of payments. Over time, however, it becomes harder to orchestrate the surprise element of expansionary policies and therefore more difficult to contain their inflationary effects. In the absence of surprise, other actors in the economy, labor unions in particular, are likely to negotiate wage bargains with built-in inflationary expectations. And thus begins an inflationary cycle that is difficult to curtail.

The institutionalization of CBI purportedly solves the time inconsistency problem and reduces inflation, according to new classical economists, by altering incentive structures that lead to inflationary expectations. CBI removes myopic politicians' access to monetary policy and gives central bank governors a mandate to protect price stability while guaranteeing them long-term positions without political interference. Generally speaking, economists consider CBI and lower inflation positive developments (Cukierman 1992). According to a policy paper that theorized the CBI–price stability nexus, "having an independent central bank is almost like having a free lunch: there are benefits but no apparent costs in terms of macroeconomic performance" (Grilli, Masciandaro, and Tabellini 1991, 375).

Other scholars, however, have raised questions about the causes of price stability and the consequences of CBI. It is difficult to show unambiguously that CBI causes low inflation (Cukierman 1992; Berger, De Haan, and Eijffinger 2001), although it may do so, given other conjunctural conditions (Loungani and Sheets 1997; Cukierman, Miller, and Neyapti 2002). Some also argue that CBI per se does not lead to price stability, but that societal consensus, wage bargaining institutions, or financial interests support low inflation (Posen 1993, 46; 1995b; Hall and Franzese 1998; Grabel 2003). Others have shown that CBI might make disinflations more costly because of the onus independence puts on central banks to prove their anti-inflationary credentials (Posen 1995a; Eijffinger and De Haan 1996). Finally, there is no evidence that CBI contributes to growth (Alesina and Summers 1993; Maxfield 1997), although high levels of inflation, exceeding 40 percent annually, can adversely affect output (Kirshner 2001).

Historically, monetary policy and CBI have been the source of political conflict because of their hypothesized relationship to unemployment, inflation, economic stimulus, and national sovereignty. And in postcommunist countries, debates about CBI were based on exactly such concerns. Political parties fought about weighing price stability and the high interest rates it required against preserving industry, jobs, and redistribution. For societies accustomed to banks as political tools, it made little sense to concentrate monetary policy and bank regulatory authority in the hands of a few to whom political parties or the government had no access. Indeed, at the outset of transition, the idea that central banks should exercise independent power had no precedent in CEE. Given the social dislocation caused by price liberalization and increasingly open markets, the central bank could have been used to finance industry, preserve employment, and protect banks from regulatory scrutiny of a kind that would limit their operations or put them out of business. The extended political use of the central bank was a notable feature of some postcommunist states, particularly Romania and Ukraine among the countries considered here.

Eventually, CBI also mattered for a different reason: European Monetary Union (EMU) (Epstein and Johnson 2009). Although accession to the European Union was not predicated on meeting the Maastricht criteria (concerning inflation, deficits, debt, and interest rates), it was expected that the newest member states would strive for Euro membership quickly, since joining the Euro Zone was a condition of admission to the European Union. But by 2006, when, whether, or how the 2004 entrants (with the exception of Slovenia) would be eligible to adopt the euro was unclear because of the lack of economic convergence on several indicators (Dyson 2006) and the lack of political desire (J. Johnson 2008). Moreover, although Poland and Hungary scored high on global indices of CBI, the European Central Bank (ECB) in 2006 was still insisting on additional legal changes to consolidate CBI further (European Central Bank 2006).

## THE SOCIAL CONTEXT IN CONDITIONALITY: UNCERTAINTY, STATUS, AND CREDIBILITY

The social context that gives international institutions access to postcommunist debates about financial sector reform is similar to that for the military-security apparatus (see chapters 4 and 5). The demobilization of sectors and resulting uncertainty, domestic actors' perceived subordinate status in relation to Western international institutions, and the credibility of the policies promoted by international institutions all help determine whether external actors have the power to set a reform agenda and cultivate a transnational coalition that can implement policy.[1]

Uncertainty within a sector heightens international institutional power because domestic actors who lack policy experience are likely to seek expert advice as a way of gaining confidence in their own policy choices (H1; see chapter 1 on the designation of the study hypotheses). Although central banking structures are in one sense continuous because they stem from communist-era monobanks, in more important respects central banks mark a sharp break with the past, and we can therefore expect the actors who are overseeing reform to experience uncertainty. Moreover, many central bank bureaucrats, coming from socialist-era monobanks, were policy novices. Because the administrative responsibilities of monobanks were peculiar to the functioning of a centrally planned economy, the liberalization of prices—a definitional feature of transition—mandated that central banks adopt a different role in the economy. Whether that role would be to finance government operations and keep state-subsidized industries afloat, or to pursue price stability and financial market regulation independent of short-term political concerns, was not determined by the fact of transition. That choice depended on the influence of international institutions.

Another measure on uncertainty also explains the receptivity of reformers to international institutions at the outset of transition. Where opposition movements took power, replacing figures from the former communist regime, Western organizations enjoyed greater influence and there was more congruence between international institutional policy prescriptions and early economic reforms. Some scholars have concluded that Poland, Hungary, and Czechoslovakia implemented Western-oriented reforms early not necessarily because international institutions had more access to those states owing to the uncertainty of actors, but because opposition movements were led by dissidents who had long preferred liberal principles (Bockman and Eyal 2002; Shields 2003; Vachudova 2005). If the interest in CBI predated transition, this would call into question the utility of the uncertainty hypothesis. I argue here, however, that the existence of concentrated expertise does not explain the broader acceptance of a policy such as CBI in former monobanks, parliaments, or societies.

Domestic actors' perceived subordinate status and their desire for social recognition from international institutions also gave organizations such as the IMF and the European Union access to domestic reform debates (H2). For Poland, Hungary, and Romania, "returning to Europe" was a strong political imperative from the outset of transition. Prizel (1998) notes that for certain Ukrainian nationalist intellectuals, particularly those based in the western sections of the newly independent country, "returning to Europe" was also a powerful political theme.[2]

A more refined operationalization of this variable helps pinpoint under what conditions international institutions can influence domestic reform by virtue of their elevated status. I use the quality of political competition to assess how transition states' desire for Western approbation provided international institutions with access to reform debates. Where there was robust political competition from 1989 forward, I argue that international institutions had greater power to set reform agendas, because the opposition competed on domestic issues as well as on a country's standing in relation to international institutions. This hypothesis is linked to research showing that political competition introduces greater transparency (Orenstein 2001; Grzymała-Busse 2002; Vachudova 2005). In addition to transparency and information, however, I argue that political competition, coupled with the existence of supranational organizations largely perceived as legitimate, changes the social dynamic by broadening the programmatic basis on which parties must compete.

Finally, the credibility of the policies that international institutions attempt to transfer to transition states affects how readily target actors adopt Western prescriptions (H3). I measure "credibility" by observing the degree of consensus underpinning a policy, as well as the normative consistency of Western states and international organizations. When Western states themselves enact the policies they promote in CEE, there is less discursive room for target actors to contest a particular recommendation. Of all the issues under consideration in this volume, central bank independence, as a way of organizing power relations among groups in society, enjoys the most credibility according to both measures. Consensus was institutionalized through all the major organizations, including the Bretton Woods institutions, the European Union, and USAID. Normative consistency was also strong in the central banking case by the 1990s because of western Europe's own use of CBI and, later, monetary union to achieve price stability after the sharp distributional conflicts of the 1970s and 1980s over double-digit inflation. As shown by comparing levels of CBI in central and eastern Europe during the 1990s and in selected OECD states during the 1980s (see table 2.1), it is conceivable that if the postcommunist transition had taken place a decade earlier, we would see much greater variation in the degree to which CBI was institutionalized among post-socialist economies.

Since CBI has evolved as a highly credible policy, most of the variation among countries materialized because of different degrees of uncertainty among actors in the transition and because those actors perceived the IFIs variously—as authoritative sources of information or not. According to the theory, Poland and Hungary should have been very susceptible to the CBI consensus, whereas Romania and Ukraine posed barriers to international institutional access. In the empirical sections that follow, I detail measures on my key hypotheses—uncertainty, status, and credibility—and explain how transnational coalitions either institutionalized CBI or failed to do so.

## OUTCOMES ACROSS THE REGION

In this chapter I use the index on CBI created by Cukierman, Webb, and Neyapti (1992; also see Cukierman 1992) to assess central bank independence across countries and over time. There are 16 measures grouped into five categories: who

TABLE 2.1

*Central Bank Independence: Postcommunist and OECD States Compared*

| Postcommunist Europe, 1990s | LVAW Score | Selected OECD States, 1980s | LVAW Score |
|---|---|---|---|
| **Poland**[a] | .89 | Germany | .69 |
| Estonia | .78 | Switzerland | .64 |
| Lithuania | .78 | Austria | .61 |
| Georgia | .73 | Denmark | .50 |
| Moldova | .73 | United States | .48 |
| Belarus | .73 | Canada | .45 |
| Czech Republic | .73 | Ireland | .44 |
| **Hungary** | .67 | Netherlands | .42 |
| Slovenia | .63 | Australia | .36 |
| Slovakia | .62 | Luxembourg | .33 |
| Bulgaria | .55 | Sweden | .29 |
| Albania | .51 | United Kingdom | .27 |
| Latvia | .49 | Italy | .25 |
| Russia | .49 | France | .25 |
| Croatia | .44 | New Zealand | .24 |
| **Ukraine**[b] | .42 | Spain | .23 |
| Macedonia | .41 | Japan | .18 |
| **Romania** | .34 | Belgium | .17 |
| | | Norway | .17 |

*Source:* Cukierman, Miller, and Neyapti 2002, 244.

*Note:* Countries appearing in boldface are included in this study. The LVAW (Legal Variables–Weighted) score is calculated based on the 16 measures in Cukierman, Miller, and Neyapti 2002, table 4.1. Also see Cukierman, Webb, and Neyapti 1992.

[a]This is the 1997 score for Poland, as opposed to the 1991 score, which was lower.

[b]The score probably overestimates the Ukrainian central bank's independence, given the number of features not specified in Ukrainian law. See Cukierman, Miller, and Neyapti, 2002, table 4.2.

formulates monetary policy; procedures for negotiating conflict over policy between the central bank and the government; commitment to price stability; the seriousness of limitations on central bank lending to the government; and procedures for appointing and dismissing the central bank governor (also see Cukierman, Miller, and Neyapti 2002). Measures of CBI for the countries under consideration here are summarized in table 2.2.

By 1998, the National Bank of Poland (NBP) was among the world's most independent central banks, with structures and regulations broadly consistent with OECD standards. The bank's independence and its primary goals were enshrined in Poland's 1997 Constitution as well as in legislation from 1990 and 1997. In terms of policy, the institutionalization of CBI meant the central bank's main objective was price stability through the use of open market operations. The

General Inspectorate for Banking Supervision at the NBP remained poised to regulate the banking sector independent of political party influence. In addition, NBP was, according to the European Monetary Institute, basically in conformity with the 1992 Maastricht criteria for participation in EMU, even if other economic indicators in Poland were not. International institutions' early embedding of CBI as an ideal among Polish bureaucrats and economically liberal parliamentarians was key to securing these outcomes. A transnational coalition overpowered a serious challenge to CBI in the mid-1990s, effectively depoliticizing monetary policy until a second, less serious flare-up in 2002.

Hungary shares the same measures on the explanatory variables as Poland and, as my theoretical framework would predict, manifested similar congruence between international institutional policy prescriptions and central bank institutions. According to CBI indices, Hungary's central bank was somewhat less independent than Poland's by the late 1990s. Hungary had a high degree of uncertainty among actors within the sector, and the country was overwhelmingly in favor of emulating Western institutions. Given these two variables, the international consensus behind CBI conveyed to Hungarian policymakers a strong

TABLE 2.2
*Central Bank Independence in Selected Postcommunist States: Measures*

| Feature | Poland 1991 | Poland 1997 | Hungary 1991 | Romania 1991 | Ukraine 1991 |
|---|---|---|---|---|---|
| Term of office | .75 | .75 | .75 | 0 | NA |
| Who appoints | .5 | .5 | .50 | .5 | .5 |
| Dismissal | .83 | .83 | .83 | .33 | NA |
| Other offices | 1.0 | 1.0 | 1.0 | 1.0 | NA |
| Who formulates | .33 | 1.0 | .67 | .67 | .67 |
| Final authority | .6 | 1.0 | 1.0 | .4 | NA |
| Role in budget | 1.0 | 1.0 | 1.0 | 0 | 1.0 |
| Objectives | .6 | .6 | .60 | .4 | .6 |
| Advances to government | 0 | 1.0 | .67 | .33 | 0 |
| Securitized lending | .67 | 1.0 | NA | 0 | 0 |
| Terms of lending | .33 | 1.0 | .33 | .33 | NA |
| Potential borrowers | .33 | 1.0 | 1.0 | NA | NA |
| Type of limit | 0 | 1.0 | .33 | 0 | NA |
| Maturity of loans | 0 | 1.0 | .33 | 0 | NA |
| Interest rates | .25 | 1.0 | .75 | .25 | NA |
| Primary market | 0 | 1.0 | 0 | 0 | NA |

*Source:* Cukierman, Miller, and Neyapti 2002, 257–58.

*Note:* Measures range between 0 and 1, where 0 represents least independence and 1 represents most. For a detailed discussion of what each measure signifies, see Cukierman, Webb, and Neyapti 1992, 358–59. NA, measure not stipulated in any banking law or in the constitution.

sense of who did and who did not have legitimate claims on the state, confining the central bank's mandate to protecting price stability. However, like Poland, Hungary experienced periodic political conflict around the central bank's role in the economy. Hungarian parliamentarians ultimately took some limited measures to increase their control over central bank policy in the early 2000s.

Romania differed from Poland and Hungary in two key respects: first, there was no initial turnover in the governing party at the outset of transition, limiting the effect of uncertainty in the political sphere; and second, the absence of political competition until the second half of the 1990s resulted in compromised status for external advisors. Weak political competition and the consequent lack of concern about international approbation meant that even if Romanian central bankers were reluctant to submit to political demands for industry financing, they could not use international standards to persuade politicians to pursue anti-inflationary policies. Thus the central bank during the 1990s had less statutory independence than its Polish and Hungarian counterparts, and it established a price stability agenda only after the Democratic Convention of Romania (CDR) came to power in late 1996. Exceptionally among the cases here, only in 2004, with EU conditionality looming, did Romania's socialists finally institutionalize CBI.

Ukraine has conformed least with international norms on CBI. Despite hyperinflation in the 1990s and multiple episodes of IMF conditionality aimed at limiting central bank financing of loss-making industries, parliamentarians, as of 2004, had yet to be persuaded of the need for a politically independent central bank. The central difference between Ukraine and the other three cases is that whereas Poland, Hungary, and ultimately Romania saw themselves as embedded in a hierarchy with respect to Western multilateral institutions, Ukraine—and particularly its parliamentarians—did not.

## INTEREST DEMOBILIZATION: THE UNCERTAINTY OF ACTORS (H1)
### *Poland*

Poland's openness to external technical advice on how to build an independent central bank out of the socialist-era monobank was facilitated by both domestic bureaucratic inexperience in managing a market economy and the political turnover of 1989 that brought the democratic opposition to power. My contention here is that both political leaders and the banking bureaucracy lacked certainty about how to achieve optimal results and were heavily dependent on external advisors during the transition. Sectoral discontinuity, which resulted from price liberalization and introduction of the market mechanism, meant actors faced an unfamiliar environment structured by new rules. Such uncertainty gave international institutions the opportunity to assign positive meanings to their own priorities, including CBI, price stability, and independent regulatory authority.

Contact between Polish politicians and the IMF and World Bank concerning economic reform dated back to 1986, when Poland rejoined the Bretton Woods institutions. Although Poland had been one of the founding members of these institutions in 1944, by 1950 Soviet hegemony and Poland's membership in the Council for Mutual Economic Assistance precluded its participation. In 1986 the World Bank considered a lending program for Poland, but ultimately demurred because the communist regime's commitment to reform was still unclear and the Bank's key shareholders were reluctant to assist a state-socialist country. Nevertheless, renewed Polish contact with the IMF and World Bank allowed the IFIs to forge ties with potential allies in the country and help lay plans for radical liberalization even before the communist regime was ousted and in advance of any conditionality agreements.[3]

Poland's renewed Western relations on economic issues were not limited to Bretton Woods. USAID was also building reform capacity and a network of contacts in Poland in the late 1980s. In 1989, before the revolutionary political changes gained full momentum, Poland had started restructuring its financial sector. Early that year, Poland passed the Banking Act and the Act on the National Bank of Poland—two pieces of legislation that converted the socialist monobank into a two-tiered banking system modeled explicitly on Western, capitalist principles. USAID affiliates had advised on how to design the structures and write the bylaws for the NBP (Poland's central bank) and the new state-owned banks that resulted from the legislation.[4]

With the first partially free elections in Poland in June 1989, the opposition's rise to power bolstered the influence of international institutions over Poland's reform path, because Solidarity was Western-oriented and sought out ties to a range of international institutions.[5] Not only would Western institutions enjoy the advantage over Polish banking bureaucrats of superior technical knowledge, but the changed political climate meant that dissidents with no experience in running state institutions would also seek external assistance to gain confidence in their policy choices. Within months of the banking-sector reform, the roundtable negotiations and subsequent elections set the stage for macroeconomic stabilization. The primary concern of the IFIs and Polish reformers entering office, led by Leszek Balcerowicz, was to formulate monetary policy consistent with anti-inflationary goals. The World Bank's Financial Institutions Development Loan, administered beginning in 1991, reflected the Polish-IFI goal consensus, as the loan was conditioned on the removal of interest rate subsidies and reduction of directed credit (World Bank 1997b, 11).

A second concern that emerged as early as 1992, when the fragility of the banking sector became evident, was the perceived need to build competence within Poland's banking supervision department, the General Inspectorate of the National Bank. Because of uncertainty among both politicians and banking bureaucrats, Poland turned to the World Bank and IMF. Oversight of the NBP by these institutions intensified in 1993 with the Enterprise and Financial Sector Adjustment Loan. Granted in conjunction with Poland's Enterprise and Bank Restructuring and Privatization program, the loan was designed to insulate banks with bad loans from political pressure to continue financing failing enterprises. Part of that agreement was to give the Bretton Woods institutions access to NBP's supervisory activities.[6] Over the 1990s, with foreign technical assistance, "banking supervision [in Poland] evolved to contain systemic risk in the banking sector and to support NBP's larger objective of price stability."[7]

Although the Financial Institutions Development Loan and the Enterprise and Financial Sector Adjustment Loan supported certain features of CBI, it is unlikely that this limited conditionality alone incentivized the choice for price stability and independent bank regulation. The first wave of Polish reformers wanted what the international institutions wanted. The IFIs provided a political rationale for liberal reformers, in addition to whatever technical justification they could convey. The reformers in turn used the IFIs to persuade other actors in the government that what they were doing was the best possible strategy.[8] According to an IMF official working with Poland on the Balcerowicz plan early in the transition, "They didn't need our money." Rather, it was "useful to the reformers to be able to lean on the IMF as they negotiated with the parliament."[9]

Given the degree of support that some Polish dissidents developed for "neo-liberal" policies long before transition (Bockman and Eyal 2002; Shields 2003; Ost 2005), the early adoption of CBI, price stability, and independent regulatory capacities may seem to have been predetermined in the Polish case. According to these arguments, uncertainty would have mattered very little. I acknowledge that the commitment to economic liberalization that evolved among some Polish dissidents during the Cold War helped establish the general reform trajectory. But specific areas of conflict between the IFIs and Polish bureaucrats highlight that those responsible for implementing CBI were in fact uncertain and lacked expertise. By their own accounts, banking bureaucrats depended heavily on expert advisors to put regulatory structures in place and, later, to defeat domestic challenges to CBI.[10]

Disagreements and misunderstandings between Polish banking bureaucrats and their foreign advisors illustrate how domestic inexperience and uncertainty allowed international institutions to promote technical policies and the values they contained. Ewa Śleszyńska-Charewicz, appointed to head the General Inspectorate for Banking Supervision in 1992, recalled that early in the transition Poles did not know what a supervisory board was for and doubted it was necessary. Senior officials believed it "had to do with police, militias and judges . . . in fact they learned that the opposite was true."[11] Even harder to convince of the merits of independent regulation were the managers of the newly created state-owned commercial banks. Whereas theories of CBI generally assume that financial interests have the most to gain—from both price stability and regulation that prevents peer institutions from cheating—Polish financiers did not see it that way. A USAID advisor reported that he and his colleagues had trouble "convincing bankers in Poland that supervision would be good for them . . . that it would strengthen and protect the banking sector" and that "it wasn't just a nuisance."[12] The idea of government deposit insurance was a third source of friction. Although the IFIs ultimately prevailed here too, Polish resistance stemmed from the similarity between deposit insurance and the "soft budget constraint" under socialism that was believed to have caused widespread economic distortion.[13]

Hanna Gronkiewicz-Waltz, appointed president of the NBP in 1992, also underwent a significant ideational transformation during her tenure as a consequence of international institutional advising. Her reorientation provides additional evidence of domestic actors' openness to external advice, given the novelty of a market-based central bank. Having done doctoral research on legal banking issues, as late as 1991 Gronkiewicz-Waltz had advised President Wałęsa to veto legislation that would have enhanced CBI. By the mid-1990s, however, when it was Gronkiewicz-Waltz's own monetary policy and "excessive" independence that members of the communist successor governing coalition were criticizing, she had become a staunch defender of the institutional arrangements she had earlier tried to undermine. Although one could argue that Gronkiewicz-Waltz was simply adapting to her professional position and maximizing her power within it, she could have done so more effectively by agreeing to politicians' demands. This is one example of the closing cognitive gap between Polish actors and international norms governing CBI, driven by IFI-funded coaching and elite socialization.[14]

The particular importance of uncertainty in the earliest stages of transition is borne out by the fact that when experience accumulated, the domestic political debate about CBI intensified. For although the finer points of open market operations might have been lost on parliamentarians and the public, the cost of credit could not be concealed. Nor could the effects of cutting off industry from financing. Thus by the mid-1990s, the communist successor parties were not the only actors objecting to what they perceived as overly austere monetary policy: political groups from across the spectrum privately lobbied the central bank for concessions that would assist particular constituencies.[15]

## Hungary

Hungary's uncertainty regarding the possible outcomes of economic reform mirrors that of Poland. Hungarian central bankers at the outset of transition were novices in the same sense as their Polish counterparts (J. Johnson 2002, 11). In addition, Hungary's informal political competition between the communist regime and the opposition that ultimately resulted in new leaders rising to power gave international institutions greater access to economic reform debates than in countries where renamed communist parties persevered. Much as in Poland, there was a broad societal consensus around the desirability of rejoining Europe and emulating institutions that were integral to achieving that goal (Balassa, Berend, and Vértes 1990). Consistent with a Western orientation, Hungary based its banking legislation on the Bundesbank and granted the central bank formal independence in 1991 (Maxfield 1997, 60; Cukierman, Miller, and Neyapti 2002).

Banking-sector reform began earlier in Hungary than in Poland. Hungary joined the IMF and World Bank in 1982. By 1987, the country had embarked on transforming the socialist-era monobank into a two-tiered system with a central bank (the National Bank of Hungary, MNB) and several specialized commercial banks (Boote and Somogyi 1991, 25–28). Hungary had its own economists embedded in international academic and professional networks (Bockman and Eyal 2002). With introduction of the New Economic Mechanism in 1968, Hungary partially decentralized the economy by placing greater economic decision-making power in the hands of enterprises. Over two decades, Hungary institutionalized some features of a capitalist economy, reintroducing private property, taxation, some international openness, and selective price liberalization—albeit all on a limited scale (Boote and Somogyi 1991).

Hungary's early accession to the IMF and World Bank, the sophistication of some of its economists, and its early market reform efforts did not, however, diminish the scope of economic change initiated in 1990. Cold War–era exchanges with

Western academics and institutions did little to cultivate widespread economic expertise among reformers, parliamentarians, and the public—particularly in the technically arcane field of central banking. Despite liberalization under communism, in the early 1990s the "internal central banking culture and structure [were] better suited to a command than a market economy" (J. Johnson 2003, 309). A public uninformed about economic policy also encouraged choices based on emulation rather than on interest—not because interests would not be affected by CBI or its alternatives, but because in the early 1990s lack of experience necessarily meant that public knowledge was low. The same was true among journalists and even parliamentarians (Nagy 2003, 14–15; J. Johnson 2006). There was also little evidence in the 1990s that publics preferred low inflation for its own sake, as central bankers tend to do (Ábel, Siklos, and Székely 1998, 168).

The rise of the Hungarian Democratic Forum (MDF) and the ousting of the previous regime also boosted the influence of international institutions in Hungary. Where new governments had no previous experience in power, they sought the assistance of international actors to bolster their confidence in their own policy choices. Hungary was as open as Poland to external technical assistance, which the IMF provided intensively in the early 1990s. And the new Hungarian government, like its Polish counterpart, brought in foreign experts to mobilize political support for CBI. This included Alexandre Lamfalussy, at that time director of the Bank of International Settlements, whom one Hungarian central banker credits with persuading Hungarian lawmakers of the virtues of price stability and legal independence (J. Johnson 2002, 25–26). International institutions and credit markets further encouraged central bankers to act independent of government wishes, not because of conditionality but because central bankers appointed by both center-right and center-left governments shared external actors' convictions that domestic spending should be curtailed (Ábel, Siklos, and Székely 1998, 158–59).

## Romania

The role of uncertainty about how to restructure the central bank in Romania was compromised by the strong continuity in the regime through the transition. Thus Romania differed from Poland and Hungary in how it managed the transition and, by extension, in central bank policy. In Poland and Hungary there seemed to be an eagerness among central bankers to learn Western ways of organizing power relations between monetary and regulatory authorities and politicians. While this was also true among central bankers in Romania, the same could not be said of Romanian politicians between 1990 and 1996. The central difference was that in the transition, marginalized members of the former communist regime took power to lead the first governments. The ouster and execution of Nicolae Ceaușescu, president and general secretary of the Romanian Communist Party, were secured by marginalized members of the communist regime. So although central bank bureaucrats faced considerable uncertainty in how to conduct policy in a chaotic and evolving environment, the basic continuity in the regime meant that Romania's new leaders did not seek external advice as a way of gaining confidence in their own policies. They were also unwilling to invest the central bank with independent authority, setting the stage for conflict between central bankers and political parties that would seek to influence central bank policy.

Romania had been a member of the IMF since 1972 and therefore had the same degree of access to foreign expertise as Poland or Hungary. Romania did move to make the central bank more independent of government than it had been under state socialism. Like Poland and Hungary, Romania created a two-tier banking system, breaking the former socialist monobank into a central bank and several state-owned, specialized savings and commercial banks. However, largely in keeping with what my theoretical framework would predict, the degree of independence granted to the National Bank of Romania (NBR) was initially substantially less than that granted to the central banks in Poland or Hungary.

Bucking international trends, Romania modeled its 1991 central banking law on that of France, before that country institutionalized CBI (in 1993)—one of the last in western Europe to do so. The Romanian central bank governor and board members were to be appointed by the parliament. There were no provisions protecting them against arbitrary removal. A mandate for the central bank—centered on price stability, the value of the domestic currency, or anything else—was not established. The law also allowed the central bank to finance government operations at a level of up to 10 percent of the government's planned budget (Maxfield 1997, 61).

In Romania, the lack of political receptivity to international trends or foreign technical advice meant poor expertise persisted in ways that eventually wreaked havoc on the economy. Subject to political control, the NBR's actions in the early 1990s were also symptomatic of a collective disregard for the accrual of international legitimacy. Later in the decade, after political party turnover, the IFIs would gain access to Romanian reform debates, including those concerning monetary policy and inflation, bank regulation, and the central bank's prerogative to discontinue financing or subsidizing dependent sectors of the economy.

Until the late 1990s, however, the NBR behaved in ways largely consistent with the political role assigned to it by the 1991 legislation. The central bank continued to finance loss-making industries and recapitalize banks. Real interest rates were maintained at negative levels. Without a strong supervisory mandate or capacity, managers of the state-owned banks and other government officials were allowed to engage in self-lending or asset-stripping of their own institutions (Cernat 2006). By 1992 inflation had reached 200 percent, and by 1993 it was close to 300 percent (Dăianu 1997, 160). Although inflation receded in 1994 and 1995, it picked up again in 1996 in near perfect conformity with predictions of the dynamic inconsistency thesis for a politically dependent central bank.[16] According to one Romanian economist, the deteriorating macroeconomic situation in 1996 was "the result of major blunders of macroeconomic policy and reflect [the NBR's] subjugation to political interests in an election year" (Dăianu 1997, 160). This same economist lamented that failing to educate politicians about the need to maintain positive real interest rates in order to curb very high inflation was an obstacle to achieving stable macroeconomic outcomes (156).

The access of international institutions to Romanian economic reform debates increased after 1996 because the measure on uncertainty was strengthened. In November of that year, a coalition of opposition parties within the CDR defeated the communist successor parties. The relative inexperience of that center-right and liberal government, coupled with Romanian central bankers' own desire to advance macroeconomic stability, contributed to a greater level of conformity of economic policy with international institutional policy prescriptions. The coming into play of this new degree of policy inexperience at the same moment that political competition emerged would mark a turning point in Romania's openness to external influence.[17]

## Ukraine

The uncertainty variable was weaker in Ukraine than elsewhere. When it declared independence from the Soviet Union and embarked on transition, Ukraine had measures in place similar to those of Romania, except that price liberalization was more limited in 1992 when Ukrainian transition began and fuller liberalization was not achieved until 1995 (also see chapter 3). Those who would ultimately run the country's economic institutions in an environment without price controls lacked expertise, leaving them open to external advice. But the continuity in leadership from the communist period limited international institutional access to Ukrainian reform policy.

As in Romania, there was significant overlap in leadership between the communist and postcommunist periods, which limited the effects of uncertainty. During the attempted Soviet coup against Mikhail Gorbachev in August 1991, the chairman of the Ukrainian parliament (the Verkhovna Rada), Leonid Kravchuk, stood silently by to see how the situation would resolve before taking a position. Kravchuk's ambivalence sparked fury from the substantial (even if short-lived in its mass form) Ukrainian Popular Rukh movement. In response, and in advance of Ukraine's presidential elections in December 1991, Kravchuk left the Communist Party. He won the election with 62 percent of the vote, partly owing to the absence of other viable, nationally recognized candidates.

Ukraine undertook partial price liberalization in January 1992, following Russia's lead. This was the boldest part of the economic reform program, however, as Ukraine did not simultaneously implement a macroeconomic stabilization plan or a privatization scheme. A presidential-governmental-parliamentary consensus was in place in 1992 to pursue only a minimalist economic reform agenda, which was not surprising given the continuity in all three bodies with the communist regime and the still dominant parliamentary position of communists or former communists who had adopted a "socialist" moniker. The consensus did not imply harmonious relations among the governing bodies, however. Courting the nationalists, President Kravchuk initially took an aggressive stance toward Moscow. He lacked solid support in the parliament, however, and would probably have been prevented from instituting a more radical reform program even had he wanted to. Its membership in the IMF (beginning in September 1992) notwithstanding, Ukraine's manifest lack of receptivity to international institutions precluded any cooperation with the IMF until 1994.

One way to characterize the difference between Ukraine, Poland, and Hungary is that these societies had different views about where authority appropriately lies. For Poland and Hungary, it was natural in the first reform phase to turn to the IMF and World Bank for technical assistance. And when these institutions made the case that parliaments, governments, executives, and industry should invest the central bank with power, Poland and Hungary were ready to comply, albeit with conflict after the fact. In Ukraine, however, authority more naturally lies with agriculture, industry, arms manufacturers, and coal. The idea that the exigencies of production should be subordinated to price stability did not make sense to Ukrainian political leaders, just as it would not have made sense to the Ukrainian public. Given the lack of uncertainty in the political class, stemming from the absence of political demobilization in the transition, it was difficult for the IMF and World Bank to empower Ukrainian central bankers. So "there was a strong concern expressed by many of [Ukraine's] advisors that through a lack of competent staff and a very disorganized administrative structure, the National Bank would be incapable of exercising legitimate central bank authority over commercial banks, national and commercial foreign exchange operations and monetary policy" (Sochan 1996, 6).

Indeed, Ukraine's central bank, under the guidance of Ukrainian politicians and legislators, initially contravened several international norms. The first central bank law of 1991 did not so much deny the National Bank of Ukraine (NBU) statutory independence as leave key features of the bank's relationship to other government bodies underspecified (Cukierman, Miller, and Neyapti 2002, 258). According to at least one index, therefore, Ukraine's 1991 legislation established a slightly greater degree of independence than that which existed in Romania (242). But at the same time, the powers and obligations of the central bank seemed to contradict one another. Although the NBU was prohibited from financing government operations, for example, it was obliged to service government debt (Maxfield 1997, 58). And a clear limit on CBI in the early 1990s was the absence of any provision against arbitrary dismissal of the central bank governor. Other areas of ambiguity included how monetary policy would be formulated, the terms of central bank servicing of government debt, and whether there would be limits on lending (Cukierman, Miller, and Neyapti 2002, 258) (see table 2.2).

The postcommunist leadership in Ukraine, carried over from the previous regime, did not seek the advice of international institutions to gain confidence in its policy choices. The ambiguity in banking law essentially allowed Ukraine to follow its own path, unconstrained by the international normative context. The "Ukrainian way" consisted of circumventing technical prohibitions against printing rubles in 1992 and issuing what was meant to be a temporary currency in the form of rationing coupons (*karbovantsi*). These quickly gained the status of legal tender, however. In addition, the central bank extended credits to enterprises. In response to Russian credits granted to help Ukraine pay for Russian goods during the growing trade deficit, the central bank pumped still more rubles into the economy. In the fall of 1992, Ukraine left the ruble zone, at which time the NBU began printing *karbovantsi* in earnest, spurring the highest levels of inflation in 1993 and 1994 (10,000% annually) of any state in the former Soviet bloc (J. Johnson 2000; Stone 2002).[18]

As in Romania, but in contrast to Poland and Hungary, the continuity of political actors from the communist period limited the initial influence of international institutions over Ukraine's economic policy, and particularly over the conduct of the central bank. As the following section shows, low-quality political competition and therefore limited concern with Ukraine's standing in relation to international organizations reinforced the primacy of domestic forces in producing outcomes. Of course, as in the other countries considered here, central banking bureaucrats were operating in a partially liberalized environment (in terms of prices) for the first time, making them potentially susceptible to expert advice. But without additional political conditions—the uncertainty of the ruling political class and the existence of political competition among them—newly trained technocrats with a price stability agenda had little authority. Ukraine, like Romania, therefore illustrates the kinds of central bank policies that can emerge in the absence of international reference points for domestic policymaking.

## INTERNATIONAL INSTITUTIONAL STATUS AND POLITICAL COMPETITION (H2)
### Poland

Understanding the models that actors seek to emulate is key to knowing which policies they will pursue. Thus the perceived elevated status of international institutions and the desire for social recognition from them are potentially powerful drivers of liberalizing reforms. Intuitively, one would expect Poland to be susceptible to Western institutions because the country's opposition to communism was democratic, Catholic, and naturally anti-Soviet. As elsewhere in this study, in the absence of an easy way to measure a country's or a sector's desire for external social recognition, I use the quality of political competition as a proxy. Political competition was robust in Poland when governing coalitions underwent major shifts—in 1989, 1993, 1997, 2001, and 2005.

High-quality political competition and the desire for external social recognition help explain why Poland more strongly embraced liberal economic principles than, for example, the expansion of workers' rights—an organizing principle of the Solidarity movement. Although some scholars have argued that the 1993 return to power of the communist successor parties in Poland was not due to the public's rejection of shock therapy and economic reform per se (Ekiert and Kubik 1999), voters did express concern that the first wave of reformers had betrayed Solidarity's earlier goals (Powers and Cox 1997; Orenstein 2001). Indeed, by the second half of the 1990s, Solidarity trade unionists sided with the nationalist right wing in Poland because they felt that the socially more progressive intellectuals who had led the movement in the 1980s had abandoned the working class in favor of economic liberalism (Ost 2005).

Political competition introduces an adaptation dynamic in which threats of opprobrium or promises of approbation from external actors encourage political parties to either distinguish themselves from or mimic one another. In CEE, where communist successor parties had to win back legitimacy because of their associations with hated regimes, maintaining constructive relations with Western organizations was an electorally effective way of competing. In both Poland and Hungary, the communist successor parties were particularly malleable with respect to international institutional policy prescriptions, according to this logic of distinguishing or mimicking. Thus, when the communist successor Polish Democratic Left Alliance (SLD) began agitating for more political control over the central bank and its regulatory functions in 1994, international institutions successfully discouraged politicizing legislation by playing on the SLD's sensitivity to accusations about its central-planning proclivities.

## Hungary

With Hungary having the same measure on political competition as Poland, international institutions had similar access to Hungarian economic reform debates by virtue of the status variable. Indeed, there is strong evidence that Hungarian political parties emulated or deviated from one another in part based on how international institutions responded to the previous government's initiatives. Where a previous administration had ruptured relations with international institutions, the subsequent government pursued policies aimed at repairing those relations, elevating the country's international standing and, in the process, improving the political party's status, both domestically and internationally.

Hungary saw coalitional shifts in the elections of 1990, 1994, 1998, and 2002. In each instance, a new political grouping took power. In 1990 the MDF ousted the communists, while in 1994 the communist successor Hungarian Socialist Party (MSzP) prevailed, replacing the first opposition government. In 1998 the center-right Fidesz-MPP (Fidesz–Hungarian Civic Party) led the government, and in 2002 the socialists again returned to power. Thus, as in Poland, between each election the political parties were critical of one another, in part based on how their policies either advanced or damaged the country's status vis-à-vis international institutions.

There is evidence with respect to both monetary policy and CBI and bank privatization (see chapter 3) that the MSzP, which returned to power in 1994, acted in greater conformity with international institutional preferences than did the MDF that had led the government from 1990 to 1994 (Hanley, King, and Tóth János 2002). Just as the MSzP sought to improve bilateral relations with Hungary's neighbors and alleviate tensions over minority rights in response to the MDF's more provocative policies (see chapter 5), so the socialists were more receptive to international economic trends. In both foreign policy and economic reform, the MSzP, in attempts to disassociate itself from the discredited state-socialist regime, embraced the policy prescriptions of international institutions—in some instances more fully than did the democratic opposition that had initially come to power.

One example of the MSzP using international standards to elevate its own status was its apolitical approach to appointments at the central bank and attempts to reform fiscal policy in response to the bank's admonitions. Although Hungary, like Poland, had institutionalized a high degree of CBI early in the transition, central bankers and politicians were in conflict from the beginning. For example, the MDF elected not to reinstate MNB Governor György Surányi with the implementation of the new central bank law, effective from December 1, 1991. The MDF replaced Surányi for political reasons, despite his many achievements, including consolidation of the country's hard currency reserves, de facto convertibility of the Hungarian forint, and winning the respect of IFIs and central bankers the world over.

In September 1991 Surányi had signed the "Democratic Charter," a document, supported by critics from across the political spectrum, that expressed concern with what its authors believed were authoritarian tendencies in the new government. Surányi's insistence on central bank independence and price stability, as well as his history with the World Bank, where he had worked for two years, actually encouraged the MSzP to reappoint him as central bank governor in 1995.[19] His closer association with economic liberals from the opposition demonstrates that international standards, rather than political affinities, take on greater significance where political competition revolves in part around issues of international standing. The MSzP in turn won the IMF's praise for its management of macroeconomic policy through the 1990s.[20]

## Romania

As noted earlier, the first major difference between Romania and both Poland and Hungary was Romania's lower receptivity to IFIs due to the absence of party turnover at the time of transition. The relative certainty of Romanian politicians, having governed continuously through the transition, did not provide external actors with access to Romanian reform debates until late 1996, when the Party of Social Democracy of Romania (PDSR) was replaced by a government led by the opposition CDR. From that point on, Romania experienced regular political turnover, with the socialists returning to power in 2000 and the opposition (led by the center-right Justice and Truth Alliance) taking control of both the presidency and the government in December 2004.

Greater political competition strengthened the country's embrace of international economic norms after 1997, but not because new parties in power were an unmitigated force for liberalism. There were Western-oriented reformers among them, and their economists brought both a new intellectual openness to the financial institutions and greater economic expertise. But as I show in later chapters, even after the 1996 elections decidedly nondemocratic practices endured. More than a few reforms were enacted by presidential decree, the government politicized segments of the bureaucracy (including the Ministry of Defense), and corruption scandals proliferated.

Nevertheless, a distinguishing feature of the new government was its headlong rush to revive relations with international actors. Negotiations with the IMF began in January 1997, just a month after the new government was sworn in. The IMF's head, Michel Camdessus, visited Bucharest even earlier, in December, to set the stage for a new relationship with the non-communist-affiliated government. In contrast to the prior ruling party, which had allowed a previous agreement with the IMF to founder within months, bankers and analysts alike remarked that the new government seemed willing to take advice, was committed to reform, and looked determined to reach agreement with the IMF.[21]

That advice included efforts to fight inflation on multiple fronts. The central bank governor, Mugur Isărescu, expressed relief that the CDR seemed ready to undertake reform that would allow deepening debt instruments, pursuing tighter monetary policy, and improving banking supervision. The government complemented these central bank measures by increasing fuel and public utility prices, signaling other actors in the economy to do the same, and reducing support to industry and agriculture.[22] Although some of these measures were expected to boost inflation in the short term, the longer-term intention, in connection with currency devaluation, was to reduce consumption, especially of imports, and to encourage foreign investment and exports. The CDR, in compliance with World Bank advice, even agreed to put off welfare provisions it had promised during the campaign—including increases in child and pension benefits.[23]

The CDR's willingness to embrace IFI advice was not without cost. The stabilization program led to economic contraction; high interest rates led to a decline in output, down 7 percent in 1997 and 4 percent in 1998.[24] While the central bank stayed the reform course, the government ultimately gave way, pursuing fiscal policy that the IMF judged too directly at odds with monetary austerity for the central bank to control inflation on its own. Structural reform, including privatization sought by the IMF and World Bank, was put on hold.

Yet Romanian central bank objectives were aligned with IMF, World Bank, and EU policy prescriptions beginning in 1997, in keeping with the theory that the desire for social recognition and the uncertainty of actors maximize international institutional influence over policy debates in transition states. Those low-inflation objectives were initially supported by a new government willing to restrain fiscal policy and dampen domestic demand. The governing inexperience of the CDR led its leaders to seek certainty in the advice of external policy experts. At the same time, the new dynamic of political competition heightened the salience of Romania's international standing. Proof of the power of international institutional status and the extent to which political competition leads to political party mimicking is provided by the communist successor party, the PDSR. Rather than return to prior practices of pressuring the central bank to do the government's bidding, the PDSR (by then renamed the Social Democratic Party, PSD), more fully institutionalized CBI in 2004.

## Ukraine

Ukraine did have political competition beginning in 1994, but its quality was compromised because the alternatives mostly stemmed from the former communist regime. Compared with Romania after 1997, Ukraine's political system was still relatively (though not entirely) immune to international opinion in the second half of the 1990s. That immunity was sustained in Ukraine's third set of political contests of the decade in 1998 and 1999, when the incumbents, including communist successor parties and Kuchma, won control of the parliament and the presidency.

Two conditions limited the status of international institution. First, both presidential contenders in 1994, Kravchuk and Kuchma, had been part of the communist apparatus from the previous regime. Second, the ongoing weakness and fragmentation of the noncommunist opposition limited diversity across the political spectrum. For example, the Rukh opposition movement won 20 of 338 parliamentary seats in 1994 and 46 seats of 450 in 1998. Overall, noncommunist nationalist parties attracted 20 to 30 percent of the vote through the 1990s, but given stark differences in nationalist programs, the bloc was never a serious challenge to those who inherited the communist mantle (Abdelal 2001, 115).

There was nevertheless a real choice between Kravchuk and Kuchma in the presidential race of 1994.[25] Thus, if my theory is correct, the rise of a challenger in the form of Kuchma should have prevented Kravchuk from focusing exclusively on domestic conditions to the exclusion of international opinion. And indeed, the 1994 presidential race was politicized along both economic and foreign policy lines (Abdelal 2001, 120). Whereas Kravchuk continued to woo nationalists by at least talking about economic independence (even if his efforts to achieve that independence had already failed), Kuchma was calling for the rebuilding of economic and political ties with Russia. This basic disagreement notwithstanding, both candidates simultaneously supported, at least rhetorically, European integration and Western outreach. It is no coincidence that Ukraine signed the NATO Partnership for Peace and established its first agreement with the IMF in the election year. The hypothesis on the connection between political competition and the elevated status of international institutions receives some confirmation in the Ukrainian case.

But elevated status for external actors on account of political competition was not limited to Western organizations, as it was in Poland, Hungary, and Romania. Although political competition coincided with greater levels of attention to Ukraine's standing with NATO, the European Union, and the Bretton Woods institutions, Russia was an additional, competing authority. With Ukraine's weak measure on the uncertainty of the political class and ambiguous measures on the country's desire for social recognition from international institutions due to low-quality political competition, it would prove difficult for the IMF or World Bank to win compliance from Ukraine.

## CREDIBILITY OF POLICIES AND CONSENSUS (H3)

Central bank independence as a means of ensuring the prominence of price stability among competing policy goals enjoyed the strongest consensus of any issue examined in this book. Not only did western European states strongly endorse the idea, but those that had joined EMU in 1999 were also normatively consistent insofar as each had given up control over monetary policy—not just to a state institution, but to a supranational one. And even in those EU states that had opted out of EMU in the 1990s, CBI was increasingly the norm—particularly after the United Kingdom made its own central bank independent in 1997 (Gamble and Kelly 2002). There was also consistency across international institutions—the IMF, the World Bank, USAID, and the European Union (once it became involved in postcommunist policy debates) all supported the same objectives.

Unlike defense planning, in which different postcommunist countries were affected differently by the credibility of Western security guarantees, there was little such variation in central banking. But even though the credibility of the policy in question cannot account for substantial variation across postcommunist Europe, credibility is nevertheless important to explain why proponents of CBI prevailed when and where they did. Normative consistency potentially limits target actors' space for disagreeing with a particular prescription if international institutions or states can point to their own consistent use of the policy. Consensus is powerful in a slightly different way—it has the effect of conveying to states in transition which groups do and do not have legitimate claims in distributional struggles. Importantly, external supporters of CBI did not view their own advocacy as political and thereby reinforced the message that what they were prescribing was technical instead.[26] Despite the variation, the credibility hypothesis receives support from the fact that nearly *every* postcommunist country increased its central bank's independence in the transition. Even where CBI remained relatively weak (as in Ukraine), formal measures rivaled or exceeded the independence of OECD central banks in the 1980s (see table 2.1).

One area of inconsistency and thus weakened credibility, however, concerned the nature of banking supervision. While some industrialized states assign supervision to the central bank, others have a separate supervisory body. It is therefore not surprising that whether to leave supervision under central bank jurisdiction or to remove it was one of the controversies that emerged in later debates on the structure and function of central banks in postcommunist Europe. In general, however, by the 1990s (and in contrast to even a decade earlier) CBI had become "a stamp of economic respectability" (Cukierman, Miller, and Neyapti 2002, 245).

## TRANSNATIONAL COALITIONS AND OUTCOMES
### *Poland*

In September 1993, the parliamentary elections in Poland marked the end of the first Solidarity era. Two reformed communist successor blocs, the Democratic Left Alliance and the Polish Peasant Party (PSL), formed a governing coalition. Both groups had direct links to the communist regime: the SLD stemmed from the SdRP (Social Democracy of the Republic of Poland), which was in turn the direct successor of the PUWP, the Polish United Workers' Party (Poland's communist party). The peasant party had been the communist party's partner in power. But there was also a great deal more continuity between the ex-communists' and Solidarity's economic reforms than might have been expected from the ex-communists' campaign rhetoric that had been sharply critical of shock therapy. While some scholars (e.g., Stone 2002, 111) have attributed the continuity in liberal economic policy to a combination of "good sense" and a redefinition of domestic interests, a more detailed analysis shows that the new center-left government faced significant international pressures to stay the liberalizing course (also see chapter 3 on bank privatization).

The challenge to CBI began with the appointment of Grzegorz Kołodko to deputy prime minister and minister of finance in early 1994. By that time the distributional consequences of CBI were becoming apparent. Although Kołodko was technically not a member of the SLD, he was among the vocal critics of the Solidarity reforms. The new minister of finance had insisted at several points that CBI should be protected (Kołodko 2000b, 35–36), but he also took exception to many of the NBP's policies under Gronkiewicz-Waltz. Moreover, in 1995 his coalition would sponsor legislation to undermine central bank authority. Although the exact provenance of the legislation was never determined, it was widely believed that Kołodko was crucial to the initiative's content.[27]

Kołodko leveled several criticisms against the central bank regarding monetary policy and bank supervision, starting in 1994. Pointing out that a central bank president's responsibilities "are not confined to those of God and History" but also include "society and the national economy," he first took aim at what he called "excessively restrictive monetary policy." Among the adjustments he called for were a reduction in interest rates in connection with a more gradual devaluation of the zloty and a reassessment of lending rates in accordance with anticipated rather than past inflation. Both adjustments would have reduced the cost of credit. Kołodko also claimed that because lending rates were too high, the central bank bore substantial responsibility for dissatisfaction with government spending, a lack of state resources, and the budget deficit, given the "enormous" costs of servicing the domestic debt. Finally, he called for the removal of supervision from the central bank, citing among other reasons Gronkiewicz-Waltz's own support for separation in her doctoral research![28]

Disagreements between the Ministry of Finance (MoF) and the NBP intensified in early 1995. Not only did Kołodko and his colleagues object to Gronkiewicz-Waltz's restrictive monetary policy, but they resented never being consulted in advance of important policy shifts. Whereas Kołodko believed that lending rates should be lowered in connection with slowing devaluation, the central bank raised bank refinancing rates to 35 percent, arguing that higher rates would encourage savings and sustainable, noninflationary growth. Kołodko countered that restrictive central bank policies were instead eliciting speculative capital inflows that themselves had inflationary effects. Moreover, the cost of financing the budget deficit would continue to rise. To make his point that rates were too high, Kołodko arranged a cash loan from a Paris branch of a Polish bank to help pay government bills.[29] Gronkiewicz-Waltz did nothing to enhance her reputation with the government when she decided, against the advice of the NBP's external advisors, to run for the Polish presidency in the summer of 1995.[30]

In keeping with Kołodko's long-standing criticisms of the NBP and of Gronkiewicz-Waltz in particular, the SLD-PSL coalition submitted two pieces of legislation—one on the NBP itself, the other on banking supervision—in August 1995. The NBP bill sought to reduce the central bank president's power by creating an "NBP council" subject to political control. The government and Sejm (parliament) would each appoint three members, and the Union of Polish banks would be entitled to appoint two. The ninth member of the council, the NBP president, would be appointed by the Sejm in consultation with the prime minister and would essentially be one among equals in deciding issues of money supply, credit policy, and exchange rates. All members would serve six-year terms. The bill would also have enabled the central bank to finance up to 5 percent of the state budget.[31] Not only did the bill dramatically undermine the central bank governor's power, but it also made appointments subject to government rather than executive control.

The legislation on banking supervision proposed a separate agency more closely linked to the MoF—not least by allowing the prime minister, in consultation with the NBP president, to appoint its head. The SLD-PSL coalition defended this proposal in part by arguing that the NBP should not supervise banks whose recapitalization it was overseeing. Gronkiewicz-Waltz responded that the situation would not be improved by increasing MoF authority, since most of Poland's banks had yet to be privatized and were in large measure owned by the MoF.[32] Her case was not helped by a critical government report, released in 1995, arguing that there was a conflict of interest in the NBP's recapitalization of the same banks it was charged with monitoring.[33]

The SLD-PSL legislation was ultimately defeated by a three-pronged attack from a transnational coalition of international and domestic actors. First, central banking bureaucrats, whose lack of experience before the transition had been reversed by IFI technical training, were the first to respond to IMF, World Bank, and USAID concerns. Second, international institutions contributed to legislation providing a clear alternative to the SLD-PSL proposal and helped prepare CBI proponents for their encounters with the Sejm. Third, international institutions unequivocally weighed in on the side of those defending CBI—both in written statements and in public appearances. It was ultimately the transnational coalition's strong convictions, coupled with the SLD-PSL's fears of international opprobrium, that ensured the rejection of the politicizing legislation.

On learning of the SLD-PSL initiative, Poland's foreign economic advisors mobilized their domestic partners. USAID officials called on the World Bank and IMF to assist their Polish allies to defeat the legislation.[34] By 1995, none of these organizations had conditionality agreements pending with Poland. And while Polish politicians debated the merits of the competing proposals with reference to the Maastricht criteria, Polish accession to the European Union was not premised on meeting the criteria prior to membership. In fact, EU representatives had repeatedly stressed that candidate countries should first and foremost focus on fulfilling the Copenhagen criteria (democratic stability, the rule of law, human rights, respect for and protection of minorities, and a functioning, competitive economy) (Wallace and Mayhew 2001, 6). Thus the transnational coalition in favor of CBI had to rely on argumentation and legitimacy rather than incentives to make its case.

NBP Governor Gronkiewicz-Waltz repeatedly stressed in media interviews that Kołodko's proposals would threaten Poland's standing abroad. In what became a battle over the credibility of the CBI consensus, she emphasized that not only was the NBP council inconsistent with how most OECD countries designed their central banks, but that it violated the Maastricht criteria.[35] Leszek Balcerowicz, chairman of the Freedom Union (Unia Wolności, UW), supported her position and further argued that CBI and price stability should be written into the Polish Constitution. And in fact, in 1996, the UW would submit alternative legislation reinforcing CBI that had been written with the assistance of external advisors.[36]

Poland's foreign advisors also helped prepare their allies for the political struggle before parliament and the public. Polish officials point to the particularly crucial role played by World Bank consultant Robert L. Clarke, who was asked to advise Poland in the early 1990s. A trusted advisor to Ewa Śleszyńska-Charewicz (NBP's head of supervision), Clarke provided the commentary, language, and arguments for the NBP to defend itself.[37] He told NBP officials what he believed they were risking if they allowed monetary policy to be politicized and supervisory functions to be removed from the central bank. NBP officials then deployed these arguments to persuade their domestic critics. USAID prepared NBP officials (including the governor) to convey competence and professionalism in making pro-CBI arguments before appearances in the Sejm.[38]

The IMF and European Union also left little doubt about whose side they were on. An IMF report stated that the SLD-PSL legislation was "worrisome," that the central bank's independence should be strengthened, and that the creation of a separate agency for banking supervision should be strongly resisted (Ugolini 1996, 40). Although both this report and a USAID official acknowledged that supervisory functions were assigned to central banks in some industrialized countries and not in others, the USAID official maintained that postcommunist states were more volatile. Appealing to international consensus, IFI officials argued that institutionalizing supervision separately "goes against the international trend toward independent supervision and close cooperation with monetary authorities."[39]

The European Union also weighed in on the side of CBI more publicly. At a 1996 press conference at the NBP, the president of the European Monetary Institute, Alexandre Lamfalussy, announced that Poland was "a credible partner for membership of the European Union and the Monetary Union." But he emphasized, with NBP President Gronkiewicz-Waltz standing at his side, that striving for lower inflation and preserving CBI were important for Poland's quest to join.[40] Poland's membership of the European Union was still not explicitly tied to the structure of its central bank institutions. However, this event clearly delegitimized SLD-PSL's claims that its legislation was more consistent with EU norms than that of Balcerowicz. Lamfalussy conferred credibility on NBP's governor, strengthening her position in relation to the MoF and the Sejm: no longer could they credibly claim that the European Union would be just as willing to support their plans as not.[41]

After more than a year of wrangling, the SLD-PSL proposals were "quietly shelved" in 1997.[42] The rival legislation proposed by Balcerowicz's UW prevailed.[43] Instead of an NBP council appointed by the government, Sejm, and Union of Polish Banks, the legislation created the Monetary Policy Council to be staffed by experts appointed by the Polish president, the Senate, and the Sejm. The Polish president, not the prime minister, would select the central bank president, who, with Sejm approval, would chair the Monetary Policy Council. The legislation also created the Commission on Banking Supervision, organizationally autonomous but still housed within the NBP.[44] In the same year, the Sejm institutionalized some features of CBI in the 1997 Constitution, including the Polish president's role in selecting the NBP head and the banning of government borrowing from the central bank.[45] Although the UW's legislation allowed the SLD and PSL to save face by diffusing the bank president's powers, international observers were pleased because there were no meaningful behavioral changes and CBI had been reinforced.[46] In fact, on all indices, Polish CBI was greater in the wake of the UW legislation and the 1997 Constitution than before (Cukierman, Miller, and Neyapti 2002, 242) (see table 2.2).

Three additional constitutive effects show how the combination of electoral competition and the pressures of winning international legitimacy contribute to political party mimicry. First, the legislative outcome on CBI is all the more remarkable for the fact that the SLD-PSL reversal took place when the coalition enjoyed an overwhelming majority in the Sejm. Having together won close to 36 percent of the vote in 1993, the SLD and PSL parties controlled nearly 66 percent of Sejm seats (Krok-Paszkowska 2000, 81). Second, after SLD-affiliated Aleksander Kwaśniewski was elected president of Poland in 1995, he sided with the NBP and its internationalist orientation, not with Kołodko. This might seem surprising because as the Communist Party's minister for culture and youth and former chairman of the SLD, Kwaśniewski might have been expected to identify with SLD economic goals. But the SLD leadership became leery of appearing too far left for both its domestic and its international constituencies.[47] Finally, after an eighteen-month campaign against the NBP in an effort to win lower interest rates, Kołodko was replaced by Marek Belka at the MoF. Thus the confrontation over CBI changed the goals of the SLD, a major political force in Poland at the time.

Close cooperation between international institutions and the first wave of Polish economic reformers was facilitated by the inexperience of the central banking bureaucracy, the country's desire to return to Europe, and the credibility of CBI. Having institutionalized features of CBI and having mobilized central bank and liberal political leaders around its preservation, communist successor parties found it difficult to oppose the principles of price stability and independent regulation. Because international institutions conferred legitimacy on only one side of the debate, not only did the SLD-PSL coalition fail to pass its own legislation, but it ended up emulating the Solidarity reformers whose policies the two parties had long criticized.

The presence of IFI loans, as well as the ongoing negotiations from 1990 to 1993 with the London and Paris clubs of creditors, raises the question of how important the social context was in the light of material incentives for Polish reformers to comply. Although conditionality in this case coincides with early compliance, four observations cast doubt on the claim that Poland was institutionalizing price stability and regulatory capacities in the early 1990s because the country was a financial hostage. First, the reforms began before conditionality was in place. Second, all of the social conditions that, according to my theory, empower conditionality were present. The uncertainty of domestic actors, their desire for social recognition from high-status international institutions, and the credibility of CBI meant that the objectives of the first wave of reformers and the IFIs were aligned. Third, even IMF officials then working with Poland on macroeconomic stabilization acknowledged that Poland's reformers needed leverage vis-à-vis the Sejm, not IMF funds (Myant 1993; Stone 2002, 99). Finally and most importantly, the *absence* of conditionality by the mid-1990s did not prevent the pro-CBI coalition from defeating threats to price stability and independent regulation.

Banking supervision would not remain the exclusive domain of NBP and its president and staff, however. In 2006, under the leadership of the Law and Justice Party (PiS) and in consultation with the ECB, Poland adopted a law that transferred supervision to a new Financial Supervision Commission, whose head would be appointed by the president of the Council of Ministers. Although this did not contradict the terms of the treaty establishing the European Community (the Treaty of Rome) or the Statute of the European System of Central Banks (ESCB), other features of Polish law did, and would have to be changed in advance of Euro membership.[48] These included the lack of an explicit prohibition against the NBP taking advice or instruction from outside the bank and a requirement that the NBP president should send monetary policy guidelines to the MoF and the Council of Ministers (European Central Bank 2006, 228).

## Hungary

Hungary's trajectory mirrored Poland's, confirming the importance of the uncertainty of actors, their perceived status in relation to international institutions, and the credibility of the policies in question. Hungary institutionalized major features of CBI in 1991, one year after Poland. Additional legislation in 1992 and 1994 further clarified the division of powers between the central bank and other state actors—all under the auspices of the country's first postcommunist reformers. Hungary's 1991 legislation marked a milestone by giving the MNB autonomy on a par with Western central banks. It increased the bank's independence and power by lengthening the term of the president, charging the bank with responsibility for defending the currency's domestic and international value, limiting central bank funding to 3 percent of anticipated government revenue, and mandating the bank to warn the public and parliament when economic policy endangered macroeconomic stability.[49]

In 2000 and 2001, under the Fidesz-MPP–led government, Hungary passed a series of laws to further bolster CBI—this time to achieve compliance with the EMU-related *acquis*. The December 2000 law concerned the prohibition of direct public sector financing by the central bank. Although Hungary had not drawn on this facility since 1995, the legislation formalized what had become common practice.[50] The 2001 law prioritized price stability, reaffirmed the independence of the members of the MNB's governing bodies (the Monetary Council and the Board of Directors), and further depoliticized the conditions of their dismissal. The law also prohibited the public sector from enjoying privileged access to financial institutions, by no longer allowing preferred status for Hungarian government securities in the portfolios of public financial institutions.[51]

By the end of the 1990s, but before Hungary's alignment with EU standards, there were two central differences between CBI in Hungary and in Poland. First, Hungary's Monetary Council had always been subject to more political control, with half of its appointments under government prerogative. Second, the MNB had been legally allowed to finance government operations, whereas the NBP was prohibited from doing so after 1997.[52] Despite these differences, according to at least one study, Hungary's central bank behaved more independently than Poland's in the first half of the 1990s (Ábel, Siklos, and Székely 1998, 158, 165). Moreover, the two countries shared an unusual provision that, according to Maxfield (1997, 61), is even more important than price stability in conferring power on the central bank: the authority to take part in government budget formulation. Central bank power over budget policy potentially functions as another guard against inflation, because central bankers will probably use their authority to rein in government spending. Based on these measures, I conclude that similar levels of uncertainty, status, and credibility resulted in similar central bank outcomes in Poland and Hungary.

If Poland and Hungary are similar in their early institutionalization of CBI and a strong commitment to price stability in ways that clearly reflected the advice and preferences of international institutions, they are also similar in their experience of periodic conflict over exactly the same issues. Both Hungary and Poland saw significant tensions around central bank policy in the early 2000s. Whereas in Poland such conflicts were resolved without legal changes until 2006, Hungarian politicians eventually succeeded in expanding the Monetary Council by four members, all of whom would be appointed by the government. The first appointees began their tenure in March 2005. Not long after, in October 2005, Polish voters brought the right-leaning PiS to power, which was also calling on the central bank to prioritize economic growth, not just price stability, in its policy formulation. PiS was unstinting in its criticism of then-governor of the bank Leszek Balcerowicz and again acted to remove supervision from the NBP.

That these tensions and legislative changes in Hungary and Poland were taking place after EU accession raises the question of whether it was EU membership all along that provided the incentive to stay the course of CBI and price stability.

There is no doubt that the appeal of membership altered the policies of transition states in many important ways. However, the Hungarian changes did not challenge the MNB's core competencies, price stability, or any of the legislative efforts that, in their totality, signaled the country's willingness to embrace international norms defending CBI against competing policy goals. Although ECB officials might have preferred that Hungary not expand its Monetary Council, there is nothing in the *acquis* that prevents governments from making such appointments, as Romania's legislation (and EU acceptance of it) shows.[53]

As was the case with Poland, however, even if Hungary's central bank was independent enough to warrant admission to the European Union in 2004, further changes would be required to win Euro membership. In particular, the ECB expressed concern about a Hungarian law that allowed the minister of justice to review the MNB's draft legal acts. The ECB interpreted the minister of justice's authority over the national bank to be a violation of Article 108 of the Treaty of Rome, which sets out the principle of central bank independence. The ECB also requested that Hungary harmonize its law on the conditions under which MNB officials could be dismissed with Article 14.2 of the ESCB Statute (European Central Bank 2006, 222).

## Romania

Romania registered later and weaker compliance with CBI and price stability than did Poland and Hungary, because until the late 1990s the country's leaders cared little about their international standing. This changed with the rise of the CDR, which pursued macroeconomic stabilization starting in 1997 and coordinated fiscal and monetary policy to curb long-term inflationary pressures. Under the CDR-led government, Romania also passed legislation in 1998 specifying price stability as a primary goal of the central bank and limiting, but not eliminating, central bank financing of government operations. So although at this point there was evidence of a new CBI consensus forming among central bankers and politicians, the NBR was still statutorily and behaviorally less independent than either the Polish or Hungarian central banks.[54]

The year 2004 marked an even greater watershed for Romanian CBI. In June, under the leadership of the former communists, the PSD, the Chamber of Deputies passed legislation that removed provisions allowing central bank financing of the public sector. It barred the NBR from buying government bonds on the primary market, removed any obligation of the central bank to issue government securities, and freed the bank from any duty to lend to the government's deposit insurance scheme. Additional legislation again bolstered CBI by specifying that neither staff nor managers of the NBR should "seek or take instructions from public authorities or from any other institution or authority."[55] The commitment to price stability was also reiterated.

Despite the changes to banking laws in 2004 (and earlier), Romania was still not in perfect compliance with EMU-related *acquis*, even as the country was striving for EU membership by 2007. Both the 2004 and 2005 EC Regular Reports on Romania's progress toward accession point out that further legal alignment would be required. In particular, the European Union was seeking stronger safeguards against central bank "lending of last resort" to the government and capital market legislation that would "prohibit privileged access of the public sector to financial institutions."[56] The European Union also wanted to ensure that after Romania's accession, the governor of the NBR could be dismissed from his or her post only by referral to the European Court of Justice.[57]

Because both Poland and Hungary institutionalized central tenets of CBI long before the European Union insisted on compliance with its Maastricht criteria or the *acquis* (Anderson, Berglöf, and Mizsei 1996, 31), forces apart from EU conditionality were clearly at work in fomenting a desire for CBI in Poland and Hungary. In the Romanian case, all of the conditions that contributed to the institutionalization of CBI appeared much later. The uncertainty of political actors and the perceived elevated status of international institutions by virtue of political competition did not register their first effects until 1997. And while economic policy reflecting a preference for price stability started then and continued over the medium term, not until 2004 did parliament take legislative action to formally institutionalize CBI.

## Ukraine

The case of Ukraine shows the extent to which the absence of a social context defined by uncertainty and perceptions of status prevents international institutions from cultivating domestic actors' support of international standards and hinders compliance with IFI conditionality. Ukraine's lack of concern with its "standing" in Western opinion translated into repeated abrogations of IMF agreements, willful concealment of information that would bear on the formulation of subsequent agreements, and continuing use of the central bank as a political instrument through the 1990s. Not only did central banking laws not reflect the emerging international consensus favoring the principles of price stability and CBI in the first decade of transition (see table 2.2), but politicians rejected such principles until the early 2000s—and even then, politicians continued to expect extensive cooperation between the NBU and the government on economic goals.[58] Notably, Ukraine persisted in its lack of compliance despite the significant financial rewards at stake.

The communist-era political class in Ukraine was able to retain power, making it relatively impervious to international opinion. Central banking bureaucrats in a liberalized price environment, on the other hand, would be expected to show greater susceptibility. This was indeed the case, as demonstrated by the attempted changes by Viktor Yushchenko, appointed chairman of the NBU in 1993. In an effort to control the money supply, he increased reserve ratios and began a policy of distributing credits on a nonpolitical basis. Simultaneously, however, the parliament was passing budgets projecting deficits that the central bank would be obliged to service, while the Council of Ministers (a government body) presided over the allocation of credit to enterprises in need. Obligations to follow through on state purchases, a faltering agricultural sector, and both domestic and international inter-enterprise debt all conspired to put pressure on the central bank to increase credits.

The lack of CBI endured even after IMF stand-by agreements were in play. Although these did not require statutory independence per se, they did stipulate a range of policies—macroeconomic stabilization, minimum reserve requirements, fiscal restraint, privatization—that would have required the NBU to emulate independent central bank authority. But IMF conditionality did not produce its intended effect. Almost immediately after receiving the first tranche of funds in April 1995 (as part of a $1.8 billion stand-by agreement), President Kuchma began reneging on the deal, first by adjusting inflation targets upward. The substantial amount of IMF money at stake notwithstanding, some members of the government and parliament put pressure on the NBU to assist ailing industries directly or to allow commercial banks to do so by lowering their reserve requirements. And by law, the central bank was still obliged to fund government deficits and to comply with the Council of Ministers' credit allocations (Stone 2002, 181). The IMF suspended the agreement by January 1996.

Ukraine failed to meet the mutually agreed upon targets under each of four IMF agreements (stand-by agreements initiated in 1995, 1996, and 1997 and an Extended Fund Facility in 1998). The IMF suspended the 1995, 1997, and 1998 deals. A recurring theme in the lack of compliance concerned the issuing of uncontrolled credits from the central bank, presumably at the insistence of politicians. The continuing administrative function of the central bank through the 1990s was consistent with its politically subordinate status. Moreover, by 1999 and

2000, there were revelations that the NBU had misled the IMF about central bank transactions that would have borne directly on IMF decisions to continue financing in Ukraine.[59] Western influence did register with Ukraine insofar as Kuchma appointed Yushchenko as prime minister after his 1999 presidential victory, but that influence remained weak.[60] There was never a powerful reform party supporting Yushchenko, and all of the political and economic actors who had previously balked at the IMF conditions attached to aid remained skeptical.

In contrast to Poland—where government officials welcomed IMF conditionality because they agreed with its aims and because, for others, maintaining constructive relations with international institutions motivated them to go along— Ukrainian politicians, according to one NBU official, never had any intention of fulfilling IMF agreements.[61] For most Polish and even Hungarian politicians, winning IMF assistance was desirable, not just for the resources but also because compliance indicated that both countries were moving closer to becoming modern, democratic, capitalist states. This was ruled out in Ukraine because, material benefits aside, there was little openness to external advice and little perceived need for Western social recognition.

Later legislation on Ukraine's central bank was passed by the parliament on May 20, 1999, and signed by President Kuchma on July 15 of that year. Over NBU Chairman Yushchenko's fierce objections, the legislation institutionalized the bank's lack of independence by creating a supervisory council, appointed by the parliament and Ukrainian president, with the power to veto decisions by the NBU chairperson and his or her colleagues. This effectively eliminated the bank's control over monetary policy. The new legislation limited the chairperson's term to five years (corresponding to a presidential term) and left considerable room for dismissal.[62] The law was also at odds with World Bank and IMF guidelines. Although the IMF's Extended Fund Facility did resume even after passage of the new legislation (only to be suspended again after revelations about concealed central bank transactions in the 1990s and missed targets), the World Bank loan, still worth an additional $200 million, was canceled. Ongoing tensions with the IMF also prevented the European Union from following through on its previous loan commitment to Ukraine. Perhaps the only area in which IFIs were influential was in persuading Ukrainian lawmakers to prohibit the NBU from buying Ukrainian treasury bills on the primary market.[63]

Following the 1999 presidential elections and the Asian and Russian financial crises, the NBU began behaving more independent of government and parliament, even as it remained legally subordinate.[64] Reflecting the IMF's ongoing concerns about inflation, the NBU resisted calls for a devaluation of the hryvnia in

2003.[65] Having urged greater CBI in 2003, the IMF welcomed what was perceived to be greater central bank autonomy later that year.[66] Yushchenko's presidential victory in December 2004 allowed closer IMF-Ukrainian cooperation and the expansion of IMF technical assistance (IMF 2005b, 7), as well as the Ukraine-EU Action Plan aimed at structural reform. The IMF also congratulated the NBU for having reached "a more formal understanding on policy coordination between the NBU and the government."[67]

In 2005, serious points of disagreement between the IMF and Ukrainian authorities reemerged. Arguing that the policy framework would not support a low and stable rate of inflation, the IMF urged the NBU to adopt a more flexible exchange rate and tighter monetary policy to control inflation, which was moving steadily beyond 12 percent. Although the IMF would have liked the NBU to adopt an inflation-targeting strategy, the Ukrainian authorities resisted. Both inflation targeting and tighter monetary policy to counter the government's expansionary fiscal policy in the run-up to the 2004 elections were viewed by the NBU as threats to growth. In addition, the NBU was formulating plans for a long-term lending facility for banks, which the IMF staff had "firmly opposed." On these issues, neither side was persuaded by the other.[68]

## CONCLUSION

Studies of central bank independence and its wide implementation, particularly through the 1990s, tend to emphasize convergence among states (Loungani and Sheets 1997; Maxfield 1997; Cukierman, Miller, and Neyapti 2002; J. Johnson 2002, 2006; Grabel 2003; Polillo and Guillén 2005). A disadvantage of focusing on convergence, particularly through formal measures, is the risk of occluding the still substantial variation across countries and what that implies for the power and limits of international institutions. Poland, Hungary, Romania, and Ukraine differed in when they institutionalized CBI and under what kinds of international pressure and advice, in the degree of independence assigned, and in the intensity of conflict around its consequences.

Three alternative explanations potentially challenge the argument here about the centrality of a social context in ensuring the openness of domestic actors to international institutions regarding CBI: preexisting interests, hyperinflation, and conditionality independent of social context. According to the preexisting interests explanation, Poland and Hungary might have institutionalized CBI in the early 1990s because democratic movements in those countries had long favored economic liberalism (Bockman and Eyal 2002; Shields 2003; Vachudova 2005).

Romania and Ukraine, the argument continues, failed to comply with international standards because of the absence of liberally minded opposition movements. I do not dispute the presence of elite economists in the fore of Polish and Hungarian opposition movements who favored CBI. But this is not the same as there being a broad societal acceptance of locating authority in IFIs and central banks. Furthermore, if sustaining CBI was only a matter of domestic politics, then in Poland, at least, the SLD-PSL legislation would have prevailed—given the coalition's overwhelming majority in parliament at the time of its challenge to the NBP. Hungary showed similar signs of domestic ambivalence toward CBI, given its willingness to increase political control over the central bank in the early 2000s. Finally, Romania changed course dramatically, in part because of political party turnover, but in part because the new coalition and its interests were constituted by international institutions.

Experience with hyperinflation across countries is also inconsistent with variation in the timing and degree of CBI. Poland, Romania, and Ukraine all either experienced or were on the brink of hyperinflation as a consequence of price liberalization or expansionary economic policy. Although CBI might be desirable to countries threatened by hyperinflation, as institutional insurance against further such episodes, only Poland and somewhat later Romania institutionalized CBI in proximity to such a threat. Ukraine did not. And although Hungary did not experience hyperinflation, much like Poland it was an early adopter of CBI. The hyperinflation argument is linked to a "best-practice" argument in which politicians willingly cede authority over monetary policy in order to preempt inflationary cycles. Variation over time and across cases also undermines the best-practice scenario, however, particularly given Ukraine's ongoing reluctance to institutionalize CBI.

Finally, the CBI case shows that conditionality was powerful only in connection with the social context as defined by uncertainty, status, and credibility. Bretton Woods conditionality was on offer in all four countries under consideration, but it was only in the countries that had the specified social context in place—Poland and Hungary—that conditionality proved powerful and compliance was achieved. In Romania and Ukraine, by contrast, IMF and World Bank programs promising financial assistance in return for compliance did not elicit CBI. Also notable is that in the first major challenge to CBI in Poland (1994–1996), the international institutions and their Polish partners prevailed against their CBI detractors despite the absence of *any* conditionality. At the other end of the spectrum, Ukraine, which had more resources at stake in Bretton Woods conditionality than any other state studied here, nevertheless proved immovable.

Ultimate institutionalization of CBI in Poland, Hungary, and Romania but not in Ukraine raises the question of whether EU conditionality was critical. But here too we find no consistent variation for the conditionality argument. Since Poland, Hungary, and Romania all faced the same incentive structure with respect to EU accession, then according to a conditionality argument all should have been motivated at about the same time to do the same thing—that is, comply with CBI. Romania's very late compliance, which accompanied the heightening of international institutional status through political competition in 1996 and after, corroborates the argument that international institutions need more than incentives to win compliance. They also need a set of domestic conditions, combined with credibility, that constitute international institutional incentives as powerful, meaningful, and worth the costs of compliance.

The constitutive effects of international institutions in Poland, Hungary, Romania, and, to a lesser extent, Ukraine with respect to CBI have been significant, but not definitive. First, international institutions did cultivate substantial support for central bank independence and price stability, objectives that many actors in postcommunist societies would not have committed to in the absence of a transnational community dedicated to purveying the low-inflation orthodoxy. The move to CBI represented a monumental shift from viewing the central bank as a political instrument to viewing it as an independent regulatory and policymaking body. Second, debate still exists in all four countries on the central bank's current role. Although in three cases there was sufficient support to secure the legal change that international institutions favored, not everyone is content with the redistribution of power implied by CBI.

# CHAPTER THREE

# Internationalizing Bank Ownership

The willingness of central and eastern European (CEE) states to allow significant levels of foreign investment in strategic sectors during the postcommunist transition is historically unprecedented. Nowhere is this more striking than in banking, where close to 70 percent of assets in Poland, Hungary, and the Czech Republic were foreign owned by the beginning of the twenty-first century. As in other instances in this study, there was significant controversy over whether, when, and how to privatize state-owned banks. Despite some variation in the degree to which states accepted the counsel of international institutions, which without exception favored foreign investment, CEE states have overwhelmingly embraced international financial integration—to an even greater degree than their western European counterparts.

Difficult to reverse once undertaken, the foreign investment shift is surprising for several reasons. First, for countries that had only recently achieved independence from Soviet hegemony and had suffered German economic domination before World War II, maintaining control over domestic capital allocation should have been a strategic priority—as many CEE politicians stated it was at the outset of transition. Second, privatization of state-owned banks with foreign capital precluded economic policies that had long served states seeking greater domestic power and international competitiveness (Gerschenkron 1962). Third, even if a country is willing to forego a statist model of development, foreign ownership still raises the question of the logic whereby foreign banks subsequently distribute credit and whether borrowing by local entrepreneurs becomes more difficult. Fourth, given the organization of banking during the state-socialist period, CEE countries were significantly "underbanked" at the outset of transition, and the sector represented an enormous growth opportunity. But foreign investment limits the extent to which returns from banking will be realized domestically. Finally, with the exceptions of the United Kingdom and Luxembourg, western European states have tended to protect their banking sectors from extensive foreign investment, both formally and informally.[1] Thus postcommunist countries had justification for considering a similar level of protection for themselves.

There is little doubt that CEE openness to foreign investment in banking has been beneficial for Western financial institutions. By December 2004, international banks headquartered in the West owned nearly one-half of CEE banking assets. In that year alone, those banks experienced a collective 15 percent increase in the value of their assets, in part owing to growth in the region.[2] By the end of 2005, the Austrian Erste Bank and Raiffeisen were reaping well over half their profits there. While introducing new skills, products, and technology, Western banks were also able to capitalize on explosive banking growth in countries whose populations had never had access to basic services such as interest-bearing accounts, mortgages, or credit cards.

One possible explanation for postcommunist openness to foreign investment is that the combination of starting conditions and globalization gave CEE states little choice but to attract foreign capital to rescue their fragile banking sectors. Low levels of domestic capital accumulation, know-how, professionalism, and technology, along with the need to increase state revenue through privatization, might have limited reform options. Moreover, there were strong efficiency arguments in favor of foreign participation. External creditors held out the promise of ending political lending, increasing transparency, and ensuring that resources accrued to those best equipped to realize returns.

Contrary to claims that states had little room for maneuver, however, I show that the constraints in favor of foreign investment, while real, were social and ideational in nature. I argue that "economic best practice" ultimately depends on the political process through which actors negotiate its definition. There were compelling arguments on both sides of the debate on privatizing the state-owned banks that emerged from the division of socialist-era monobanks into two-tiered banking systems (see chapter 2). Protectionists could point to the longer-term developmental advantages of state, or at least domestic, private ownership. There was also a strong case for breaking up existing political and business networks, for maximizing state revenue, and for quickly initiating a more efficient method of allocating resources. But neither argument prevailed, strictly on its merits, in any country. Rather, as in other sectors examined in this study, where international institutions exercised the greatest power, domestic reformers favored privatization with foreign capital and favored it sooner. Relative openness to foreign advising allowed international institutions to frame this debate in ways that altered what postcommunist states sought to maximize—in this case, faster rationalization at the expense of power.

Although CEE levels of foreign ownership in banking are higher than the OECD average, with some exceptions, outcomes across the region reflect only partial denationalization. "Denationalization" in this case refers to the removal of state interest in or control over a country's banking sector. To be sure, selected states in postcommunist Europe—including Croatia and Estonia, with 87 percent and 97 percent foreign ownership, respectively—have almost completely denationalized their banking sectors (Naaborg et al. 2003, 26).[3] But the more usual pattern has been for states to maintain at least some domestic or even state control over banking through political intervention in the private sector, or to maintain a reluctance to privatize at all. Postcommunist states have also exercised control by limiting the share that any single foreign entity can own, thereby balancing control among multiple interests and limiting their vulnerability to other states.

But regardless of piecemeal efforts to prevent total domination by foreign entities, CEE states have been strikingly willing to use the market to resolve the political conflicts inherent in distributing state assets after communism. Whereas state ownership or the privileging of domestic buyers were viable options (which Slovenia, exceptionally for the region, exploited to a great extent), most states put their long-term strategic concerns aside (Feldmann 2007; also see Epstein 2008).[4] By opting for international bidding instead, CEE states have traded national autonomy for greater efficiency. The central question addressed in this chapter is whether postcommunist states had a realistic choice in this matter, or whether their relative poverty, indebtedness, and technological backwardness effectively precluded using the banking system for economic development and national autonomy.

## FOREIGN OWNERSHIP IN COMPARATIVE PERSPECTIVE

Despite OECD and EU regulations that allow open market access to banking sectors among member states, in reality, most industrialized countries have maintained high levels of domestic ownership. Where data are available, we find that the usual rate of foreign ownership among the wealthiest countries is below 20 or even 10 percent, with the few exceptions limited to states that are either financial centers or have for other reasons bucked international trends (see table 3.1).

TABLE 3.1
*Foreign and State Ownership in Selected Banking Sectors, 2002*

| Country | Foreign-Owned Assets, % | Government-Owned Assets, % |
|---|---|---|
| New Zealand | 99.11 | .04 |
| Luxembourg | 94.64 | 5.05 |
| United Kingdom | 46 | 0 |
| South Korea | 29.54 | 39.97 |
| Norway | 19.2 | 0 |
| United States | 19 | 0 |
| Portugal | 17.7 | 22.8 |
| Australia | 17 | 0 |
| Cyprus | 12.7 | 4.2 |
| Greece | 10.8 | 22.8 |
| Switzerland | 10.71 | 14.2 |
| Spain | 8.5 | 0 |
| Japan | 6.7 | 0 |
| Finland | 6.2 | 0 |
| Italy | 5.7 | 10 |
| Canada | 4.8 | 0 |
| Germany | 4.30 | 42.2 |
| Turkey | 3.47 | 31.82 |
| Netherlands | 2.2 | 3.9 |
| China | 1.9 | 98.1 |
| Israel | 1.2 | 46.1 |
| Denmark | 0 | 0 |
| Belgium | NA | 0 |
| France | NA | 0 |

*Source:* Barth, Caprio, and Levine 2006, 149–50, 152–53.

*Note:* Remaining assets are listed as privately owned (Barth, Caprio, and Levine 2006, 154). NA, data not available.

Although by 1990 most OECD countries had desisted from "state banking"— that is, from state involvement in direct credit allocation (Verdier 2000)—they were nevertheless reluctant to embrace full market liberalization. In the late 1990s and 2000s, industrialized states continued to use whatever informal means were necessary to prevent foreign takeovers. In a spectacular example of such interference, the Italian central bank chairman, Antonio Fazio, was caught conspiring with local bank managers in 2005 to foil a Dutch bid to buy an Italian bank. Although Fazio came under fire and the Dutch offer ultimately prevailed, both the indignant international response and the success of the foreign takeover were virtually unprecedented in the European experience.[5]

OECD trends away from state banking might suggest that changes in the global economy would also bode poorly for continued state intervention in postcommunist credit markets. Economic-development success stories after World War II, particularly from Asia, led some scholars to ask at the outset of transition why CEE states were not keener to pursue industrial policies with state financial capacity (Albert 1993; Amsden, Kochanowicz, and Taylor 1994; Bryant and Mokrzycki 1994; Chang and Nolan 1995). Traditionally, states have had four kinds of tools at their disposal: financial repression, direct credit through state-owned banks, loan guarantees on foreign borrowing, or simply reaching a *modus vivendi* with private banks—assuming they were domestically owned.[6] Even if the choice of central bank independence and price stability ruled out financial repression (see chapter 2), commercial banks remained a potential conduit of influence.

Given that states had never become competitive through the market alone (Amsden, Kochanowicz, and Taylor 1994; Landesmann and Abel 1995), and that they had often sought to improve—albeit with variable success—on the efficiency of markets through state credit allocation (Zysman 1983; Haggard and Lee 1993), it was unclear at the outset of transition how CEE states should manage their strategic assets. Amsden and colleagues (1994) argued that the Asian Tigers, which used domestically controlled credit extensively in their early economic development strategies, were poor reference points for CEE democratizers because of the authoritarian or semi-authoritarian character of those Asian states in their high-growth years. But more important than whether state-directed credit allocation is inimical to democratic governance (postwar France, Germany, and Italy would suggest it is not) was the ideological commitment to the idea in the 1990s that the two were incompatible.

Thus Bretton Woods assessments of the Asian Tigers' economic strength, highlighting how important "getting the prices right" had been, reinforced the belief that state intervention was not the source of their success (World Bank 1993). The international financial institutions (IFIs) were intent on bolstering a pervasive, if not yet dominant, liberal worldview. International institutions' own misgivings in the early 1990s about market intervention underpinned arguments in favor of internationally competitive privatization.

## THE SOCIAL CONTEXT IN CONDITIONALITY: UNCERTAINTY, STATUS, AND CREDIBILITY

External actors supported rapid privatization of state assets in CEE as an essential component of transition to a market economy. There was also powerful domestic impetus for privatization in some states (especially the Czech Republic), even if others (such as Romania) showed much less appetite for it. But across the postcommunist region, foreign ownership was still highly controversial. Nevertheless, with the help of their domestic interlocutors, international institutions could shift the terms of debate in favor of liberal economic principles and overcome opposition to the loss of national control.

But that capacity was contingent. International influence and the role of foreign capital were generally greater where domestic actors were uncertain and sought confidence in their policies by opting for IFI-backed solutions. The elevated status of international institutions and the desire of domestic actors for social affirmation facilitated the access of external advisors to reform debates. The degree of international consensus and normative consistency on international bidding for state-owned assets also affected bank privatization outcomes.

The operationalization of these social variables is the same as for central banking (see chapter 2). The central factors to bear in mind are, again, uncertainty, status, and credibility. First, being new to office, the theory implies, leaders sought an external imprimatur for their choices (H1; see chapter 1 on the designation of the study hypotheses). Commercial banking, like central banking, has a high measure on uncertainty. For although managers of state-owned commercial banks might have been employed by the socialist-era monobank, price liberalization and market-based lending require quite different expertise. The second variable—the elevated status of international institutions and domestic actors' desire for social affirmation—is again measured according to the quality of political competition (H2). Not only does political competition bring additional information to light, but it allows international opinion to assume greater salience in domestic settings and enables international institutions to encourage political parties to emulate or deviate from one another in the light of international approbation. Finally, the credibility of bank privatization with foreign capital is measured in terms of international consensus and normative consistency (H3). The consensus behind internationally competitive bids for state assets was strong, as reflected in both OECD and EU rules. But industrialized countries have also violated the spirit if not the letter of open market rules. The credibility hypothesis would therefore predict friction around foreign investment in banking to be linked to what other countries have done, creating unevenness in the degree to which postcommunist states cede control over bank ownership.

Although positive measures on all three variables rarely combined in the four countries of the study, most of the conditions were met in Poland and Hungary in the early 1990s and in Romania a decade later. In Poland and Hungary, international institutions were able to forge transnational coalitions before 1995 that facilitated heavy foreign investment in commercial bank privatization. Poland

and Hungary reveal political party mimicry, as well. Communist successor parties in both countries realized, after their returns to power in 1993 and 1994, that liberal economic policies would help them maintain constructive relations with international institutions. Thus, as in other cases in this study, international institutions weighed in on domestic debates to affect outcomes but also to constitute actors. They helped change the orientation of postcommunist parties, making them economically more liberal and accepting of bank privatization with foreign capital that narrowed the capacities of postcommunist states.

## OUTCOMES ACROSS THE REGION

From the outset of the transition in Poland, there were competing views about when and how to privatize state-owned enterprises. Linked to these debates were disagreements about what role the state should play in the economy. Because a key conduit of economic influence had traditionally been control over domestic credit allocation, a particularly sensitive issue was the privatization of state-owned banks, fourteen of which resulted from transforming the socialist monobank into a two-tiered banking system in 1989 and 1990. In early 1991, the assumption was that only a 10 to 20 percent stake in any bank would go to a foreign strategic investor, with 30 percent remaining with the Polish treasury and the rest distributed among bank employees and other private investors. By the early 2000s, that original vision had clearly given way to other priorities, as close to 70 percent of the Polish banking assets were foreign owned (see table 3.2). But at that time, Poland's enthusiasm for strict efficiency wavered, leading to multiple delays in the privatization of the state savings bank, Powszechna Kasa Oszczędności Bank Polski. In a reversal of earlier policy, Poland resolved to keep this, the country's biggest bank (in terms of assets), in national hands. An initial public offering in November 2004 limited foreign access to the dispersed 40 percent stake that went on the market while the state maintained its controlling share.[7]

The preference for Polish ownership has had many manifestations.[8] In the mid-1990s, the Democratic Left Alliance–Polish Peasant Party (SLD-PSL) coalition made a serious bid to exercise state influence over the course of bank privatization—specifically to ensure greater domestic control. That effort failed—the result, I argue, of the cultivation of a transnational coalition, spearheaded by the IFIs and the European Bank for Reconstruction and Development (EBRD), which shifted the balance of power in favor of foreign capital. After institutionalization of a free market policy orientation early in the transition, the barriers to reversing it in the banking sector were to prove prohibitive. External actors did

TABLE 3.2
*Foreign and State Ownership in Postcommunist Banking Sectors, 2002*

| Country | Foreign-Owned Assets, % | Government-Owned Assets, % |
|---|---|---|
| Estonia[a] | 98.9 | 0 |
| Czech Republic[a] | 90 | 3.8 |
| Croatia | 89.3 | 5 |
| **Hungary**[a] | 88.8 | 9 |
| Slovakia[a] | 85.5 | 4.4 |
| Lithuania[a] | 78.19 | 12.16 |
| Bulgaria[b] | 74.56 | 17.6 |
| Bosnia-Herzegovina | 73 | 10 |
| **Poland**[a] | 68.7 | 23.5 |
| Latvia[a] | 65.2 | 3.2 |
| **Romania**[b] | 47.3 | 41.8 |
| Albania | 46 | 54 |
| Moldova | 36.7 | 13.6 |
| Belarus | 26 | 74 |
| Kyrgyzstan | 24.7 | 16 |
| Slovenia[a] | 20.6 | 12.2 |
| Kazakhstan | 17.9 | .5 |
| Serbia-Montenegro | 13.2 | 3.8 |
| **Ukraine** | 10.5 | 12 |
| Russia | 8.8 | 35.5 |
| Azerbaijan | 4.6 | 58.3 |

*Source:* Barth, Caprio, and Levine 2006, 149–50, 152–53.
    *Note:* Countries appearing in boldface are included in this study. Remaining assets are listed as privately owned (Barth, Caprio, and Levine 2006, 154).
    [a]Countries admitted to the European Union in 2004.
    [b]Countries admitted to the European Union in 2007.

provide material incentives for Polish politicians to stay the liberalizing course. But those incentives were important only by virtue of their power to reinforce or destroy relationships—a power invested in them by a particular social context. Understood in this way, extensive state intervention in the banking sector became politically rather than financially untenable.

Ironically, although Hungary seemed even more explicitly determined to maintain a large stake in domestic banking, by the early 2000s it had proved even less able to do so. By 2002, 88.8 percent of Hungary's banking assets were foreign owned, compared with Poland's 68.7 percent (Barth, Caprio, and Levine 2006, 152–53) (see table 3.2). In most respects, the outcomes in the two countries are comparable, although by retaining a stake in the country's largest bank, Poland proved marginally more able to resist international pressure. The equivalent outcomes are in accord with my theoretical framework, starting with the fact that both countries were relatively open to IFI influence owing to strong measures on uncertainty and a desire for external social recognition.

Hungary and Poland also differed in important respects. In banking, Hungary was much slower to implement an effective system of regulation, experienced earlier foreign participation and on a larger scale, and had a more protracted and costly bank bailout than Poland (Hjartarson 2004). Moreover, whereas all Hungarian political parties basically believed that a strong domestic presence in banking was essential (Hjartarson 2004, 17), at least a few Polish liberal reformers with key positions in the Ministry of Finance (MoF) and the central bank argued that foreign investment would be better than just any form of domestic ownership.[9] Variation along these dimensions notwithstanding, both countries had comparably denationalized banking sectors by the early 2000s. Consistent outcomes highlight the importance of similarities between the two in why they were susceptible to external influence—namely, the uncertainty of actors and their desire to be identified as members of the Western community.

Before the 1996 elections, Romania was a very different case from Poland and Hungary. But political competition and ultimately EU accession would raise the status of international institutions and ultimately bring Romania into line with both Hungary and Poland. Indeed, by 2002 the share of foreign ownership in Romanian banking was at 47.3 percent and climbing, up from just 10 percent four years earlier. In keeping with my theory, Romania was both slower to allow foreign investment and more determined to maintain domestic ownership. The initial lack of uncertainty among the governing class and Romania's insouciance toward international opinion limited the salience of external policy prescriptions as reference points.

In the early 2000s, Ukraine had the lowest level of foreign investment in banking of the four countries. Foreign holdings of banking-sector assets were around 10 percent. Reflecting the enduring weight in Ukraine of agriculture, heavy industry, and certain branches of the state, the centrality of domestic credit control prevailed through the 1990s. Of the five banks formed from the monobank, two remained state owned. The other three—serving agriculture, heavy industry, and social and municipal services—had in a certain sense been privatized in the early 1990s, but remained under the direction of state-owned enterprises and subject to substantial political influence (Sochan 1996). Foreign banks were in principle allowed to operate in Ukraine from the late 1980s and early 1990s, and much previous discriminatory legislation against them was reversed by legislation in 1997 and 2001. By March 2001, however, still only 6 foreign banks were operating, of a total of 156 banks (OECD 2001, 19–20). Following the Orange Revolution of late 2004, foreign participation in the banking sector increased significantly.

## PRIVATIZING BANKS WITH FOREIGN CAPITAL: THE UNCERTAINTY OF ACTORS (H1)
### Poland

Both measures on uncertainty in the banking sector were high in Poland at the outset of transition. Leaders from Solidarity replaced the communist regime in June 1989. This was also a period of enormous uncertainty and fluidity—a time of "extraordinary politics" (L. Balcerowicz 1995). As elsewhere in the region, the onset of price liberalization and credit markets made neophytes of employees in the newly formed state-owned commercial banks whose competencies under the centrally planned economy had been essentially administrative.

Uncertainty, coupled with the desire of first-wave reformers for international recognition, allowed international institutions and Solidarity reformers to set a liberalizing course for reform in 1989. Although the IFIs began advising Poland on financial reform somewhat earlier (in 1986), the opportunity for dramatic change widened after the opposition came to power in 1989. One of the first foreign interventions in banking reform occurred late that year at a conference near Warsaw.[10] Jeffrey Sachs, the Harvard economist who also figured prominently in Poland's macroeconomic stabilization plan (Kuroń 1991; Myant 1993), argued that it was imperative to modernize and privatize Poland's banks. He suggested enlisting IFI assistance to create a training program with Western bank involvement, to provide Polish banks with much-needed know-how and to generate Western investor interest among banks in Poland. Sachs was not the first to imagine pairing banks to promote transfer of knowledge and possibly investment from West to East. But it was his impetus that first established a liberalizing frame and set things in motion.

In response to Sachs's Warsaw lecture, the Polish deputy minister of finance in charge of banking reform got in touch with an International Finance Corporation (IFC) official later the same day to discuss the plan's feasibility.[11] The IFC, and this particular official, had been active in building independently financed business networks in Poland. Both men had attended the Sachs event. Thus began the formation of an ideational coalition among Polish and foreign actors that ultimately launched the "Twinning Arrangements" in the spring of 1991. The Twinning Arrangements were only modestly successful. Only one bank, Allied Irish Bank, ultimately invested in its "twin" in Poznan, Wielkopolski Bank Kredytowy, and none of the other partnerships led directly to business ventures. However, both the Italians and the Dutch, who had participated in the program, did invest elsewhere in Poland's banking sector at later dates—and on a large scale.[12]

Another indication that Poland was moving toward denationalization in commercial banking with IFI assistance was the design and implementation of the bank bailout plan that began in 1991. Familiar with the IFIs' priorities and orientation, Polish MoF officials devised a bank restructuring and recapitalization scheme that they hoped would win IMF approval.[13] The IMF subsequently agreed to reallocate a substantial portion of the unused zloty stabilization fund (originally worth $1 billion) to the proposed bank bailout program. The IMF added one informal condition to the reallocation: that the MoF make a good-faith effort to privatize six of Poland's state-owned commercial banks by the end of 1996.[14] Not coincidentally, it was also in 1991 that the Polish MoF went from planning a relatively minor role for foreign strategic investors to allowing them a 25 percent stake in privatized banks (Abarbanell and Bonin 1997, 37–38), a maximum allowable share that would continue to increase over time.

Poland opened its banking market to foreign participation in yet another way. Believing that foreign competitors would accelerate bank reform, the government went to some lengths to encourage greenfield investment. Early, liberal licensing allowed foreign firms to set up and enjoy three years of generous tax relief as well as flexible arrangements concerning foreign currency holdings and capital mobility (National Bank of Poland 2001, 51). By 1993, however, these incentives were eliminated, and licensing, especially for new domestic banks, was tightened in an effort to bring greater stability to the system. Nevertheless, the number of foreign banks continued to increase. Internationalizing the banking market by opening it to foreign participation and allowing foreign investment in state assets was broadly consistent with foreign advisors' and IFIs' counsel (Bonin et al. 1998).

Uncertainty stemming from interest demobilization in banking facilitated Poland's openness to international advising early on. The Twinning Arrangements (supported by the IFC and World Bank), the bank bailout plan (funded by the IMF), an early start to privatization (buttressed by the EBRD), and the acceptance of a larger role for foreign strategic investors than originally planned revealed the full embrace by political leaders of IFI initiatives. The IFIs provided ready prescriptions favoring a rapid rationalization of the sector, at the expense of state control, national autonomy, and domestic ownership.

Other analysts have strongly challenged the notion that "neoliberal" reformers in CEE were uncertain about economic reform (Bockman and Eyal 2002; Shields 2003). They argue that liberal economic policies followed naturally from opposition to communism (Vachudova 2005). While a liberal agenda certainly was not imposed without the consent of domestic actors, my concern here is with the origin of that consent. Economic expertise was very narrowly held. It is unclear why financial denationalization ultimately prevailed when many reformers initially opposed it and preferred a nationalist approach to domestic banking (Abarbanell and Bonin 1997; E. Balcerowicz and Bartkowski 2001, 17–19). Moreover, in Poland, some of the most nationalist reformers were found in Solidarity, and disagreement about economic policy was an important reason why the movement eventually fragmented. Opposition to a despised regime is one thing, but to claim that any number of economic policies logically follow from that fact—including policies, such as foreign domination of finance, that many industrialized states have frequently rejected for themselves—is quite another.

## Hungary

International institutions could also influence Hungarian banking reform because of political turnover and the uncertainty of banking bureaucrats (Balassa 1992, 12–14),[15] as indicated by two key developments. First, and in keeping with its international advisors' counsel, Hungary introduced a liberal regulatory framework that allowed foreign banks to begin operating almost immediately (Hjartarson 2004, 18). Theoretically, this was to spur domestic banking innovation, a point on which Hungarian politicians and international institutions concurred.[16] Second, the first major banking law—the Law on Financial Institutions of 1991— foresaw a reduction of state ownership to less than 25 percent of state-owned banks by 1997,[17] and that even if ownership remained above 25 percent, the state would nevertheless restrict its voting rights to that level (Piroska 2005, 114, 118, 127). In 1992, Hungary established a bank privatization committee expressly for removing the state from credit allocation functions.

But regardless of these laws, privatization proceeded slowly because Hungarian politicians preferred to find domestic buyers. The catalyst for an acceleration seems to have been the publication of two *Financial Times* articles in May 1993. Based on IMF and World Bank sources, these reports painted a gloomy picture of Hungary's banking sector (Piroska 2005).[18] Noting high levels of bad loans and insufficient provisioning, the articles' use of the term "insolvency" put Hungarian policymakers on the defensive. Within five months the Hungarian Democratic Forum (MDF)–led government launched a bank recapitalization plan with World Bank assistance and charted the privatization of two of the country's largest commercial banks—Budapest Bank and the Hungarian Foreign Trade Bank (MKB).[19] A few months later, in April 1994, the Bayerische Landesbank

Girozentrale and the EBRD agreed to buy 25.01 and 16.7 percent, respectively, of MKB. The state cut its own holding from 49 to 25 percent, with the remaining shares being widely dispersed.[20]

Despite the MDF's apparent sensitivity to the international business press and the IFIs, there was a wide-ranging debate in Hungary over how to manage bank restructuring, and foreign advisors did not dictate the terms of privatization. Conservative MDF members were committed to encouraging small-business participation in bank privatization and preventing socialist bureaucrats from gaining access to state assets. Members of the liberal party, the Alliance of Free Democrats (SzDSz), were more enthusiastic about limiting the state's role and allowing markets greater jurisdiction—and their sentiments had the most explicit support of the IFIs. But the laws on foreign access expressed contradictory preferences, both in prohibiting limits on foreign participation and in declaring a central role for state ownership in the transition (Piroska 2005, 113–19). Even as the first freely elected government sought deals with foreign interests keen to buy Hungarian banks, those deals ultimately foundered in the first three years over precisely these issues of long-term strategic control (Hjartarson 2004, 17). Indeed, by the end of the MDF's first term, the government and population alike were growing anxious about what conservatives viewed as excessive foreign investment. By the second half of 1993, further measures were in place to encourage domestic purchase of state assets, although notably not in the banking sector (Hanley, King, and Tóth János 2002, 153–57).

## Romania

Romania's measure on uncertainty was compromised by the continuity of the regime, although bankers were operating in a liberalized price environment for the first time. Banking functions had been concentrated in the monobank and linked to fulfilling the centralized economic plan. The Romanian monobank issued currency, directed credit, and handled deposits. To the extent that interest rates were ever applied, this was done without regard to the scarcity of money or the presence of risk. The only area in which Romanian bankers operated in a liberalized environment was in foreign exchange—not an insignificant realm, given the scope of Romanian borrowing on Western capital markets (Ritson 1989). Nevertheless, when Romania liberalized prices in 1991 (with the exception of some heating, basic food, and housing prices), most bankers in the original four commercial banks and the national savings bank separated off from the National Bank of Romania (NBR) had little to no exposure to a market environment.[21]

As in the case of the Romanian central bank, however, the potential access of foreign advisors to banking reform was limited by the continuity of the regime. For even if some bankers were eager to upgrade their skills in line with Western standards, they would find it difficult—foreign assistance notwithstanding—to mobilize the political class in favor of privatization. Romania's hesitation, not unlike that of Poland and Hungary, stemmed from the sentiment that "banks [were] considered to be among the most important, strategic assets of the state" (Tsantis 1997, 201). But the principal way in which Romania differed from Poland and Hungary was in the desirability of EU preaccession reforms and the meaning of Bretton Woods conditionality. Whereas Poland and Hungary were wary of breaking ranks with the IFIs, Romanian politicians entered readily into agreements with which they had no intention of complying.[22] According to one former minister of finance, Romanians thought "there must be another way" than that being pushed by the IFIs.[23]

Indeed, there was no shortage of IFI engagement with Romania, as attested to by the many conditionality agreements between the country and Bretton Woods institutions (Ghizari 1992, 115, 121; Tsantis 1997). Given only little liberalization in Romania in the early 1990s, the IMF predicated its 1994 stand-by agreement on the drafting of a bank privatization law. Subsequent agreements linked to banking reform included the IMF's 1995 stand-by agreement, which called for commercial bank restructuring and privatization of the Romanian Bank for Development (BRD), and the World Bank's 1996 Enterprise and Financial Sector Adjustment Loan, which also called for privatization of the BRD in addition to a tightening of conditions for the NBR's providing banks with refinancing credits (Tsantis 1997, 173, 200).[24] Romania nevertheless avoided significant banking reform, engaged in ad hoc refinancing, and held on to the BRD as well as other majority state-owned banks. IFI conditionality failed to elicit compliance because the Romanian governing class did not perceive the need for IFI advice to gain confidence in its policies.

Despite the absence of compliance, Romania did adopt some internationally sanctioned policies. The two-tiered banking system, introduced in 1990, was consistent with market-based reforms throughout the region. Four foreign bank subsidiaries were already operating in Romania when the transition began.[25] And the 1991 legislation on foreign investment seemed to be nondiscriminatory.[26] But such measures did not result in levels of foreign participation similar to those in Poland and Hungary, due to simultaneous countermeasures. Whereas Poland and Hungary actively encouraged early entry of foreign banks into their markets, Romania maintained rigorous capital and regulatory requirements that discouraged new entrants—whether foreign or domestic. Romania initially preferred to consolidate domestic banking (including state-owned banks) without excessive competition.[27] And although ostensibly nondiscriminatory, the 1991 foreign investment law did require interested parties to seek permission, which was granted to a foreign bank (the Dutch ING) for the first time only in October 1994.

But like Poland and Hungary, Romania did enlist the financial and technical assistance of the IFIs and also sought EU membership. Nevertheless, although the availability of new information and incentives did not vary across these countries, Romania was decidedly less receptive to external advising. Banking-market outcomes for much of the 1990s therefore reflected Romanian priorities rather than international norms. Due to the weakness of IFI influence, the primary goal of banking through the decade was not the efficient or even profitable allocation of resources, but the continued financing of state-owned enterprises. Not until the end of the decade did Romanian authorities even accept that banks could go bankrupt—regardless of whether the bank in distress was publicly or privately owned (Doltu 2002, 291, 301).

## Ukraine

According to the uncertainty variable, international institutions should have exercised the least influence over banking in the case of Ukraine. Ukraine experienced significant continuity not only in terms of governance—with many of the same leaders that dominated under Soviet leadership maintaining power through elections—but also in the preservation of some core socialist economic principles. Whereas Poland, Hungary, and, to a lesser extent, Romania liberalized prices at the outset of transition, Ukraine took a more gradual approach. Because the price environment remained largely under government control until as late as 1995, bankers and ministry officials in Ukraine were even less beholden to foreign advisors on financial sector organization than those in Romania.

In all communist countries, the main "clients" of bankers had been government ministries (Sochan 1996, 4). Limited market experience among bankers is common to all four countries. But in Poland, Hungary, and Romania, price liberalization changed the logic of the economy such that government ministries could no longer provide a safety net for failing firms via the banking system. In Ukraine, however, in the absence of sweeping price liberalization, it was precisely the government ministries that continued to exercise such influence, including over banks that had only nominally been privatized.

Ukraine took a limited and then stop-go approach to price liberalization (see chapter 2). It initially followed price liberalization in Russia, beginning in January 1992, but even more reluctantly and less aggressively (Dąbrowski and Antczak 1995, 4; Sochan 1996, 10). It freed only about 20 percent of retail prices and then regulated or continued to administer most others. Two kinds of control were used. Prices for goods such as coal, petroleum, natural gas, electricity, freight, transportation, communication, rents, and basic food items remained under government control. Other items were regulated by government limits on profit margins of 25 to 40 percent.

Between January 1992 and June 1994, the state, led by the executive or parliament, made multiple changes to the price regime—adjusting administered prices up or down, further liberalizing then rolling back. It was not until the election of Leonid Kuchma in the summer of 1994 that liberalization began anew, for the first time with the assistance of an IMF Systemic Transformation Facility (Dąbrowski and Antczak 1995, 17–18). Structural changes, including price liberalization, continued through at least the end of 1995.

In keeping with the social context, Ukraine's bank reform strategy evidenced little international influence early in the transition. Five banks were carved out of the monobank. The Savings Bank (Oschadny Bank) and UkrEximBank (created in 1992 in response to the failure of Vnesheconombank) remained in state hands. The other three banks (Bank Ukraina, Prominvest Bank, and UkrSotsBank) were privatized almost immediately to state-owned enterprises and bank managers and employees. Although ostensibly private, these three banks maintained strong links with the government and were consistently subject to (often unwelcome) political control (Sochan 1996, 16–18; World Bank 2000, 18). Also in contravention to Western norms, Ukraine retained controls against most kinds of foreign participation. The business environment was sufficiently fraught with legal uncertainty, however, that it is unclear how eager foreign banks would have been to invest, even given the opportunity. The lack of legal compliance with international accounting and business practice was itself a manifestation of the country's resistance to foreign influence early in the transition.

## INTERNATIONAL INSTITUTIONAL STATUS AND POLITICAL COMPETITION (H2)
### Poland

The elevated status of international institutions in Poland, together with the uncertainty of actors, allowed international institutions to influence Polish bank restructuring early on. The quality of political competition was also strong. Communist successor parties returned to government in 1993, and further alternations in power took place in 1997, 2001, and 2005. In the area of banking-sector reform, political parties' desire for social recognition was particularly notable between 1994 and 1997 when the SLD-PSL coalition forged a state-led bank consolidation plan, which it ultimately abandoned for fear of alienating the IFIs. The details of that plan and its abandonment are recounted in later sections.

Political party mimicry shows that as international reference points come into play, policy options narrow. The SLD-PSL coalition in power from late 1993 initially viewed the diminishing scope for state intervention in the economy with concern. Although some research shows that it was not primarily economic hardship from radical reform that led Poles to put the communist successor parties back in power (Powers and Cox 1997; Ekiert and Kubik 1999), the SLD and PSL publicly urged more gradual privatization during the campaign and displayed a greater suspicion of international institutions.[28] But their skepticism was reversed during their term in office as they discovered how dependent their political reputations were on international approval of their policies, which explains why the coalition ultimately reembraced a rapid privatization policy in keeping with international institutional wishes.

## Hungary

Although the party systems of Poland and Hungary differed, the underlying competitive dynamic in both countries gave international institutions significant access to bank reform debates. In Hungary, the MDF-led government had been eager to promote privatization even if it had also been wary of allowing either former communists or foreign investors to gain control of the state's assets. First-wave economic reformers in Poland were more liberal and managed to persuade the nationalist elements of Solidarity to follow their lead, supported by an array of highly legitimate (in the Polish context) IFIs. In Poland it was the reformed communists who would have taken a more state-led approach to bank restructuring and privatization had it not been for international mobilization against such a strategy. But in Hungary, it was the Hungarian Socialist Party (MSzP), a communist successor party, that set the country on a more decisively liberalizing course.

The Hungarian socialists led a center-left coalition to victory in the 1994 elections by capitalizing on the severity of the transition recession. This was the first year of GDP growth since the collapse of communism. Given the poor macroeconomic indicators, particularly the current account and budget deficits, the country's status with international institutions as a transition frontrunner had begun to erode toward the end of the MDF's first term. In December 1993, both IMF and World Bank disbursements were delayed because of missed targets set three months earlier.[29] Tensions with international institutions over bank insolvency, macroeconomic mismanagement, and privatization gave the socialists an electoral opening.

By the first quarter of 1995, the MSzP-led coalition had begun to distinguish itself from its MDF-led predecessor by moving closer to international institutional policy orientations and prescriptions, accelerating the privatization of banks and other enterprises, and by embarking on a broader program of macroeconomic stabilization focused on the current account and budget (Kornai 1997). The MSzP also resumed constructive relations with the IMF, World Bank, European Union, and EBRD in an effort to rebuild Hungary's image as a transition leader (Hanley, King, and Tóth János 2002). And Hungary joined the OECD in 1996. While stabilization restored Hungary's standing with international financial markets, privatization—of banks in particular—ended the cycle of poor performance and state recapitalization. But the costs were high, including public "bitterness" about falling real wages (Kornai 1997, 131) and the indefinite exclusion of domestic owners from a highly lucrative strategic sector—banking.

## Romania

In late 1996, the Democratic Convention of Romania (CDR) prevailed in the parliamentary and presidential elections, allowing an opposition party to form a government for the first time. Because of the repression of opposition under communism, the CDR did not have the qualities of either the Polish or Hungarian opposition movements. It was fragmented from the outset and lacked a powerful cadre of Western-trained economists. Nevertheless, rotation in power marked a sea change in Romanian politics, including in the management of the country's banking sector.

In the run-up to the 1996 election, the governing Party of Social Democracy of Romania (PDSR) orchestrated giveaways through the central bank and through the still numerous state-owned commercial banks (Dăianu 1997; Tsantis 1997; Cernat 2006). This was either a last-minute effort to win the elections or a way of siphoning additional assets in the event of defeat. In either case, the CDR inherited many of the same banking problems that had troubled the sector from the outset of transition. Banks issued credits without conditionality or monitoring. Lending was often done in the interest of sustaining loss-making enterprises. The central bank was under constant pressure to provide backup financing should loans prove unrecoverable.

Unlike its predecessors, but much like the socialists in Hungary after 1994, the CDR responded to the banking crisis by facilitating exit and privatization, rather than by state financing. The first such privatization was of the BRD, which had been targeted for sale as early as 1994. After several false starts under its predecessors, the CDR finally oversaw the bank's controlling purchase (51%) by Société Général in 1998. General Electric Capital Corporation, in partnership with Banco Portugues de Investimento, bought 45 percent of Romania's Banc-Post. Preparations were also made for Banca Agricola's privatization. In all, under CDR leadership, foreign bank ownership in assets grew from 15.2 percent in 1998 to 43.56 percent two years later (Doltu 2002, 289). In addition to privatizations, the exit of several Romanian banks from the market due to bankruptcy (which previously had not been enforced) altered the relative share of domestic and foreign ownership.[30]

The theory of political party mimicry based on the increased salience of international sources of authority would also predict that in the wake of the CDR's relative success, the socialists—who assumed power again in late 2000—would continue to pursue privatization. And indeed, by the time Prime Minister Adrian Năstase and President Ion Iliescu's party controlled the government and executive for the second time since the revolution, the socialists followed the privatization path, much to the West's surprise.[31] Banca Agricola was sold to Austria's Raiffeisen in 2001. The state also sold a controlling share of BancPost to EFG Eurobank (53%). Under conditions of new openness, the EBRD was allowed to become an active player in the banking market.[32]

But the emergence of political competition in Romania and the consequent elevated status of international standards did not translate into unlimited IFI control over banking reform. Indeed, the CDR was demonstrably less keen to do the IMF's bidding than were the socialists in Hungary. Thus, although the IMF and World Bank stipulated that solving the Bancorex crisis was a key condition for maintaining Bretton Woods assistance in 1999, the Romanian solution was not the one favored by the IMF.[33] Whereas the IMF sought Bancorex's liquidation, the Romanian government chose consolidation with another bank instead, hoping to avoid absorbing the potential losses from outstanding assets held by foreigners (Cernat 2006). Nevertheless, the CDR was willing to accept bank bankruptcy, curtail central bank financing of state-owned enterprises, and countenance foreign ownership in what was still believed by all to be a strategic sector, all of which suggests that political competition had in fact extended policy options in a Western, liberal direction.

Although the socialists went from rejecting bank privatization in their first term to embracing it in their second, they nevertheless manifested a lingering reluctance to cede this strategic sector. Both the EBRD and IMF were active in encouraging the privatization of Romania's banking "crown jewel," the Commercial Bank of Romania (BCR). Despite pledges to privatize the bank, the government demurred, keeping it in state hands. Romania also opted to retain its Eximbank and use it as a strategic tool for export promotion. The socialists also neglected to privatize the national savings bank (Casa de Economii si Consemnatiuni) during their 2000–2004 tenure.[34] Thus state-owned assets in banking remained at 40 to 50 percent until 2004 (Barth, Caprio, and Levine 2006).

## Ukraine

Between 1991 and 2000, Ukraine showed only weak compliance with international institutions' financial prescriptions because these institutions were not viewed as authoritative sources of information, which allowed domestic norms and priorities to prevail (World Bank 1999, 15). Starting in 2000, however, compliance increased, particularly in rationalizing the business environment to attract large-scale foreign investment in banking. The key questions for this study are whether Ukraine's perceptions of the status of international institutions changed between the first and second periods, and whether political competition in the 1999 presidential elections and protests against the government starting in the early 2000s are a good proxy for such a change.

As noted in chapter 2, international institutional status in Ukraine measured in terms of political competition is ambiguous. Both leading presidential candidates in 1994, Kuchma and Leonid Kravchuk, were from the same political background, thus the extent to which either would compete with respect to Western reference points was limited. Indeed, Ukraine differed not just from Poland and Hungary in this respect, but also from Romania. Political competition had a quite different character in Ukraine, given the enduring prominence of political figures that had emerged from the state-socialist apparatus and ideology.

Nevertheless, the evolution of political competition in Ukraine did increase the power of Western actors and norms. Although in 1994 Kuchma had run as a pro-Russian candidate, during his first term he signed partnership agreements with the European Union and NATO. He also made agreements with the Bretton Woods institutions, even if Ukraine rarely complied with their conditions. By 1999

Kuchma was running as the only ostensibly pro-Western candidate against a field of mostly pro-Russian contenders. Not only did the latter have central planning instincts, but some favored rebuilding a union with Russia and Belarus. Kuchma's victory in the run-off election in November 1999 against Communist Party candidate Petro Symonenko, using pro-Western and pro-market rhetoric, suggests—in line with the status argument—that Western institutions would subsequently be more persuasive in economic policymaking. Given Ukraine's increasing compliance with foreign technical advising on banking reform after 2000, the correlation between increasing political competition and greater compliance lends support to this hypothesis.

A rival hypothesis to status deserves consideration here, however. Increased compliance could also be explained by short-term exigencies. Ukraine suffered severe fallout from the Russian financial crisis in 1998 and 1999 (World Bank 1999, 14). By the time of the 1999 election, Ukraine was more than $3 billion in debt to the IMF, the World Bank, and foreign creditors, also perhaps compelling compliance. A financial-pressure hypothesis would suggest, however, that it would not have mattered who won the 1999 presidential election—either candidate, whether Communist Party member (Symonenko) or rhetorically pro-Western (Kuchma), would have registered stronger compliance with international institutions by virtue of indebtedness. In the light of Symonenko's Russian orientation and celebration of centralized authority and state planning, however, this seems unlikely. In addition, Ukraine had spent most of the 1990s flouting Bretton Woods conditionality. There was little reason a Communist Party president could be expected to dramatically Westernize his orientation and cooperate with the IFIs. The more likely explanation of compliance post 1999 is that Kuchma had positioned himself as pro-market and in line with Western institutions as a means of defeating his Communist Party opponent. Themes of Western economic and political integration were even more explicit in the 2004 presidential campaign, when Viktor Yushchenko's victory in the Orange Revolution ushered in a phase of heightened foreign investment in Ukraine's banking sector.

## COMPROMISED CREDIBILITY AND RESISTANCE TO COMPLIANCE (H3)

The measure on credibility in bank privatization is mixed for all four countries—Poland, Hungary, Romania, and Ukraine. Credibility has two possible dimensions: consensus and practice. There was a strong international consensus among Western actors and international institutions that state assets should be divested

via internationally competitive bids. But consistency in practice among the same
actors and organizations was rather weak and undermined the credibility of the
policy. While most OECD countries maintain little to no state ownership of
banks (an exception is Germany), most industrial democracies have preserved
domestic control of their banking sectors for both geostrategic and economic
reasons.

Noting Western protection against high levels of external investment in banking, and having a nationalist sensitivity to foreign domination, the postcommunist
countries received international advice on the matter with measured cynicism. To
be sure, there were free market enthusiasts in every CEE country who believed
that the advantages of inviting foreign capital outweighed the more traditional
security concerns. But the credibility of the claim that postcommunist states
should sell their strategic assets to the highest bidder, regardless of origin, was a
source of controversy and variation in outcomes, both within and across countries.

In Poland, despite early harmonization of the liberals' economic policies with
IFI prescriptions, other forces in the government restricted foreign investment.
Wary of foreign domination, in 1991 the Polish Council of Ministers put a 30 percent limit on the share any single foreign investor could acquire in a domestic
commercial bank.[35] While conservatives favored some foreign participation, they
originally wanted to limit it to 10 to 20 percent, keeping a larger state share and a
still greater private, domestic component.[36] In fact, throughout the first fifteen
years of postcommunism, there were numerous episodes in which high-ranking
policymakers, normally sympathetic with international institutional views, questioned giving untrammeled access to foreign capital. When a founder of the
Warsaw Stock Exchange vented his concerns about the long-term costs of diminished domestic economic control and ownership to the international press, he was
pressured into silence by government officials.[37]

By far the most consequential expression of dissent in Poland was the SLD-
PSL's bank consolidation plan of the mid-1990s. The coalition was wary of privatizing banks quickly and primarily with foreign capital. The leaders of the
communist successor parties took a more nationalist approach to commercial
bank restructuring (E. Balcerowicz and Bartkowski 2001). Not having been party
to the first negotiations with the IFIs on bank restructuring and contingent use of
the zloty stabilization fund for bank recapitalization, the SLD-PSL coalition was
prepared to test the limits of its maneuverability vis-à-vis international actors by
proposing programs with new priorities, including an increased role for the state
in the economy.

According to Grzegorz Kołodko, the SLD-appointed minister of finance from early 1994, the rush to privatize Poland's banks was a mistake.[38] Noting that many other industrialized and developing countries in North America, Europe, and Asia had protected domestic ownership in banking, Kołodko believed there was no technical reason to privatize state-owned enterprises sooner rather than later.[39] He pointed out the lack of correlation between a country's rate of privatization and its economic performance, and also claimed that rapid privatization would complicate the institution-building that was essential for enhancing state regulatory capacity. He further argued that the rapid privatization of Poland's banks would mean de facto sale to foreign interests, because the domestic market was still too capital-poor to absorb such investments. While Kołodko acknowledged that privatization was one way to boost state revenues, he also thought that delaying privatization would ultimately make state-owned banking assets more valuable.

Kołodko wanted to commercialize six to eight of the state-owned commercial and regional banks, consolidate them into two groups (around Bank Handlowy and Pekao SA), and postpone their privatization—for two reasons: to maximize state revenues from the sales and to facilitate purchase by Polish interests. Moreover, Kołodko had two developmental goals in mind: to maintain the state's role in bank management and credit allocation and to create a Polish-owned, internationally competitive banking conglomerate—a capacity that other industrialized countries had routinely preserved for themselves. These objectives were set out in a bank consolidation plan that the Polish MoF, under Kołodko's direction, made public in late 1995.[40] But IMF, EBRD, and US Treasury pressure would ultimately prevent the SLD-PSL coalition from implementing this plan.

In Hungary, the lack of credibility underpinning calls by international institutions for the country to privatize its banks quickly—even if that meant sale to foreign interests—was subject to greater debate in the first postcommunist term, from 1990 to 1994, than thereafter. International institutions and the states that served as models for Hungarian reformers were consistent in abdicating state ownership over banks. But the fact that OECD countries limited high levels of foreign ownership in their own banks gave Hungarian reformers pause. The dilemma for market reformers across postcommunist Europe was essentially the same: how to conform to the Western norm of removing the state from the economy while also maintaining domestic control over resources and development.

The MDF-led government failed to implement a coherent strategy, tending instead to prevaricate until the embarrassment of insolvency made rapid privatization more tolerable. More surprising than the MDF reversal, however, was the socialists' subsequent rapid and indiscriminate privatization of the country's banks. Hungary's bank privatization strategy in the latter part of the 1990s and early 2000s showed little concern for maintaining a domestic presence—a quite remarkable outcome given scant European precedent for unbridled liberalization with foreign capital. So while political conflict over bank privatization between 1990 and 1994 confirms the importance of the study's credibility hypothesis, the MSzP's acceptance of foreign ownership casts doubt on the importance of credibility after 1994.

Romania's initial resistance to banking reform was also based on the belief that banks were strategic assets, but its debate on reform differed in that the principal concern was with privatization as such. Through much of the 1990s, banking was considered strategic for supporting critical enterprises. Thus the reluctance to privatize banks with foreign capital was not born of a sense of injustice, as in Poland, but from concern about economic management capacity in the absence of control over domestic credit.

The measure on credibility changed over the course of Romania's bid to join the European Union, however. Instances in western Europe of domestic ownership protection continued to contribute to the IFIs' compromised credibility. But international institutions strengthened their case for foreign ownership in finance by uniting in their calls for reform and by orchestrating their efforts, thereby increasing the consistency of their message over the course of the transition.[41] In addition, by the late 1990s and early 2000s, when Romania began to clean up its banks and search for foreign investors, much of CEE (Romania's peer group) had already taken the plunge. The foreign investment option had been chosen more often than any other, and among EU accession candidates, all but Slovenia had high levels of foreign ownership in their banking sectors (see table 3.2). The IFIs' growing credibility on the inclusion of foreign capital strengthened Romanian politicians' resolve to internationalize ownership of the banking sector.

Ukrainian reluctance to denationalize its banking sector corresponds more closely to tendencies in both Western countries and the Commonwealth of Independent States to preserve domestic ownership. It became increasingly "normal" for EU accession states to auction off their banks during the 1990s. But for Ukraine, a country with concentrated economic power and a leadership committed to keeping it that way, control was more important than efficiency, and given the social context, international institutions had little power to change the Ukrainian view until the early 2000s.

However, it must also be noted that international institutions' normative inconsistency on banking was never as politically salient in Ukraine as in Poland, because the same degree of coercion was never applied. Although some international institutions and foreign advisors noted that an evident weakness of Ukraine's economy was its very low level of foreign ownership in banking, the country was never directly sanctioned over the issue. Even if IMF agreements with Ukraine were consistently tied to privatization (as in the 1995 and 1996 Standby Agreements and the Extended Fund Facility of 1998) and financial assistance was made contingent on privatizing some state-owned firms, neither banks nor the role of foreign investors were singled out for particular attention. By the time of the Extended Fund Facility of 2000, the IMF had shifted its focus from the number of enterprises to be privatized to the "quality" of privatization—that is, making tenders more transparent and open to foreign investors (Elborgh-Woytek and Lewis 2002, 14). But no special demands were made regarding banks, in part because three of the five state-owned banks had already been nominally privatized, albeit exclusively to their managers, employees, and state-owned enterprises, and because other issues such as inter-enterprise debt and nonpayment were prioritized over bank privatization.

Rather than treat foreign investment as an end in itself, Ukraine's advisors tended to focus on creating a more stable business environment amenable to foreign investment. Noting that low levels of foreign participation in finance were symptomatic of Ukraine's lagging economic performance, the World Bank, OECD, and US Treasury all recommended reducing nonpayment in the economy, rationalizing the tax structure, improving the financial sector's regulatory framework, ending political protection for weaker banks, and limiting arbitrary political interference (see OECD 2001; Roe et al. 2001; Brown 2004; Duenwald, Gueorguiev, and Schaechter 2005). Research indicated that foreign investment would naturally follow from better business conditions—which it did, beginning in late 2004.

## TRANSNATIONAL COALITIONS AND OUTCOMES
### *Poland*

In the first four years of transition, international institutions exploited uncertainty and status to forge a transnational coalition in favor of privatizing Poland's banks quickly, even if it meant a significant role for foreign capital. The coalition comprised international institutional representatives, Western and Polish bankers who had participated in the Twinning Arrangements, and Solidarity-affiliated liberals, who by 1994 were once again in opposition. International institutions cultivated this pro-privatization coalition by exploiting the uncertainty of transition and the desire for social recognition among first-wave, Western-oriented reformers. The

IFC and World Bank established the primacy of Western know-how and capital with their training program, the IMF used the MoF request for bank bailout funds to extract a goodwill commitment to privatize rapidly, and the EBRD consolidated the coalition by investing in Polish banks and pushing privatization forward. But the compromised credibility in the recommendations of international institutions was an ongoing source of friction, and ultimately led to the SLD's bank consolidation plan to end rapid financial privatization with foreign capital.

When the SLD government announced the specifics of that plan in the fall of 1995, the IMF and EBRD were among the first to object. As previously noted, the plan involved consolidating six to eight banks into two conglomerates for sale to domestic interests. The most alarming aspect to foreign actors was that one of the banks slated for consolidation, Bank Przemysłowo-Handlowy of Krakow (BPH, which was to have been merged with Bank Handlowy), had already been partially privatized by, among others, the EBRD, and divided between four major shareholders: the Polish State Treasury (46.6%), the EBRD (15.06%), ING Bank (10.1%), and Daiwa (4.57%). GE Capital and other Polish banks had also expressed interest in investing in BPH not long before the consolidation announcement. The other group proposed for consolidation included Pekao SA (the lead bank), Bank Depozytowo-Kredytowy (Lublin), Powszechny Bank Gospodarczy (Łódź), and Polski Bank Rozwoju (in which Citibank was already a minor shareholder).[42]

While domestic support for the plan was mixed,[43] international misgivings were immediately made known to the press and the Polish MoF.[44] Kołodko did not change course, however, until he and his deputy, Vice Minister of Finance Krzysztof Kalicki, came under direct pressure from members of Poland's bank recapitalization fund steering committee, which included Larry Summers and David Lipton. US Treasury officials in Washington, DC, who were in this instance the final arbiters of IMF policy and who were also acting on behalf of the EBRD, urged Kołodko to drop the program.[45] Building on criticisms Kołodko had already received at home, they argued that state-led consolidation was at odds with the basic principles of a market economy, that such plans were anticompetitive, that it was inappropriate to seem to be "picking winners," and that these were protectionist policies designed to favor domestic over foreign investors. This was especially problematic in Poland, they argued, where it was the communist successors who were pursuing policies that resembled central planning of the previous era. The US Treasury warned that this would raise concerns among foreign investors more generally and that the Polish government could not afford to slow privatization, in the light of the government's budgetary priorities. And, given that

bank consolidation was not in the spirit of the agreement with the IMF to privatize state-owned banks by 1996, US Treasury officials threatened to withhold the
next installment of recapitalization funds.[46]

In 1996, Kołodko and the SLD dropped the greater part of the bank consolidation plans and shifted strategy back to privatizing the banks, one by one, inviting
foreign capital to participate.[47] The intensity of the conflict with the IMF, EBRD,
and US Treasury, coupled with the criticism at home, provoked a sufficient sense
of opprobrium and isolation in Kołodko and his colleagues at the Polish MoF that
they proceeded with a series of pro-market policies well beyond the bank consolidation issue. Not only did the SLD government drop bank consolidation and
the push for domestic ownership, it also initiated a fast-track privatization scheme
for the banks that had previously been slated for consolidation, and sought out
foreign capital for the task. Seeking "a way out," Kołodko justified this policy shift
with a purported need to raise revenue through privatization sooner rather than
later, and then used that revenue to promote a tax cut.[48] SLD deputies further
supported legislation outlawing the consolidation of any bank that was not 100
percent state owned.[49] Kołodko went on to become a visiting scholar at IMF
headquarters in Washington, DC, after his tenure as Polish minister of finance
ended.

The return to denationalization illustrates the causal and constitutive effects
of transnational coalitions. External pressure carried significant causal weight
through material threats. Kołodko emphasized how central the risk of losing IMF
and US Treasury support was in his reasoning. But the social context, which
constituted the meaning of Western financial aid, was equally important. If funding had been the only consideration, the Polish government most likely could
have financed the remaining bank recapitalization itself. The $400 million legis-
lated at that time by the Sejm for emergency adjustment assistance to sensitive
enterprises was instead provided by the World Bank, for example, giving the
government financial leeway to recapitalize Poland's banks. The SLD could also
have refrained from cutting taxes. Moreover, the existence of the zloty stabilization fund for bank recapitalization, engineered by the first post-Solidarity
reformers, was completely fortuitous. Other countries in Poland's position would
have had to find domestic solutions for bank insolvency, which would have meant
going to national legislatures and marshalling political support for that purpose.
Of course, Kołodko could have done that as well. But given the choice between ap-
proaching the Sejm for additional funds after rupturing relations with multilateral
lending institutions or repairing relations with international actors by changing
course on bank privatization, Kołodko chose the latter.

This series of interactions around banking had additional causal and constitutive effects. As noted, the conflict elicited a more market-oriented approach from the communist successor coalition, pushing it programmatically toward its post-Solidarity rivals. To the extent that political parties eventually professed the same preferences around key issues and then proceeded to institutionalize them in that manner, a new role for the state in the economy was defined that became increasingly difficult to contest. The barriers to reversing privatization in banking were compounded by the political disruption it would have caused, particularly for the SLD-PSL coalition.

After the fact, Kołodko continued to maintain that state control over domestic credit allocation was a potentially powerful developmental tool.[50] What matters to political outcomes, however, is what actors do, not what they think. Because political forces threatened to portray him as an unreconstructed communist (even though he was not even a member of the SLD), in a country where state socialism had been thoroughly discredited, Kołodko felt more or less obliged to comply with IFI prescriptions.

Subsequently, Polish policymakers changed course yet again by maintaining state ownership of two banks, including the country's largest, the state savings bank Powszechna Kasa Oszczędności Bank Polski. Even in 2005 it was majority state-owned, having only late in 2004 floated less than 50 percent of its shares on the Warsaw Stock Exchange in a bid that limited foreign investment. The Law and Justice (PiS)–led government was also trying to mute the political effects of large-scale foreign investment by requiring Citibank and ING to reduce their stakes in two Polish banks to 75 percent each. It also tried to stop UniCredito's plans to merge Pekao and BPH, arguing that the consequences for the sector's competitiveness had not yet been sufficiently well examined.[51] However, more than fifteen years after transition began, Poland's banking sector was largely, if not entirely, denationalized, and PiS was able to adjust foreign ownership only at the margins.

## Hungary

In keeping with the uncertainty, status, and credibility hypotheses, Hungary's first MDF-led government set a trajectory that would ultimately, albeit inadvertently, favor foreign ownership of its banks. As in Poland, liberal licensing laws allowed foreign banks to enter the market. Although the objective was to increase competitiveness and force domestic banks to improve their skills and services, the more immediate (if unintended) effect was to encourage politically based lending and repeated bank bailouts. Not only did Hungarian banks fail to update their skills fast enough, but the presence of advanced competitors in combination with decentralized and insufficient regulation put Hungarian banks at a competitive disadvantage (Hjartarson 2004; Piroska 2005). The first reformers were reluctant to sell Hungarian banks to foreign investors outright, preferring Hungarian owners who were not *nomenklatura* insiders.

But after 1994, the socialist-led government, in coalition with the liberals, undertook large-scale privatization in the financial sector. The MDF did prepare Budapest Bank for sale and sold the foreign trade bank (MKB) in response to international pressure: Bayerische Landesbank bought a 25 percent share in MKB in 1994 and eventually acquired a controlling stake, while the EBRD purchased another 17 percent. But the socialists went much further in privatizing commercial banks during their 1994–1998 tenure. Beginning in 1995, the state began selling shares of the country's biggest retail bank, National Savings and Commercial Bank Limited (OTP), to portfolio investors, although foreign strategic investors were not allowed a controlling stake. Portfolio investors also bought portions of Postabank in 1995, with the state temporarily maintaining a major stake. GE Capital and the EBRD bought shares of Budapest Bank in the same year, with GE eventually acquiring close to 70 percent. In 1996, Dutch ABN-Amro bought Hungarian Credit Bank (MHB), and the Belgian Kredietbank/Irish Life consortium invested in Kereskedelmi- és HitelBank. Hungary also sold Takarekbank to German interests and Mezobank to Austria's Erste Bank in 1997.[52]

When a new center-right government (Fidesz–Hungarian Civic Party) came to power in 1998, it continued along the privatization path, but less vigorously than its socialist predecessor. In 1999, 14 percent of OTP was offered by the Hungarian State Privatization Agency, through which the EBRD acquired a stake. But one of the state's largest remaining banks, Postabank, was once again in need of substantial recapitalization, stimulating new privatization plans.[53] And it was the socialists, once again, who accelerated the process from 2002. Further sales of Kereskedelmi- és HitelBank, Földhitel- és Jelzálogbank (a mortgage bank), Konzumbank, and Postabank were targeted at foreign buyers or listed on the Budapest Stock Exchange.[54] To the extent that Hungary had promoted domestic ownership, it was in the form of portfolio holdings. The state did not retain a strategic interest in any of the banks, but did retain a small share in OTP.

The outcome in Hungary is largely what my theory would predict. But two rival hypotheses might explain Hungary's approach to bank privatization as well as or better than my social context argument. The first is that a combination of indebtedness, IFI conditionality, and EU accession rules constrained Hungary's room for maneuver (Hanley, King, and Tóth János 2002). The country's loose regulatory framework that put its banks at a competitive disadvantage arguably also demanded multiple, taxpayer-funded bailouts (Hjartarson 2004; Piroska 2005). The material costs of bad management could have been a more powerful constraint than the social conditions I outline.

Nevertheless, it is unlikely that indebtedness or conditionality, independent of the social context, "forced" Hungarian bank denationalization (Hanley, King, and Tóth János 2002, 161). Financial constraints, in the end, were not overwhelming. Although Hungary had one of the highest levels of per capita debt in postcommunist Europe, Slovenia faced a similar constraint and yet chose not to privatize its banks as a partial remedy (Piroska 2005, chap. 3). The IMF and World Bank did express concern about Hungary's current account and budget deficits in late 1993 and halted financial assistance (Hanley, King, and Tóth János 2002, 156), but that interruption was likely due less to IMF–World Bank concern than to Hungary's ability to draw external financing from international capital markets to which the MDF government had carefully retained access. Hungary was therefore hardly desperate for Bretton Woods support.[55] Also, although a rationalist explanation might be that bank privatization was driven by the need to reduce budget deficits, privatization revenues were already very high at 135 billion forint in 1993 and further privatizations would not have solved the deficit problem (van Elkin 1998, 64).

When the socialists came to power in 1994, their "stabilization" plan, for which they enlisted the assistance of international institutions, was a preventive plan (Kornai 1997). Moreover, although EU accession did call for a harmonization of market access rules, both Poland and, to an even greater extent, Slovenia found ways of preserving domestic ownership. Conditionality was no doubt important to securing bank denationalization in Hungary—but not because material constraints left no other options. Rather, the socialists effectively and voluntarily used international conditionality from 1994 until 1998 to redefine their image.

It is more difficult to dismiss the other rival hypothesis, that rapid privatization was the most attractive option given regulatory failure and degradation in the domestic banking sector (Hjartarson 2004; Piroska 2005). In Hungary, it was the relatively early and large-scale entry of foreign banks that immediately put its banks at a competitive disadvantage. Creditworthy borrowers and consumers in turn flocked to foreign banks, while Hungarian banks attracted a less desirable clientele (Hjartarson 2004, 20). After a protracted and costly series of bank bailouts, one possible long-term solution was to finally sever political relations between the state and banks by encouraging still more foreign investment. The wisdom of the IFIs and the socialists' strategy of selling the banks to foreign investors were only confirmed in 1998 when the scope of Postabank's troubles was revealed.

There are two ways in which a social context argument complements, but does not necessarily supersede, the regulatory failure argument. First, early Hungarian debates about privatization were not about whether but about how to privatize state-owned banks. The narrowness of perceived policy options, in addition to the MDF's willingness to open the Hungarian banking market to foreigners, reveals Hungary's receptivity to IFI counsel—particularly on what would produce the greatest efficiencies and that efficiency, as opposed to state power, should be maximized. Second, as the 1990s progressed, it was the socialists who promoted bank privatization most aggressively. Although the second center-right government of 1998–2002 ostensibly planned further privatizations, including that of the troubled Postabank, no major bank privatizations took place on its watch. In keeping with the social context argument, the socialists were more beholden to international opinion than were conservative nationalists. Regulatory failure and the costs of repeated bank recapitalization strengthened arguments in favor of privatization, irrespective of uncertainty, status, and credibility, but did not absolutely oblige it.

## Romania

Initial conditions in Romania during the transition limited the influence of international institutions. As in other sectors, impenetrability in banking is explained by the continuity in regime personnel and the absence of international status seeking until the competitive elections of 1996. In a social context in which neither the Bretton Woods institutions nor the European Union were credible authorities, Romanian politicians made commitments to international institutions about which they were ambivalent. Politicians were reluctant to privatize state-owned banks, even those that suffered insolvency problems and required repeated bailouts, because government officials and their allies in the private sector used banks for their own financial and political purposes. Domestic interests prevailed in Romania, despite a series of international financial agreements that were linked in part to bank privatization.

By early 2006, however, the picture had changed dramatically: Romania had sold all but two of the formerly state-owned banks. State ownership of banking assets had declined from 75 percent in 1998 to 8 percent in 2006. Moreover, the larger of the two remaining banks, the national savings bank (Casa de Economii si Consemnatiuni), was slated for privatization by the summer of 2006. Thus

TABLE 3.3

*Major Increases in Foreign Ownership in Banking: Selected States, 1998–1999 to 2002*

| Country | Foreign Ownership, 1998–1999, % | Foreign Ownership, 2002, % |
|---|---|---|
| South Korea | 0 | 30 |
| **Romania**[a] | 8 | 47 |
| Mexico | 20 | 83 |
| Czech Republic[b] | 26 | 90 |
| **Poland**[b] | 26 | 69 |
| Brazil | 17 | 30 |
| Lithuania[b] | 48 | 78 |
| Chile | 32 | 47 |
| **Hungary**[b] | 62 | 89 |
| Venezuela | 34 | 43 |
| Estonia[b] | 85 | 99 |

*Source:* Barth, Caprio, and Levine 2006, 153.
Notes: Countries appearing in boldface are included in this study.
[a]Countries admitted to the European Union in 2007.
[b]Countries admitted to the European Union in 2004.

between 1996 and 2006, Romania had completely shifted its strategy—not only in favor of privatization but in favor of foreign strategic investors. Romania, like Hungary, Slovakia, the Czech Republic, and Bulgaria, was headed for record high levels of foreign ownership in banking, which hovered above 80 percent by 2006.

International institutional pressure and assistance, *preceded* by a changed social context, explains the radical shift toward internationalization of the banking sector in Romania. The changed social context included the heightened status of international institutions that accompanied the competitive elections of 1996 and arrival in power of the inexperienced CDR. Although in some respects ineffectual as an opposition to the socialists, the CDR promoted itself in part on the basis of improving Romania's international standing, even if repairing relations with the European Union and the Bretton Woods institutions meant short-term austerity measures. In banking, this stance led to the opening of Romanian markets, and majority foreign capital ownership jumped from 8 to 47 percent between 1998 and 2002 alone (see table 3.3). When the socialists returned to power in 2000, compliance included an economic strategy for EU membership that called for still further bank privatization, even if that policy was originally put in place by the CDR (Doltu 2002, 291).

Cooperation with international institutions further involved a 25 percent purchase of Romania's biggest state-owned bank, BCR, in 2004 by the IFC and

EBRD, which then successfully oversaw reorganization of the bank before its 62 percent sale to Austria's Erste Bank in late 2005. Earlier, beginning in 1998, successive Romanian governments had sold major stakes in the Romanian Development Bank, BancPost, and Banca Agricola—all to foreign investors.[56] And Bancorex, the large and long-ailing former trade bank, finally closed its doors in 1999, in part through a merger with BCR.

The international pressure to embrace internationalization is not in question. Privatization remained a key condition of World Bank and IMF support, and Romania was pursuing the earliest possible date for EU accession.[57] The 1998 Accession Partnership agreement listed bank privatization specifically (although the equivalent document a year later did not mention banking).[58] Public officials, including a secretary of Romania's national import and export association and a Romanian minister of finance, publicly acknowledged that external pressure was at work.[59] But such pressure is unlikely to secure compliance independent of a particular social context. One need only compare Romanian compliance with IFI demands for privatization in the early 2000s with the situation five years earlier to see that conditionality—a feature of both periods—is insufficient on its own to elicit compliance (Tsantis 1997, 200–205).

Another alternative to the social context argument is simply that the pressures of EU accession loomed large by the early 2000s. My argument suggests that EU conditionality did contribute to the financial denationalization outcome, but not because it offered a clear-cut promise of admission in exchange for openness to foreign investment in banks. In fact, as late as the spring of 2006, Romania was judged to be seriously out of compliance in areas of finance and agriculture. But it was nevertheless poised to join the European Union in January 2007, because thresholds for Romanian compliance in these sectors had been modified for political purposes.[60] Indeed, the extent to which EU conditionality is politically, rather than strictly, applied is well documented (Grabbe 2002; Hughes, Sasse, and Gordon 2004; Sasse 2005; Sissenich 2007). Finally, with specific respect to bank privatization, it is notable that although Poland had maintained state ownership and Slovenia had been consistently protective of its banking sector, both countries were admitted to the European Union in 2004.

A final alternative argument is that privatization with foreign capital was simply the best possible solution in the circumstances. After all, Romania's banking sector had been in near constant crisis between 1990 and 2000, and repeated bailouts necessitated by political lending had cost the state billions of dollars (Cernat 2006). Romanian consumers have benefited from recent changes, and the state is no longer compelled to bail out the sector. But this "best-practice" argument can be rejected on two grounds. First, it suggests that Romania would have ultimately settled on the same solution without the influence of international actors. But this would not explain why the same group of domestic actors—the socialists—would fund failing state enterprises and buy political loyalties in one period, but protect consumer interests and balance the budget later on. What constituted a "desirable outcome" changed dramatically between the early 1990s and the 2000s, precisely because international actors had increasing power to define an optimal outcome—and that did not include subsidizing industry or self-lending.

Second, although Romania's banking sector was undoubtedly in better condition following a number of bank privatizations, it is not clear that state-run or domestically owned banks (in CEE countries) cannot also perform well. By 2004, after much restructuring, three of Romania's banks, all still state owned, were indeed doing well: BCR, National Savings Bank, and Eximbank.[61] When BCR was finally sold to Erste Bank in December 2005, it fetched the highest price of any CEE bank in the postcommunist period—3.75 billion euros, six times its book value.[62] Poland and Slovenia also boasted well-managed state-owned banks, while Hungary's (domestically managed if not domestically majority-owned) OTP had become internationally competitive, acquiring assets outside the country.

## Ukraine

Ukrainian banking outcomes are consistent with a social context in which international institutional power was circumscribed for much of the period under consideration. Compared with other CEE transition economies, the outlook for Ukraine's banking sector was still poor but improving by the early 2000s. In 2003, the country's banking-sector capitalization was still only $2.5 billion—the equivalent of one mid-sized European bank (Brown 2004, 7–8). The sector continued to suffer from high levels of concentration, segmentation, and lack of competition. The costs of borrowing remained relatively high, particularly for small and medium-sized enterprises. The enduring very large number of banks (more than 150 at any given time) pointed to potential consolidation within the sector, and Ukraine's foreign advisors were urging the National Bank of Ukraine (NBU) to end its protection of the weakest banks.

In a signal that business conditions were improving and that Ukraine had become increasingly open to both foreign advice and investment, the pace of international banking deals in Ukraine had accelerated by 2005. In late 2004, Sweden's SEB Group had bought 94 percent of shares of Ukraine's Agio Bank. In

2005, Austria's Raiffeisen and France's BNP Paribas bought substantial stakes in Aval and UkrSibBank, respectively, two of Ukraine's largest banks. In early 2006, Italy's Banca Intesa purchased another of Ukraine's former state banks, UkrSotsBank.[63] With foreign ownership of the banking sector inching up toward 30 percent, observers expected Ukrainian banks to become increasingly competitive.[64] The adoption of more advanced technologies and the broadening of operations by some of Ukraine's stronger banks had the potential to limit market segmentation, increase competition, and make credit more widely available, particularly to small and medium-size enterprises.[65]

The Orange Revolution of late 2004 no doubt played a crucial role in changing foreign investors' perceptions of Ukraine as an increasingly democratic and Western-oriented power. However, over the previous four years the social context between Ukraine and several international institutions had already been evolving. Given the increasingly competitive political sphere and the relatively consistent technical advice provided by the Bretton Woods institutions, Ukraine manifested a higher level of compliance in 2005 than it had in 2000. In 2001, a report from the World Bank suggested that no major reforms had followed from its 1995 assessment of Ukraine's financial sector and provision of a Financial Sector Adjustment Loan of nearly $300 million (Roe et al. 2001, 4, 33; also see World Bank 2000). Among other problems it pointed to was the NBU's failure to close the weakest banks, inadequate restructuring of the two remaining state-owned banks, continued government interference in banking activity, government tolerance of barter and nonpayment among actors in the economy, arbitrary tax policy, and a generally uncertain business environment.

Between 2001 and 2005, however, Ukraine registered a higher degree of compliance with IFI advice, starting with passage of the Law on Banks and Banking Activities in 2001 that eliminated restrictions on foreign investment in the sector. Other reforms recommended by the World Bank included the liquidation of Bank Ukraina, a state-affiliated bank that had long posed a systemic risk to the banking system; improved performance and management of the two remaining state-owned banks, Oschadny and UkrEximBank; and stronger NBU regulation, including forced disclosure of banks' ownership and cross-ownership structures with other enterprises. The central bank also began enforcing tougher capital adequacy and loan loss provisions that led to improved prudential reports for the largest seven banks. This is not to say that all of the World Bank's concerns had been addressed by 2005. But the business environment had improved sufficiently to encourage foreign investment. And just as important, Ukrainian law no longer discriminated against foreign interests.

## CONCLUSION

Foreign investment in postcommunist banking sectors has transferred technology, know-how, and capital from West to East. In countries with recurring bank insolvency problems, such as Hungary and more recently Romania, foreign ownership has relieved the state of the burden of repeated recapitalization. Bank privatization has also limited the possibility for domestic political lending. With foreign ownership close to 70 percent in Poland, 80 percent in Romania, and 90 percent in Hungary, one plausible explanation for denationalized banking would be that foreign ownership was the quickest way to achieve rationalization—an outcome that international institutions universally supported.

Poland, Hungary, and Romania did have political forces that favored foreign investment because they *ultimately* came to believe that modernization precluded state and even domestic control of capital allocation. But in no country did such beliefs enjoy broad support at the outset of transition. The question is therefore why so many CEE states started the transition professing one set of goals and ended up embracing another. My argument is that where domestic actors were uncertain and perceived a hierarchical relation between themselves and foreign advisors, international institutions could frame national ownership strategies as too costly to pursue.

In Poland and Hungary, even pro-Western reformers in the first postcommunist governments had nationalist ambitions and assumed that they could limit foreign ownership to 10 or 20 percent of any single bank. But striving to refashion their image, communist successor parties in both countries proved particularly accommodating to international actors. Poland and Hungary converged on foreign ownership not because actors across the political spectrum were persuaded of "best practice." Rather, they were persuaded, however grudgingly, of where authority appropriately lay—in international institutions and not in national economic sovereignty.

Romania and Ukraine, by contrast, were much slower to yield to international authority, remained sensitive to industrial and agricultural demands, and believed there were viable alternatives to large-scale foreign investment. But the growing status of international opinion in Romania by the late 1990s, in connection with political competition, corresponded to a new acceptance of IFI prescriptions that bank rationalization was more important than strategic or even short-term political concerns. Ukraine remained the most nationally oriented of the four countries, maintaining 70 percent domestic ownership in the sector as late as 2006, but even this country registered stronger compliance with World Bank recommendations—again in line with strengthened political competition.

Nor can variation across the four countries be explained by degrees of banking crisis. It was Hungary and Poland that privatized first, while Romania suffered the greatest costs from banking-sector problems. Indeed, the degree of variation not just among the four countries but across the entire region points to the fact that some countries—including Slovenia and Russia—still perceive "best practice" in terms other than high levels of foreign investment (see table 3.2).

That the three countries with the highest levels of foreign ownership in banking have since become members of the European Union also raises the question of whether Bretton Woods or EU conditionality imposed denationalization. Bretton Woods conditionality was applied against Poland and Hungary and elicited compliance in bank privatization in the early and mid-1990s. But similar conditionality failed to produce the intended effects in Romania and Ukraine. The proximity of conditionality to policy change in Poland and Hungary attests to its power. But that power was contingent on a social context in which domestic actors sought expertise from what they perceived to be authoritative sources. Absent the same hierarchical relation between international institutions and Romania and Ukraine, Bretton Woods conditionality was not deemed worthy of compliance.

Some analysts have speculated that EU conditionality is more likely to elicit compliance than Bretton Woods conditionality, because so much more is on offer and at stake. Not only do states receive financial assistance, but they gain market access and voice within one of the world's most powerful institutions. Willful defections from EU membership criteria cast doubt on such claims, however, including defections by Romania and Bulgaria, which failed basic compliance in the 1990s and were finally admitted without fulfilling all the criteria in 2007. Turkey's and Serbia's ongoing struggles with the European Union also suggest that EU conditionality, like its Bretton Woods counterpart, must be constituted as desirable and authoritative before states can be expected to comply.

Romania complied more closely with EU banking demands in the run-up to accession with the privatization of BCR, a clear signal that it was willing to do what Brussels wanted. Since compliance was preceded by a changed political environment in which international opinion became more salient, this suggests that even EU conditionality demands a particular social context. But the independent power of EU conditionality is difficult to test, given that it is imposed unevenly. The continuing role of the state in banking in Poland and Slovenia provides two examples of EU flexibility.

The combination of technical advising and conditionality on display in bank privatization highlights the importance of constitutive and regulatory rules. As in other aspects of this study, banking reveals how regulative rules constitute actors. Communist successor parties in Poland and Hungary proved to be the most active proponents of foreign investment and liberal economic policy because of the power of international institutions to assign meanings to actions. Political competition in Romania and Ukraine ultimately also revolved around each country's standing in international opinion. Further, to the extent that states complied with conditionality or were persuaded by technical advice, selling formerly state-owned banks to foreign interests indefinitely limits their role in the economy and alters the distribution of power, both domestically and internationally. The wisdom of the foreign investment decision most likely will be a theme that post-communist states return to and struggle with as actors reconsider its short- and long-term consequences.

# CHAPTER FOUR

# Democratizing
# Civil-Military Relations

The accession of Poland, Hungary, and the Czech Republic to the North Atlantic Treaty Organization in 1999 and of Romania in 2004 ought *not* to have been a vigorous test of NATO's power to win compliance from candidate states. The proven vulnerability of all four states made membership in the world's most successful military alliance a patently logical goal. The rise of democratic opposition movements under communism in Poland, Hungary, and the Czech Republic should have made the idea of democratic civil-military relations attractive to these states. Communist party armed forces that had helped prop up hated regimes might have been sufficiently discredited that in theory, at least, they would have difficulty resisting new modes of governance.

Despite these seemingly auspicious starting conditions for NATO, compliance with democratic civil-military relations proved problematic in postcommunist states, and strong compliance was ultimately the *exception*, not the rule. For although central and eastern European (CEE) states had historically been vulnerable, publics were not uniformly supportive of NATO membership. Even in the presence of democratic oppositions, CEE states were unaware of the substance of NATO's standards of democratic control. Perhaps most surprisingly, militaries were not uniformly discredited throughout the region. Their continuing legitimacy as symbols of national independence in countries such as Poland and Romania—in spite of everything—further complicated NATO efforts to transform power relations between the armed forces and their would-be civilian overseers.

To be sure, NATO pushed all states that it engaged closer to a model of diffuse democratic civil-military relations than would probably have happened in the absence of the alliance's enlargement policy. But the key challenge for NATO throughout the region was the CEE sentiment that narrow executive authority over the armed forces, which in turn allowed high levels of military autonomy, was entirely compatible with democratic governance. As postcommunist states, one after another, shifted from communist party control to an executive-led model, NATO officials attempted to show why this was not democratic enough. But the alliance's reach was uneven for reasons largely consistent with a social context informed by uncertainty (H1), hierarchical relations (i.e., status; H2), and the perceived credibility of NATO's core demands (H3) (see chapter 1 on the three study hypotheses). As these conditions varied across countries, so too did the alliance's access to reform processes.

## CIVIL-MILITARY RELATIONS IN THE POSTCOMMUNIST CONTEXT

Theorists of civil-military relations have traditionally been concerned with the military's ostensible proclivity to exercise excessive authority at society's expense. What this might mean in practice is that the military interferes in matters of policy so as to favor its material or power position relative to other groups in society, particularly civilian leaders and their constituencies. The most extreme version would be the military's full seizure of political power and establishment of a military dictatorship, as has so often occurred in Latin America and more recently in Myanmar, Pakistan, and elsewhere. In important respects, the record of post-communist military transformation has departed from these traditional concerns.

Stemming from communist-era legacies, the most serious problems in civil-military relations have generally been linked not to military interference in poli-tics (except in isolated cases) but to armed forces' struggle to win autonomy from civilian authority. Also peculiar to the postcommunist context, this struggle has at times taken place with the active or passive assistance of civilian leaders (Epstein 2005a, 2006b). For although state-socialist civil-military relations were far from democratic, there was rarely any serious breach in the norm of civilian control, even if that civilian control did not provide thoroughgoing NATO-style civilian and societal oversight.[1] In the postcommunist setting, the challenge to democra-tization has centered on the need to persuade military personnel and civilians alike of the functional and normative desirability of limiting military autonomy, where such autonomy was something that civilians and officers had long taken for granted (Cottey, Edmunds, and Forster 2002, 4).

In the light of communist-era legacies, democratizing civil-military relations in postcommunist Europe would necessitate the following: that multiple channels of civilian oversight be established and exercised; that civilians in positions of authority over the military be made democratically accountable, both to an electorate and to a free press; and that large segments of the military-security apparatus that had been the exclusive domain of military authority be significantly civilianized. Specific measures include a civilian defense minister to whom the General Staff answers, a civilianized Ministry of Defense (MoD), parliamentary defense committees that exercise military oversight, a transparent defense budget, and civilian authority over intelligence services. In sum, what NATO was asking for was a system of checks and balances in which the executive, government, parliament, and society, through the media and nongovernmental organizations (NGOs), would share in oversight—a system that had no precedent in CEE.

NATO membership requirements, including the specific features of democratic civil-military relations that candidates were expected to adopt, began to take shape in 1994 with the Partnership for Peace (PfP). The admission criteria were reinforced in the "Perry Principles" in early 1995,[2] and again with the *Study on NATO Enlargement* released in September of the same year (NATO 1995b).[3] Confounding rationalist expectations that would predict compliance on the basis of security incentives and the increasing clarity of membership criteria, there was hardly a seamless adoption of the new rules. In a particularly apt description of the reform processes, one US official deeply involved in advising CEE states on military reform conceded that "ninety percent of the battle is showing these countries that there is a problem. Ten percent is fixing it."[4]

## NATO INFLUENCE OVER CIVIL-MILITARY RELATIONS: UNCERTAINTY, STATUS, AND CREDIBILITY

In chapter 1, I argued that uncertainty among domestic actors (H1), their perceived subordinate status vis-à-vis international institutions (H2), and the credibility of international institutions' policy prescriptions (H3) shape a social context that makes compliance with incentives more or less likely. In the case of NATO and the democratization of civil-military relations, variation in the second and third hypotheses accounts for much of the difference in outcomes among the four countries under study: Poland, Hungary, Romania, and Ukraine.

The level of uncertainty among military personnel was low and posed a barrier to NATO influence in all four cases, because militaries experienced very little in the way of interest demobilization in the transition (H1). This is quite different from what transpired in the financial sector, where price liberalization and the market mechanism disoriented interest groups and led to high levels of uncertainty. Sectoral continuity in military-security apparatuses resulted in strong confidence among military personnel on how reform should proceed. Preferred reforms did not include enhanced civilian or societal oversight. Civilians in ministries of defense and foreign policy were more open to NATO's counsel, however, and it was through them that the alliance was first able to exercise influence.

Variation in international institutional status—defined by the desire among domestic actors for the approbation of international institutions—explains much of NATO's uneven influence in the 1999 and 2004 enlargements (H2). Operationalized in terms of the quality of political competition, the status variable explains why some communist successor parties were ultimately eager to fulfill NATO criteria and why democratizing reforms in Romania were put off until after the first competitive elections in late 1996 (Gheciu 2005a, 2005b). Curiously, however, and in contrast to what the status hypothesis would predict, democratic opposition under communism was not a sufficient predictor of NATO's influence. Dissident movements under state socialism, often supported by the West, used Western ideas as reference points against their own regimes (Garton Ash 1993; Thomas 2001; Vachudova 2005). But even among states with such dissident movements, there was substantial variation in the acceptance of NATO prescriptions. Hungary and the Czech Republic were much weaker compliers than was Poland, for example.

Given the consensus behind the principle of democratic control through the 1999 enlargement, NATO was acting with a high degree of credibility in the case of civil-military relations (H3). Turkey was the exception to the rule, and in keeping with the hypothesis, Polish politicians in particular raised the Turkish question with NATO: if Turkey, a NATO member, was allowed to have a direct line of authority between the executive and the armed forces, then why couldn't Poland? Turkey notwithstanding, NATO officials could point to the array of alliance members that did have democratic and diffuse control over the armed forces, reinforcing credibility.

Although uncertainty, status, and credibility are at the center of the analysis, this is not to suggest that incentives were at no point critical to outcomes—they were. But as argued in chapter 1, and demonstrated in chapters 2 and 3 for the financial sector, those incentives were never separate from a social context that imbued them, or failed to imbue them, with power. I am not testing for the effects of conditionality versus socialization (Checkel 2001b, 2005; Kelley 2004a; Schimmelfennig and Sedelmeier 2005), nor am I arguing that changes in personal convictions alone explain democratic outcomes in military governance (Gheciu 2005a; and on citizenship rights, see Checkel 2001b). The process in CEE of introducing democratic control over armed forces for the first time was not one in which the logic of consequences operated independent of the logic of appropriateness (March and Olsen 1989, 1998). Rather, the attempted transfer of value-laden knowledge to target states by international institutions provided the social context in which incentive structures either made sense or were judged unworthy.

NATO exercised the most influence in states where it could elevate the status of civilians in relation to the military by bolstering their defense expertise and corroborating their claims for the need to subject the military to diffuse and democratically accountable civilian oversight. The alliance had the most comprehensive access to military reform in Poland. Over a decade, NATO helped put elements of Poland's past aside, diminishing the salience of Polish military tradition and centralized authority. In Hungary, compliance was decidedly weaker than the theory would predict, while in Romania the initial lack of political competition resulted in delayed compliance. Ukraine manifested the weakest adoption of democratic civil-military relations by 2004, lacking most elements of a social context that would make the incentives of NATO membership meaningful.

## CLASH OF HISTORIES: MILITARY LEGACIES AND NATO INFLUENCE (H1)
### Poland

The case of civil-military relations, as noted above, is marked by a consistent *lack* of uncertainty; the absence of interest demobilization across the armed forces in postcommunist Europe posed a barrier to NATO influence. Polish officers, for example, had a strong military tradition that provided institutional guidance on how to conduct reform coming out of the Warsaw Pact. Even if their command experience was limited by the Soviet Union during the Cold War, Polish officers were anything but uncertain about the military's role in an independent Poland. Moreover, the Polish armed forces were never purged in the wake of communism (as they were, for example, in Czechoslovakia), a testament to their perceived independence from the Soviet Union and their professionalism and national loyalty. No doubt, the military's embrace of the transition and independence in Poland was essential to the pacific nature of otherwise revolutionary events (Barany 1993, 155). But as NATO encroached and began suggesting reforms, the military more often than not resisted the terms of NATO membership.[5]

By contrast, civilians in the foreign and defense ministries lacked experience in governing the military because, under communism, party leaders awarded the armed forces operational autonomy in exchange for their political subservience.

Uncertainty was thus stronger on the civilian side of the defense apparatus, and thus it was through civilians that NATO initially exercised the most influence. In Poland, a sharp divide between civilians and military officers emerged, with civilians proving susceptible to NATO's arguments about the value of democratic accountability. Normally, the lack of civilian expertise is judged to be a factor inhibiting constructive reform.[6] And admittedly, in Hungary and the Czech Republic, to the extent that civilian ignorance translated into neglect, civilian inexperience initially did harm the reform process and for a longer period than in Poland. But in Poland, where social support for military power was high, the lack of strongly held ideas among civilians about how to structure reform ultimately bolstered NATO influence.

Polish officers began the transition with long experience in matters of defense. During the Cold War, the Polish military was, although by no means entirely, uniquely autonomous within the Warsaw Pact in ways that allowed Polish military tradition to exist alongside compliance with Pact requirements.[7] The military's circumscribed "autonomy" from the Soviet Union included the capacity to expel Soviet officers from Poland after 1956 and to limit the number of Soviet garrisons on Polish soil; the use of pre- and noncommunist military victories and "glorious" defeats in sustaining Polish military mythology; the rejection of Soviet political indoctrination on the comity of Polish and Soviet interests; the professionalization of the armed forces; the maintenance of a number of officers that was excessive by purely military standards; the pursuit of independent foreign policy initiatives such as the Rapacki Plan;[8] and the 1967 law decreeing universal commitment to defense of the Polish "fatherland."

Perhaps most important, the Polish military's autonomy during the Cold War was evident in its perceived unreliability, from the Soviet perspective, as an instrument of domestic repression.[9] To the extent that Polish nationalists were able to maintain some room for maneuver in relation to the Soviet Union, it was at least in part by preserving Poland's military tradition (Jones 1981; Sanford 1986; Michta 1990). Public opinion reinforced the army's perceived (by the Soviets) unreliability by continuing to celebrate the life and achievements of Marshal Josef Piłsudski, who led Polish forces in the defeat of the Soviet Union in 1920 and governed the country through much of the interwar period, albeit from behind the scenes, after staging a military coup.

The preservation of military prowess and tradition under even the most adverse conditions long predated the Cold War, and has its origins in the "aristocratic military ideal" that began under the three partitions of Poland beginning in 1772 and continuing through World War I.[10] In the course of resisting foreign invasion and occupation, the Polish soldier demonstrated loyalty first and foremost to the military leader, not to a government. During decades of attempted socialization within the Warsaw Pact by the Soviet Union, the Polish military tried to preserve its character while simultaneously placating a superpower. It is thus not surprising that for the Polish military, the collapse of the Soviet empire represented an opportunity to finally win back Polish independence, and this did not necessarily include a readiness to submit to new civilian authorities or to collective security arrangements. Even among civilians early in the transition, what would later become accepted in Poland as the NATO standard of civilian control was neither understood nor championed.

Indeed, the first set of civil-military reforms, resulting from the Żabiński Commission report, reflected Polish tradition more than NATO norms in maintaining separate military and political guidance and in failing to make the General Staff accountable to the MoD or parliament (Michta 1997). A series of crises in civil-military relations between 1992 and 1995 in which politicians failed to sanction civilian and military misconduct further strengthened the military's autonomy and signaled the myriad ways in which the idea of democratic civilian control had not yet taken hold.[11]

Lacking uncertainty, the national experience informed civil-military relations in Poland in the first years of transition. In the Parys affair of 1992, Poland's first civilian defense minister, Jan Parys, came to the job intent on de-Sovietizing the armed forces and consolidating ministerial oversight. But at the same time, President Lech Wałęsa was trying to expand the scope of executive authority over foreign policy and security affairs—in part by exchanging high levels of military autonomy for the loyalty of the General Staff. In 1992, these competing objectives came to a head. Parys accused Wałęsa of planning new martial law contingencies and of promising to assign General Tadeusz Wilecki to the post of chief of the General Staff without consulting key civilian bodies, or even the MoD (Simon 1996, 62–65). The Sejm (parliament) committee concluded that all of Parys's claims were spurious. Wałęsa's unvetted appointment of Wilecki stood, while Parys was forced from office. Most Polish politicians still adhered to the idea that the military should be run by military personnel.

The Drawsko affair in 1994 was also an example of ministerial weakness and parliamentary passivity—and therefore consistent with Polish history. High-ranking officers were increasingly willing to disregard MoD authority—as in the vote taken at Drawsko by high-ranking military officers, at Wałęsa's instigation, on the competence of the minister of defense, retired Vice Admiral Piotr Kołodziejczyk.[12] Although the vote of no confidence had no legal status (and violated Poland's

"Little Constitution" of 1992), Kołodziejczyk felt sufficiently undermined that he accepted Wałęsa's subsequent request for his resignation. There was never any formal reprimand of the generals involved, however, or any sanction of Wałęsa for his role. Wałęsa was later able to issue promotions and monetary rewards to the very generals who had violated democratic principles (Simon 1996, 82–83; Michta 1997, chap. 4; 2002, 170). Again, the failure to punish this breach of democratic accountability, parliamentary passivity, and the circumvention of MoD authority demonstrated a lack of recognition for NATO standards of civilian control.

Between 1989 and 1995, other symptoms of civil-military tensions included attempts to politicize the military during the 1995 presidential election (the Komornicki affair)[13] and the repeated public criticisms by high-ranking military figures of civilian leaders and their policies. While in many instances civilians were complicit in the exercise of military overreach, as civilians competed with each other over jurisdiction military leaders exploited that conflict and aggrandized their own authority. Simon argues that by 1995 the military's exploitation of civilian weakness "brought the military an independence not found anywhere else in Central Europe. As a result, the General Staff has acquired enormous influence vis-à-vis the defense ministry in personnel policy, financial policy, military information (intelligence), professional military education and the press" (1996, 115).

President Wałęsa plays a special role here, partly undermining the uncertainty hypothesis, for although he was a civilian, he also resisted what NATO was telling him about the need for diffuse democratic control. This exceptionalism can be explained first by a worldview governed by a sentimentality about the Polish military, close to that of the Polish public generally. For despite the military's previous role in propping up the communist regime, Wałęsa believed that a competent state needed a strong, effective military and that the armed forces should basically be run by their own people.[14]

But the general pattern of civil-military relations in the early 1990s shows a military eager to exploit civilian conflict and incompetence and civilians generally unaware that they could or should be exercising more authority. One foreign and defense policy expert, in explaining the difficulties in trying to persuade Prime Minister Jan Olszewski of why Poland should appoint its first civilian defense minister in 1991, noted that at the time, "nobody believed in civilian control in this part of the world."[15] But equally relevant is that no one knew what democratic civilian control was—or at least, no one was familiar with NATO's definition of it. Only after NATO made decisive moves to enlarge its membership after 1994–1995 would the alliance finally begin communicating what it meant by democratic civilian control.

## Hungary, Romania, and Ukraine

The continuity of the armed forces across much of the postcommunist region ensured that NATO would encounter some friction in every state where it tried to democratize civil-military relations. Whether countries had strong military traditions and independent armed forces or not, NATO was consistently dealing with military officers opposed to systems of democratic oversight. Their civilian counterparts were unaware of NATO's version of democratic civil-military relations and, when they ultimately found out, were ill-equipped to implement it, due to a lack of authority and expertise. But consistency in sectoral continuity notwithstanding, more minor points of variation among the countries are worth noting.

Hungary's measure on uncertainty most closely resembles Poland's. The military in Hungary had been firmly embedded in the Warsaw Pact, but it also had a prior independent military tradition; as in Poland, civilians had been removed from operational control of the armed forces. The most notable difference between the two countries was in the strength of military traditions: Hungary's had been thoroughly undermined by the Soviet Union whereas Poland's had not. But in both cases, the consequences of certainty and sectoral continuity were clear: military resistance to democratic innovation and initial civilian acquiescence. As in Poland, civilians in Hungary, early on, supported military reform that left the armed forces with far more autonomy than was acceptable to NATO. Once the alliance's admission criteria became more specific, however, a struggle ensued in which civilians, backed by NATO training, tried to submit Hungarian officers to a more thorough oversight than they wanted.

Romania's military also had a command system incompatible with NATO's principles of democratic civil-military relations. But compared with Poland and Hungary, Romania's military was more independent from the Soviet Union during the Cold War, and Romanian civil-military relations were more strained than elsewhere in the Warsaw Pact. In the early 1990s, neither Romania's military nor its political leadership was receptive to NATO's coaching on the importance of democratizing civil-military relations. Although the communist successors, the Party of Social Democracy of Romania (PDSR; formerly the Democratic National Salvation Front, FDSN), did appoint a civilian minister of defense in 1994, and the 1991 Constitution forbade military participation in political activity, little had changed in terms of democratic accountability. Both the defense and interior ministries were largely militarized, and the division of authority between the government, executive, and parliament was not clear.

Romania had proved more skillful than Poland in securing political and military autonomy under the Warsaw Pact, potentially limiting NATO influence further. Autonomy had been possible for Romania in part because, from the Soviet perspective, it was strategically less significant than Poland or even Hungary. Romania's growing independence from the Soviet Union took multiple forms. Romania took a curiously (by the standards of the time) neutral position in tensions between communist China and the Soviet Union; it developed closer ties to Tito's Yugoslavia, even after the Soviet-Yugoslav split; it deployed an extensive territorial defense program (which the Soviets had prevented in Poland); and it invested heavily in its domestic arms industry in order to limit dependence on Soviet technology and supply. Most exceptionally for a Soviet satellite, the Ceauşescu government was openly critical of the 1968 invasion of Czechoslovakia, when other regimes in the region had come to the Soviet Union's military aid (Watts 2003).

But while Nicolae Ceauşescu used the armed forces to insulate his country from Soviet domination, his own political failings also contributed to the dysfunctional civil-military relations, which would have implications for NATO compliance in the post–Cold War period. By denying the armed forces material support while also deploying them in public works projects, Ceauşescu alienated the military leadership and inadvertently encouraged military institutions to become more autonomous, nationally oriented, and less susceptible to communist party indoctrination (Watts 2002, 14). Mistrust between the civilian leadership and the officers intensified, especially through the 1970s and 1980s, which made it more difficult for civilians to exercise oversight in the 1990s.

The continuity of Romanian leadership in the postcommunist regime also limited uncertainty and muted NATO's democratizing power in the early 1990s. Even though marginalized actors from Ceauşescu's own cohort exploited public dissatisfaction and managed the revolution (including Ceauşescu's trial and execution), this did not create a unified front between political leaders and military officers. On the contrary, civilian-military estrangement was a powerful legacy in Romania that complicated NATO's agenda. NATO therefore faced enormous challenges in cultivating a new consensus around the desirability of democratic civil-military relations.

Ukraine also had a low level of uncertainty in the armed forces that would limit NATO influence. As elsewhere, the Communist Party of Ukraine and the Communist Party of the Soviet Union traded complete political control over the armed forces for operational independence. Due to the Ukrainian armed forces' total integration into the Warsaw Pact, military legacies were an even more powerful barrier to change than in Poland or Hungary. The Soviets had incorporated Hungarian and Polish armed forces into military plans in ways that would keep national capacities in those states weak, but Ukrainian officers were present at some of the highest levels of command, creating not just institutional legacies but also entrenched "attitudes about authority, society, national security and the role of the Military in defending it" (Sherr 2005, 158).

But in other respects the Ukrainian armed forces should have been relatively open to institutional change. Ukraine had very little in the way of an independent military tradition.[16] With just a brief period of statehood following World War I, Ukrainians had spent the preceding centuries as either a junior partner in federation with Russia or as minorities within the Polish or Austro-Hungarian empires (Prizel 1998). Adapting Russian military traditions and methods of organization was therefore the most natural course for many senior Ukrainian officers, and almost fifteen years after independence Ukrainian military personnel still failed to understand what Western advisors meant by "civilian control."[17] However, NATO did provide an alternative model, given that Ukraine was engaged in a state-building process from 1991 forward and given the country's sporadic efforts to escape Russian hegemony. By 2004, according to one NATO official, at least some of Ukraine's military leaders had developed an interest in reform in connection with NATO standards.[18]

As in Romania, potential civilian openness to NATO in Ukraine was undermined by the continuity in leadership from the communist era to post-independence, beginning in 1991. Ukraine was not so much a newly liberated state as a new state, implying a degree of inexperience among civilian leaders in how to conduct foreign and defense policy. However, within the Soviet Union, Ukraine did have some of the trappings of statehood, including a seat at the United Nations and republic-level control over the tools of domestic repression— including the security services. So when Leonid Kravchuk, a former secretary for ideology in Ukraine's Communist Party and later its head, perceived the inevitability of the Soviet Union's demise, he quickly acted to ensure his party's survival, albeit in a slightly more nationalist form (Prizel 1998, 359–65). In this case, the lack of an MoD worked to Kravchuk's advantage. In the hyper-presidential system that Ukraine subsequently adopted, the executive would be the only body with the institutional channels to govern the military, however inadequately.

## ACCOUNTING FOR VARIATION: NATO'S UNEVEN STATUS (H2)

States are more likely to comply with an international institution's policy prescriptions when they perceive themselves as subordinate within a hierarchy. The status hypothesis suggests that postcommunist states with democratic opposition movements under communism and political competition in the postcommunist period should have been more receptive to NATO's principles than those without political competition and party turnover. Among the countries considered here, political competition is theoretically linked to higher status for international institutions because membership bids give these institutions the opportunity to weigh in on which political parties are fulfilling the necessary criteria. Thus international opinion becomes a reference point around which political parties compete.

Although the quality of political competition is a useful proxy for the status hypothesis across the cases in this book, it is an imperfect proxy in the area of civil-military relations. According to the political competition proxy, for example, one would expect Poland, Hungary, and the Czech Republic to be equally strong compliers with NATO prescriptions, but they were not. Instead, Poland was ultimately the strongest complier (although not until after 1997), and Hungary and the Czech Republic were weak compliers, especially before the 1999 enlargement. Political competition as a proxy for status corresponds more predictably to the beginning of Romania's compliance with some of the NATO prescriptions in the late 1990s, after the Democratic Convention of Romania (CDR) unseated the communist successors in the elections of late 1996.

An additional operationalization that helps capture status dynamics between candidate states and NATO is public support for NATO membership. A public support proxy would seem to come very close to corroborating a neoliberal explanation of compliance with incentives—the more a country wants to join NATO, the more receptive it is to the alliance's demands. Variation across countries and over time does not bear this out, however. If a measure of public support was *all* one needed to predict compliance, then Poland and Romania should have been strong compliers by the early 1990s (which they were not), and Hungary and the Czech Republic might never have complied with anything that NATO wanted (but they did). (Table 4.1 shows data on public support for NATO membership.) The neoliberal interpretation of public support also does not answer the more basic question of why countries with similar experiences of military vulnerability and foreign domination had such divergent public perceptions of the value of NATO membership, even if elites across countries were uniformly committed to joining.

Measuring the perceived status of an organization in terms of measures of political competition and public support for membership is one method of systematizing historical differences among states. Contrary to what a neoliberal or realist approach would predict, the history that mattered most in understanding which publics would support NATO membership most fervently was not geostrategic vulnerability but military-society relations. Tables 4.1 and 4.2 highlight

TABLE 4.1
*Opinion Data on NATO Membership, 1995 and 1997*

| Country (year of accession to NATO) | In Favor, % | | Undecided, % | | Against, % | |
|---|---|---|---|---|---|---|
| | 1995 | 1997 | 1995 | 1997 | 1995 | 1997 |
| **Poland** (1999) | 69 | 61 | 12 | 18 | 6 | 4 |
| **Romania** (2004) | 64 | 67 | 12 | 11 | 4 | 9 |
| **Hungary** (1999) | 32 | 47 | 22 | 22 | 22 | 15 |
| Czech Republic (1999) | 33 | 36 | 23 | 21 | 23 | 22 |
| Slovakia (2004) | 30 | 31 | 26 | 24 | 18 | 17 |
| Slovenia (2004) | 44 | 45 | 16 | 13 | 18 | 23 |
| Bulgaria (2004) | 30 | 37 | 14 | 22 | 28 | 14 |
| Estonia (2004) | 47 | 32 | 29 | 37 | 13 | 12 |
| Lithuania (2004) | 38 | 31 | 23 | 28 | 8 | 16 |
| Latvia (2004) | 34 | 36 | 29 | 34 | 14 | 10 |

Source: European Commission, *Central and Eastern Eurobarometer*, March 1996 (no. 6), fig. 31; 1998 (no. 8), fig. 35.

Note: Countries appearing in boldface are included in this study. The question asked was, "If there were to be a referendum tomorrow on the question of (our country's) membership of NATO, would you personally vote for or against membership?" Respondents included only those who have the right to vote. Respondents who gave no answer or who answered "don't know" are not represented in the data.

the covariation between high levels of support for NATO membership and strong military-society relations. The surprising consistency between trust in militaries and the desire to join NATO again points to the centrality of social context in shaping outcomes. There are no objective means by which publics assess national security. Rather, public judgments about how and whether to ensure military preparedness are rooted in nationally based beliefs about the utility of the armed forces and, by extension, the value of NATO membership. Where the alliance enjoyed elevated status, states engaged in early and overcompliance, public pressure to comply was powerful, and political party platforms converged in response to NATO standards.

## Poland

All dimensions of the status hypothesis receive strong confirmation from Poland. The value of becoming more like a NATO member—initially with or without membership—corresponded to democratic opposition under communism. NATO had enormous symbolic value in Poland, stemming from the association between the United States' leading role in the alliance and its strong public stand against the Soviet Union and communism. While the Germans pursued

TABLE 4.2

*Public Confidence in the Armed Forces: Selected Postcommunist States*

| | | Response rate, % | | | | | |
| Country | Year | A Great Deal | Quite a Lot | Not Very Much | None at All | Do Not Know | No Answer |
| --- | --- | --- | --- | --- | --- | --- | --- |
| **Poland** | 1990 | 22.2 | 40.9 | 26.1 | 6.5 | 0 | 4.3 |
| | 1997 | 23.4 | 51.7 | 15.6 | 3.7 | 5.6 | 0 |
| | 1999 | 18.7 | 45.7 | 26.1 | 4.9 | 4.5 | .1 |
| **Romania** | 1993 | 36.9 | 44.6 | 15.0 | 2.6 | .9 | 0 |
| | 1998 | 34.7 | 45.2 | 14.7 | 2.8 | 2.6 | 0 |
| | 1999 | 35.3 | 44.9 | 14.3 | 2.6 | 2.2 | .7 |
| **Ukraine** | 1996 | 17.6 | 44.9 | 22.2 | 7.2 | 8 | 0 |
| | 1999 | 19.9 | 44.9 | 22.3 | 7.0 | 5.0 | .8 |
| **Hungary** | 1991 | 9.1 | 41.5 | 38.7 | 8.6 | 0 | 2 |
| | 1998 | 12.8 | 43.7 | 32 | 9.1 | 2.1 | 0 |
| | 1999 | 5 | 39.6 | 38.5 | 13.9 | 2.7 | .3 |
| Czech Republic | 1991 | 6.9 | 33.4 | 48 | 10.9 | 0 | .8 |
| | 1998 | 2.7 | 39.5 | 41.2 | 13 | 3.7 | 0 |
| | 1999 | 2.5 | 22.2 | 60.5 | 12.5 | 1.6 | .7 |
| Slovakia | 1991 | 9.9 | 45.2 | 34.6 | 8.9 | 0 | 1.5 |
| | 1998 | 12.1 | 53.6 | 24.6 | 5.9 | 3.8 | 0 |
| | 1999 | 13.4 | 58.6 | 17 | 4.6 | 6.5 | 0 |
| Bulgaria | 1990 | 23.2 | 44.8 | 22.7 | 8.2 | 0 | 1.1 |
| | 1997 | 35.4 | 40.4 | 13 | 4.4 | 6.9 | 0 |
| | 1999 | 11.3 | 42.3 | 32.1 | 7 | 6.8 | .5 |

*Source:* World Values Survey, Public Confidence in the Armed Forces,
www.worldvaluessurvey.org.

*Note:* Countries appearing in boldface are included in this study. The question asked was,
"I am going to name a number of organizations. For each one, could you tell me how much
confidence you have in them: is it a great deal of confidence, quite a lot confidence, not very
much confidence, or none at all?" The military was one among several institutions listed.

"normalization" with Warsaw Pact capitals via Ostpolitik, and western Europeans
generally sought accommodation rather than confrontation between East and
West, it was the United States that insisted on funding dissident movements in
CEE and spending the Soviets into the ground (Garton Ash 1993).

Another such source of legitimacy was that the West had clearly prospered
under the conditions of cooperation, peace, and domestic transformation that
NATO had cultivated and sustained over decades. According to one Polish observer, NATO represented the "civilizational standard" to which he believed
Poland should aspire, as a means of escaping what he considered more primitive
traditions of military political power.[19] NATO's status with respect to how a liberal, democratic country should balance authority between the military and civilians was admittedly only relevant to a narrow section of Polish society in the early

1990s. Nevertheless, the Polish elites who aspired to institutionalize a range of liberal rules proved instrumental in multiplying NATO's power.

Evidence of the perceived status of an international institution can be found in actors' overcompliance with the terms of membership or early, preemptive emulation. The Atlantic Club in Poland, founded in October 1991, is an example both of how NATO exploited its status and of how domestic actors formulated policy when seeking identification with international institutional values. Although the Atlantic Club was a post–Cold War innovation, NATO had influenced the thinking of Club members over decades.[20] One of the Club's leaders was Zdzisław Najder, founder in exile of the Polish League for National Independence during the Cold War and frequent contributor to the subversive journal *Kultura*, a literary, political, and cultural precursor to Solidarity.

At a time when NATO still ruled out enlargement, in large measure because the United States was skeptical about adding new members, the notion of Poland in NATO was radical—both for Western officials and for the Polish public.[21] Nevertheless, Najder and his colleagues used NATO as a reference point for reform and ultimately succeeded in convincing Prime Minister Olszewski in 1991, against his better judgment and against President Wałęsa's wishes, to appoint Poland's first civilian minister of defense. Certainly the Atlantic Club's emphasis on democratic civilian control was partly in hopeful anticipation of one day joining the alliance. But according to Club members, civilianization of the security apparatus was desirable by virtue of its association with Western democracies, and they would have pursued it irrespective of NATO's enlargement strategy—but not irrespective of NATO's embodiment of it.

The 1993 Onyszkiewicz/Grudziński reforms, which would have moved Poland away from the more traditional command set up under the Żabiński reforms toward a Western model, were also an attempt at early conformity with democratic standards.[22] Although they were not implemented in 1993, because of the Suchocka government's collapse, these reforms evidenced a growing awareness among Western-oriented reformers that traditional patterns of civil-military relations were incompatible with NATO's "civilizational standard." Importantly, these efforts were made before the Partnership for Peace was announced, before the Perry Principles were articulated, and two years before NATO clarified its intention to enlarge. Multiple missions between Brussels and Warsaw in the early 1990s were clearly aimed at sharing information so that Polish reformers would have the necessary tools to begin democratizing military governance (Bobrowski, Każmirski, and Waszczykowski 2006).

In another instance of overcompliance, civilians adopted models of command that were better suited for signaling their solidarity with the alliance than for governing the Polish armed forces. Based on the US system of separate commands for land, sea, and air, their applicability to Poland was questionable given the realities of the Polish military—namely, that some commands far outweighed others in number and importance. Military personnel resisted, noting that the new command structure was more of a "caricature" of the US system than an effective organizational strategy for the Polish armed forces.[23]

Another determinant of NATO's status in postcommunist states was public support for membership. Although elites in CEE all lobbied equally hard to join NATO, the greater public enthusiasm in Poland than in Hungary and the Czech Republic explains why the latter two countries manifested lower levels of compliance than Poland on everything from democratic oversight to Target Force Goals—the process whereby new members essentially redesign their force structures and develop new capabilities (Wallander 2002). The variation in public perceptions is particularly important for showing the social as opposed to exclusively strategic dynamics that facilitate compliance with international institutions, because equally vulnerable states had very different public perceptions of joining NATO—some much more strongly in favor than others (see table 4.1). Hungarian and Czech publics in particular were not overwhelmingly in favor of joining, while Polish and Romanian publics were.

The importance of high and low public support for NATO membership is borne out by two kinds of evidence in Poland. The first is the way in which public opinion and concern about NATO accession pressured the military into compliance. Public awareness about the link between military-security reform and admission to NATO had grown over the course of the early 1990s. One indicator was the media reaction to a 1995 US Congressional Research Service (CRS) report (Collins and Meyer 1995) that argued that Poland, while fit for peacekeeping, was not competent to fight a war; that because officers had not taken part in important Warsaw Pact decisions, their professional growth was stunted; that NATO accession hinged on a democratic constitution and the legal basis for civilian control; and that the minister of defense and many of the senior officers who set policy and shaped opinions had become mired in political wrangling over control of the armed forces.

The CRS's critical findings were widely reported in Poland, raising the public's anxiety about whether the country was qualified to join the alliance. There were competing interpretations. *Gazeta Wyborcza*, the country's leading newspaper, founded by members of Solidarity, reported that "NATO cannot trust the Polish

Army officers, because . . . no personnel changes have been carried out since the change of the political system,"[24] but the deputy minister of defense, Andrzej Karkoszka, argued that the report contained "more praise than reproof" and that "the treatment it was given by the Polish media is grotesque."[25] Nevertheless, the Polish General Staff, recognizing public support for NATO, understood that the ongoing argument over civil-military relations might jeopardize membership.

Public enthusiasm for NATO (if not for the finer intricacies of democratic control) also narrowed the political spectrum. The most powerful communist successor parties of the early 1990s, the Polish Peasant Party (PSL) and the coalition that would eventually become the Democratic Left Alliance (SLD), were initially skeptical of NATO membership.[26] Amid widespread disillusionment with economic hardship and the sense that Solidarity had betrayed its earlier agenda (Powers and Cox 1997; Orenstein 2001; Ost 2005), in the 1993 elections the communist successor parties ran on a platform of easing economic reform and slowing integration with the European Union and NATO. With specific respect to NATO membership, PSL and SLD party members variously argued that it should be contingent on Russian approval or that if NATO were to enlarge it should also include Russia and Ukraine. Aleksander Kwaśniewski, who would in 1995 become the SLD's presidential candidate, also favored reopening the question of NATO membership in 1993.[27] Another SLD member complained that "there was never any debate on Poland's future security possibilities or about NATO membership and its implications . . . We don't say no, but we believe it would be wise to explore other possibilities."[28]

In an example of how international institutions in combination with public support and political competition can change party platforms, the postcommunists' apparent ambivalence was short-lived. Within a month of forming an SLD-PSL coalition after the 1993 elections, the new Polish government began expressing its steadfast support for membership in NATO, and the SLD began denying that its members had ever equivocated on the issue.[29] Two developments explain the reversal. First, the leading coalition parties came under immediate pressure from their political enemies and from the press.[30] Those who were willing to debate the issue of whether Poland should join NATO were accused of being against membership.[31] Second, on coming to power, the postcommunists were assured by their contacts in multiple international organizations that they could continue to work together, as long as the new government protected democratic governance.[32] Although collaboration with the former communists was distasteful to (among others) Americans working on Polish-US and Polish-NATO bilateral relations, they conceded that cooperation would "make the SLD behave better than it otherwise would."[33]

The perceived status of NATO in Poland had both regulative and constitutive effects on actors, including the military and postcommunist parties. NATO's power was regulative insofar as the political context put pressure on actors to reject national tradition. But the alliance also changed the *properties* of actors. The Polish military went from wanting autonomy to wanting NATO membership even at the expense of autonomy. The SLD went from wanting to distinguish itself from its political rivals to wanting to cultivate constructive relations with organizations that had been its enemy only a few years earlier. In recognizing new sources of authority, actors were also adopting new political objectives.

## Hungary, Romania, and Ukraine

The status hypothesis receives only partial confirmation in the Hungarian case. Hungary is much like Poland in having had a democratic opposition under communism and party turnover in the transition. In Poland, competitive political dynamics resulted in a strong identification with NATO's values and preemptive compliance with its democratic norms. In Hungary, there was some initial emulation of Western models of democratic civil-military relations, including the appointment of a civilian defense minister, attempts to subordinate the military to the government, and civilianization of the MoD (Simon 1996, 145–48). But when the socialists returned to power in 1994, some of these apparently pro-NATO reforms were weakened, contradicting what the status hypothesis would predict about the effects of political competition. In particular, whereas the Hungarian Democratic Forum (MDF) had civilianized many offices in the MoD, the Hungarian Socialist Party (MSzP) reappointed military officers (Jacoby 2004, 140).

Different levels of societal support for NATO membership help explain the variable responses to the alliance's policy prescriptions. Hungary's elite fought hard to have the country included in the first post–Cold War NATO enlargement, which was not an obvious choice for the alliance: Hungary' geography was discontiguous with NATO and its military was in a poor state.[34] But the Hungarian public was decidedly more ambivalent. In April 1996, less than a year after NATO's commitment to enlarge became firm with release of the *Study on NATO Enlargement* (NATO 1995b), a poll showed that only 38 percent of the Hungarian population supported NATO membership and 27 percent had a negative view (Simon 1996, 172) (also see table 4.1 for 1995 and 1997 figures).

NATO's relatively low status in Hungary (compared with Poland or Romania) stemmed from widespread public disillusionment with military power as a means of advancing national goals. Such disillusionment had its origins in the nation's history. During World War II, in alliance with Nazi Germany until 1945, Hungary's ill-equipped and outnumbered forces suffered decisive defeats by their Soviet enemies (Barany 1993, 31). Military-society relations would never recover. From that time forward, the role of the Hungarian military went from that of "defender of the nation-state to that of protector and guarantor of the continued domination of the Communist party"—a thoroughly illegitimate regime in the eyes of much of the Hungarian public (Barany 1993, 29). The only point at which the military might have improved its status with the population was in the 1956 Hungarian uprising. But rather than defend the Hungarian people against Soviet crackdown, the army, not wanting to support the Stalinist regime against the population, simply disbanded (Dunay 2002, 68).

Ensuing hostility and mistrust between civilians and the military also hindered reform of the kind NATO demanded. Indeed, only a narrow band of Hungarian elites actively pursued "Western models of military organization" (Jacoby 2004, 134), and it proved difficult to bring high-level military officers on board. Whereas Western criticism of civil-military relations in Poland caused a public outcry and conveyed to the General Staff that its conflicts with civilians jeopardized public loyalty, one could not expect commensurate public pressure in Hungary. Instead, NATO and the Hungarian government had to fund a media campaign to ensure a successful referendum in favor of NATO membership (Jacoby 2004, 144). The public relations campaign resulted in stronger Hungarian support for membership by 1997 (table 4.1 shows public opinion before and after the campaign).

Romania provides stronger support for the status hypothesis. The lack of party turnover in the transition and the absence of robust political competition until 1996 initially limited the appeal of democratic civil-military relations. As previously noted, there was strong continuity between the leadership of the communist era and what came after. Marginalized elements within Ceaușescu's own apparatus orchestrated his capture, trial, and execution. These "managers" of the revolution in December 1989 went on to seek their political fortunes through the newly created National Salvation Front (FSN), prevailed in the first "free" elections of May 1990, and then ruled continuously, sometimes in coalition with other nationalist or communist successors, until late 1996. So even though among the first countries to express interest in NATO membership, Romania (together with

Ukraine) was the least receptive to the alliance's principles of democratic civil-military relations in the first half of the 1990s.

With the competitive elections of 1996 and the replacement of the socialists with the CDR in coalition with the Social Democratic Union (USD) and the Democratic Alliance of Hungarians in Romania (UDMR), the status of international institutions increased. Political competition enhances the likelihood of policy transfer from West to East because international sources of legitimacy matter to contenders. In the absence of political competition, the ruling party can choose the basis on which it cultivates public support. With two or more groups vying for power, international institutions can take sides, define interstate relations, and assign status. Democratic civil-military relations had no stronger precedent in Romania than anywhere in CEE. But it was under CDR leadership that the first far-reaching democratizing reforms in line with NATO prescriptions were attempted (Gheciu 2005a, 2005b).

Once political competition was in place, NATO could also exercise power over Romanian reform by virtue of public support for membership. Public confidence in military power was even stronger than in Poland and eventually facilitated Romania's compliance with some aspects of NATO prescriptions more than in either the Czech Republic or Hungary. The public commitment to bolstering the armed forces stemmed in part from the revolution and from the longer-term perception of the military as the necessary guardian of the country's independence. Because the Romanian armed forces were thought to have fought valiantly in both world wars and because they sustained casualties in the struggle against Ceauşescu, the military was among the most trusted of Romanian institutions (Encutescu 2002, 46; Watts 2002, 9–13). High levels of social support translated into relatively high levels of defense spending, a keen interest among some defense specialists in learning about NATO, and fairly consistent public enthusiasm for Romanian membership.

In Ukraine, by contrast, the lack of party turnover in the transition, the poor quality of political competition until the early 2000s, and low levels of support for NATO membership all inhibited significant policy transfer. Although membership in NATO had ostensibly been a goal of Ukrainian policy from the 1990s, in 2004 the country was still registering low levels of compliance. There are additional reasons for the low levels of Ukrainian compliance that are somewhat removed from the status hypothesis. While public support for NATO membership in Hungary was initially low and conceivably linked to similarly low confidence in military power, Ukraine's strategic, cultural, and economic position is much closer to Russia than in the other cases studied here. In western and central

TABLE 4.3
*Ukrainian Public Opinion Data on NATO, 1998*

| Survey Statement | Agree, % | Disagree, % |
| --- | --- | --- |
| Ukraine must attempt to join NATO as soon as possible. | 22 | 30 |
| Ukraine must try to enter in a military union with Russia and other CIS countries, but not with NATO. | 34 | 24 |
| In the nearest future, Ukraine must remain a neutral country. | 41 | 16 |
| The "Partnership for Peace" is the best framework of cooperation for both Ukraine and NATO. | 35 | 9 |

*Source:* Galin 1999, 25–28.
*Note:* Respondents who neither agreed nor disagreed or who did not know are not represented in the data.

TABLE 4.4
*Ukrainian Public Opinion Data on NATO
Membership, 2000*

| Ukraine Should Join NATO . . . | Response, % |
| --- | --- |
| . . . in 5 to 10 years. | 23 |
| . . . in 10 to 15 years. | 9 |
| . . . never. | 51 |
| It's hard to say. | 17 |

*Source:* Bychenko and Polyakov 2000, 15.

Ukraine, support for NATO membership in 2004 was considerably higher (although still not in the majority) than in eastern and southern regions of the country. But a full third of generals serving in Ukraine at independence were of Russian origin. And while many of them pledged loyalty to the new Ukrainian state, many did so only after thoughtful hesitation (Strekal 1994).

Moreover, in southern and eastern Ukraine, much of the public in 2004 still perceived NATO as a hostile, aggressive organization, which limited the alliance's influence on the country (Razumkov Centre 2004, 174–75). The burning in effigy of a NATO soldier during President Yushchenko's Brussels summit with North American, European, and NATO leaders in February 2005 was one indication of the public opinion challenge facing the alliance in Ukraine. Although by 2005 some members of the governing elite had developed a desire for NATO's social recognition, much of the Ukrainian public still did not see the country's identity or security as profitably tied to membership (see tables 4.3 and 4.4).

NATO'S DEMOCRATIC CREDIBILITY:
ASSESSING NORMATIVE CONSISTENCY (H3)

Through the first post–Cold War enlargement in 1999, NATO maintained strong, though not complete, credibility around the ideal of democratic civil-military relations. Both the consistency in democratic practice across alliance members (with the exception of Turkey) and NATO efforts to portray enlargement and compliance as democratic choices among candidate states bolstered its credibility in Poland and Hungary. Credibility and its absence explain much about whether and how the process of policy transfer is likely to unfold. In civil-military relations, the credibility hypothesis predicts the grounds on which actors were likely to resist and how the alliance ultimately diminished dissent.

## Poland and Hungary

Beginning with the way in which NATO introduced the idea of enlargement, it is evident the alliance was aware of the advantages of maintaining credibility. Even for Polish leaders with roots in Solidarity and a strong Western orientation, making NATO membership an official objective too early was risky. In September 1991, on his trip to Washington, DC, Polish Prime Minister Jan Krzysztof Bielecki did argue for formal links to the alliance (Bobrowski, Każmirski, and Waszczykowski 2006). But NATO was still undecided on enlargement, and parts of the US government were hostile to the idea. Few in Poland were eager to publicly pursue membership only to be rejected by the West and left diplomatically exposed in a historically dangerous region. Then in early 1992, Polish officials received the signals that some had been hoping for. Jan Parys recalls that as Polish minister of defense, he first received strong encouragement for pursuing membership from US Secretary of Defense Richard Cheney, German Minister of Defense Volker Rühe, and NATO Secretary General Manfred Wörner.

When Wörner visited Poland in March of that year, he told Parys privately that the Cold War division of Europe had been "artificial and misguided" and that any new security architecture in Europe should include those states unjustly exiled by Yalta.[35] But early Western supporters of enlargement also coached Poles on how to broach the question. Because the Americans, Germans, and NATO itself were unable to credibly raise it first, the initiative would have to seem to come from sovereign states acting on their own volition.[36] It was important to project an image not of NATO wanting to expand, but rather of sovereign states wanting to join.[37] Following these private revelations, Parys publicly pressed Wörner on NATO reform and enlargement at a conference on central European security.[38] The secretary general finally conceded—for all to hear—that NATO's doors were open to Poland.

NATO efforts to project credibility, by orchestrating a series of exchanges in which CEE states would ask to join and NATO leaders would say yes, produced two kinds of results—one domestic and one international. Domestically, adhering to an open-door policy (consistent with Article 10 of the Washington Treaty) showed Poles they were not "knocking on closed doors"—one early critic's claim.[39] It also organized the debate in Poland's public sphere about how best to achieve membership and further provided the foundations on which reformers could argue their case for democratization of the security sector. Internationally, Wörner and Parys's combined strategy created a context in which it was hard to argue with the legitimacy of NATO enlargement. The order of events and the respective roles of actors, coupled with the spreading belief—even in Russia—that sovereign states should have the right to formulate foreign policy independently, belied claims that NATO was an imperialist organization.

NATO's reluctance to openly coerce candidate states, and its refusal to shame them publicly for transgressions of basic principles of civilian oversight, bolstered the impression that postcommunist states were entering a democratic organization that would not bully even its weakest members.[40] Similarly, NATO's insistence that there was no single model of democratic civil-military relations (even if there were core concepts) suggested that the alliance would uphold the principle of national autonomy. Finally, NATO's repudiation of Western arms manufacturers' claims that new weapons systems were essential for eastern European membership demonstrated that the alliance's apparent preoccupation with democratic governance was not simply a subterfuge to conceal commercial interests.[41]

The objective of such normative consistency was to bolster credibility and elicit national ownership of policy. In this regard, NATO officials explicitly acknowledged their efforts to produce interests at both the elite and public levels that might not otherwise come about. For example, Target Force Goals were upgraded only incrementally, and at the alliance's behest. NATO encouraged slow change in this area, in part for technical reasons, but also because "from the political perspective too, nations need to be persuaded that changes are necessary for them. National governments may then have to begin a process of explaining the reasons for change to their publics" (Boland 1998, 33).

NATO often pursued credibility even at the expense of efficiency. CEE reformers eager for rapid modernization expressed frustration at the alliance's timidity. Even when NATO officials had ample opportunity to shame those who were obstructing reform into complying, more often than not the alliance failed to act by any public means.[42] Even some within CEE defense establishments, eager to use NATO membership as a vehicle for internal renovation, were disappointed that the alliance was not more insistent on better and quicker political assimilation.[43] Publicly stated directives might have produced more immediate compliance, but the alliance framed its prescriptions merely as suggestions.

The almost universal institutionalization of democratic civil-military relations among "old" NATO members also contributed to the alliance's credibility. In direct response to Western models, for example, Hungary appointed a civilian defense minister, formally subordinated the General Staff to the government, and civilianized the MoD—all with the backing of the Hungarian constitutional court (Szenes 2001, 79). Admittedly, the MSzP (the socialists) began undermining these reforms in 1994 by downsizing the civilian presence in the MoD, by resisting the merger of the General Staff with Army Command, and by appointing a retired colonel as minister of defense. But even as the MSzP tried to reassert its authority over the military, it was careful not to reject the formal democratic premises on which the original reforms were based. And before the end of their tenure in government, the socialists relinquished part of their agenda in response to Western pressure (Simon 1996, 169; Szenes 2001, 84).

The perceived credibility of policies also sets the parameters for how actors argue their case. Given Turkey's notable lack of diffuse democratic civilian control over its military and yet its membership in NATO, Wałęsa defended his own predilection for executive authority by pointing to the inconsistency in the alliance's position.[44] CEE leaders also portrayed NATO's early reluctance to expand the alliance as normatively inconsistent with Western claims about wanting to transcend Europe's Cold War divisions (Schimmelfennig 2003). Normative inconsistency also explains why military-to-military contacts between CEE officers and their Western counterparts failed initially to have the desired effect (from NATO's perspective) of persuading the former of the necessity of democratic civilian control. Instead, given ongoing tensions between Western military authorities and their own civilian interlocutors, postcommunist military officers concluded that civilians everywhere were insufficiently competent to govern the military and should be excluded from sensitive matters such as defense planning and intelligence gathering.

## Romania and Ukraine

The degree of NATO's consistency and thus credibility changed during Romania's bid to join the alliance. A strong Western (if not international) policy consensus still underpinned the idea of a decentralized and democratically accountable system of civilian oversight through the 1999 enlargement. In fact, the alliance increased its efforts at socializing new security elites in candidate states by boosting training and educational programs and by creating or expanding programs aimed at achieving interoperability, including the Membership Action Plan after the 1999 enlargement. These efforts were made because the alliance learned from Hungary and the Czech Republic that liberal, democratic values in the military-security apparatus were not obvious even to Western-oriented reformers in post-communist states (Gheciu 2005a, 158). But by the early 2000s, largely in response to the terrorist attacks on the United States on September 11, 2001, the alliance's conception of security was shifting, as were its standards of the optimal balance between democratic accountability and security maximization. According to NATO officials, the definition of security broadened as a consequence of the perceived terrorist threat. The events of 9/11 sharpened the alliance's concern about mental interoperability—that is, the shared commitment to particular values that makes possible consensus-based decision-making in large organizations.[45]

But if NATO's emphasis on mental interoperability was increasing in the early 2000s, its substance was different than in the run-up to the first round of enlargement. As the West's, and particularly the United States', sense of vulnerability increased, the alliance became less demanding of democratic accountability and more solicitous of foreign policy solidarity (Barany 2003, 144, 173–74). Although the post-9/11 shift did not imply a new *de jure* policy on democratic civil-military relations, NATO's emphasis changed such that more energy was devoted to bolstering CEE support for the wars in Afghanistan and Iraq (Jacoby 2005). This meant that less attention was paid to thoroughgoing domestic reform (Gheciu 2005a). In addition, NATO became less concerned with ensuring broad operational compatibility in favor of encouraging each new or candidate state to produce something—no matter how small—for multilateral missions (Watts 2002, 22; Jacoby 2005). The partial erosion of the Western consensus around democratic principles of military oversight, and NATO's failure to apply the same expectations to Romania as to Poland, would lead one to expect a lower level of Romanian compliance with democratic civil-military relations—which was indeed the case.[46]

For Ukraine, there is little doubt that by the early 2000s it could have exploited the alliance's willingness to forego some democratic accountability in exchange for increased foreign policy solidarity. Indeed, NATO was courting Ukraine on this basis. The alliance was highly motivated to bring Ukraine into the Western fold, believing that "converting" one Slavic state with deep ties to Russia could mark the beginning of a more sweeping transformation of the entire postcommunist region.[47] But in fact, Ukraine was still so far out of compliance with minimum NATO standards on democratic civil-military relations and most other measures that the alliance, although keeping its doors open to Ukraine, was also rebuking the country for particular policies.[48]

Kuchma, for example, might have sensed that the 9/11 attacks altered NATO's priorities to favor strategic allies over like-mindedness among NATO members. The embarrassment of his exclusion from the Prague Summit changed not only Kuchma's perceptions, but also those of his ministers, and brought to their attention NATO's insistence that it still had democratic standards.[49] And, in addition to the problems implied by the Kolchuga scandal over selling radar equipment to Iraq and the murder of the investigative journalist Heorhiy Gongadze, NATO was still concerned in 2002 about Ukraine's commitment to democratizing civil-military relations, enforcing the rule of law, and subjecting both the security services and interior ministry to parliamentary and democratic oversight. Even as the Ukrainian government was frustrating NATO efforts to Westernize Ukraine's policies, the alliance was having an impact, in part through a growing group of NGOs that, by the mid-1990s, were interested in what they perceived as NATO's transformative capacity.[50]

## THE SOCIAL CONTEXT AND TRANSNATIONAL COALITIONS: COMPLIANCE WITH NATO

Uncertainty among domestic actors, their perceived subordinate status in relation to international institutions, and the credibility of policies prescribed by international institutions—all contribute to a social context favorable to compliance. The stronger the measures on uncertainty, status, and credibility, the more robust the coalition in favor of policy transfer. In the case of civil-military relations, no country had consistently strong measures and no country underwent a seamless transition from state-socialist methods of military governance. Variation in uncertainty, status, and credibility informed the power of transnational coalitions, the contours of conflict over policy, and the timing and extent of compliance with NATO's standards of democratic civil-military relations.

### Poland

The evidence from Poland supports the explanatory power of all three hypotheses. The Polish armed forces were not uncertain about which policies to pursue, because the military endured through the transition largely intact and Poland had maintained its own military tradition. Civilians were relatively open to NATO's educational efforts on the benefits of diffuse democratic control, however. NATO enjoyed elevated status in Poland because of the public's high esteem for military power and because political competition made NATO standards a central feature of political discourse. And finally, the perceived credibility of NATO policies strengthened the pro-reform coalition and marginalized those opposed to democratization. All of these factors help explain why Poland developed a particularly strong coalition in support of democratic civil-military relations, why civilians supported reform and the military resisted, and why Poland registered strong, but not complete, compliance by the time of NATO accession in March 1999.

Some of the means through which NATO mobilized a transnational coalition in support of its policies have already been examined. Putting Polish accession on the agenda by merely conceding the possibility of NATO enlargement signaled to members of the Atlantic Club and Solidarity sympathizers that they should become more like alliance members. NATO responded by providing seminars for civilians, funding for officer training, and multiple missions between Warsaw and Brussels.[51] One Polish official recalled that in closed educational seminars on improving civil-military relations, Poland was repeatedly used as a model that should not be emulated.[52] The CRS report that was sharply critical of Poland's failings (Collins and Meyer 1995) also spurred defense and foreign policy personnel to action, while putting Poland's military commanders on notice.

NATO at times also inadvertently undermined its own supporters. The PfP, launched in 1994, is now recognized as a useful tool for training a range of militaries in technical compatibility and NATO's operational procedures. At the time of its initiation, however, the PfP was an argumentative weapon for those opposed to reforming the armed forces and their governing structures. The PfP seemed to create second-class affiliates rather than represent a commitment to enlarge, and it sparked bitter disappointment among civilian leaders.[53] Experienced officers, for whom Polish independence and military tradition served as central reference points, saw little reason to adopt a new and unfamiliar system of power relations, given that the PfP did not make a clear commitment to admit Poland.

Starting with the 1995 *Study on NATO Enlargement*, however, the alliance used it status and credibility to empower civilian reformers to implement reform. Earlier statements that enlargement was a question of time, not of fact, were finally concretized in a document that clearly articulated the "how and why" of expansion. Like the CRS report, the 1995 study backed up Polish civilian claims about the desirability of reform against officers who had resisted compliance with

NATO norms. The study's plainly stated aims put pressure on those who favored military autonomy to stop making their case, both publicly and privately.[54]

More decisive to the internal workings of the Polish defense establishment, however, was the early release to Poland of the "Defense Planning Questionnaire" in mid-1996, which made clear that the alliance was throwing its support behind pro-reform figures.[55] Although initially a dry run, this NATO-restricted document had until that time been reserved for NATO members only. The questionnaire required respondents to be forthcoming about force structures, capabilities, the country's commitment to democratic values, civilian control, and collective security procedures—all of which structured Poland's reform agenda thereafter. That it was civilians who had the authority to author the responses raised their stature relative to military officers—and also strengthened the imperative for the armed forces to accurately inform civilians about Polish military holdings.[56] NATO was thus according civilians the authority to earn a prized place in the alliance—an authority they would have otherwise not enjoyed.

The importance of the status hypothesis is also corroborated by the ways in which political parties competed to win NATO's approbation. The Law on the Office of the Ministry of Defense, vetoed by Wałęsa in 1995 but signed soon after by his ex-communist successor, Aleksander Kwaśniewski (an early NATO skeptic), was among the most important developments in recasting Polish civil-military relations. NATO accession criteria structured the law's content. Its passage reflected a consensus among politicians that the military should be subordinated to broad-based civilian authority, and led to other critical changes in the way civil-military relations were structured. The new consensus was also reflected in the 1997 Constitution, which carefully specified the division of powers between the executive and government, rendering any future president's grab for power commensurate with Wałęsa's impossible. It was NATO guidelines that shaped many of the Constitution's new provisions, including subordination of the armed forces to elected leaders across the governing apparatus (Kramer 1999, 429).

The consensus that NATO had constructed in favor of decentralized and democratic civilian control was shared by a range of governing bodies that together, through 1996 and 1997, conveyed a consistent message to Poland's General Staff. Among the changes imposed was Defense Minister Stanisław Dobrzański's resubordination of intelligence to the MoD, which in 1993 had been subjected to General Staff authority. Dobrzański also undermined the General Staff's powers in finance and acquisitions, reduced the size of its bureaucracy, established the NATO Integration Department that would be embedded in the MoD, and created a new commander of Land Forces. Other key figures who cooperated in the broad-based efforts to improve civilian oversight were Jerzy Milewski of the National Security Bureau, Jerzy Szmajdziński of the Sejm Defense Committee, and Danuta Waniek, head of the President's Office.[57]

In the face of continuing resistance in the military to some reforms, however, Polish and external actors alike exploited NATO's status in support of a new model of civilian control. In cultivating and directing NATO assistance, First Deputy Minister of Defense Andrzej Karkoszka was among the most important figures. He was a principal mediator between NATO and the Polish armed forces through the mid-1990s and was uniquely prepared for the job. During the Cold War, Karkoszka was repeatedly nominated by the Polish Communist Party to attend NGO arms control conferences in the West, where he played the role of a scholar pursuing military-strategic research. In an unusual case of inadvertent interest-formation, even as a Communist Party member, Karkoszka's thinking and experience had been shaped by NATO over decades. He was able to serve as Poland's main liaison to NATO through the 1990s, including at the Madrid Summit in July 1997, precisely because he was so familiar with Western civil-military structures and norms. He was also adept at inspiring the trust, confidence, and respect of NATO officials, because of his extensive experience in talking to and dealing with the Western academic and policymaking elite throughout much of the Cold War.[58]

Most important, with the backing of Kwaśniewski, Dobrzański, Szmajdziński, and Western officials and with the alliance's support, Karkoszka implemented the legislation that finally broke the lock on military autonomy over the course of his two years as deputy defense minister. The Dobrzański/Karkoszka reforms came into force on February 14, 1996, and substantially recast governing institutions. Karkoszka was the MoD's point person who had to cajole the military into accepting reforms that imposed a new command structure designed to weaken the General Staff. Based on the US model of separate commands for land, sea, and air, this new structure resubordinated the General Staff to the MoD, "forcing it to relinquish its most immediate control over the armed forces, thereby also losing its relative weight in the country's domestic politics" (Michta 1997, 105).

Karkoszka, who had the sympathy and support of many in the alliance, had also repeatedly requested the removal of the chief of the General Staff, General Tadeusz Wilecki. Because of Wilecki's role since his appointment in 1992 in trying to shield the military from political control, Karkoszka was convinced that continuing reform of the armed forces required Wilecki's dismissal. Thus Karkoszka, using the social context and transnational support for greater democratic control over the armed forces, brought about one more dramatic change before the Madrid Summit in 1997.

In a clear case of domestic actors trading domestic sources of authority (in this instance, traditions protecting military power) for international ones (NATO norms of civilian oversight), the Polish presidency finally exercised its full authority over the General Staff, starting in 1997. Like Wałęsa, President Kwaśniewski was somewhat politically dependent on the military because of the vast network of political support it had traditionally represented. Kwaśniewski's reluctance to heed domestic and international calls to remove Wilecki led NATO officials to apply their own pressure. Insisting that the decision was out of his hands, one senior US official who had advised Poland on how to restructure civil-military relations in compliance with NATO's expectations repeatedly told President Kwaśniewski that if General Wilecki stayed on as chief of the General Staff, he (the US official) could not guarantee that Poland would be included in the first round of NATO enlargement.[59]

The proximate cause of Wilecki's removal, however, was a *New York Times* article that detailed the ways in which Poland's generals, and specifically Wilecki, were resisting the terms of NATO membership.[60] Without President Kwaśniewski's knowledge and fully aware of the pressure it would generate, Karkoszka served as the main source for that article.[61] Kwaśniewski was then left with a choice. Months before the Madrid Summit, where NATO would issue invitations to join, Kwaśniewski could fire Deputy Minister Karkoszka, who in NATO's estimation was essentially responsible for Poland's preparedness for NATO. Or he could dismiss General Wilecki, who since his appointment as chief of the General Staff in 1992 had done little other than rupture relations with the West. Kwaśniewski "rotated" Wilecki out of office in the spring of 1997.[62]

Institutional reform of the kind outlined above is of course not the same as thoroughgoing behavioral compliance. And, in keeping with what the hypothesis on uncertainty and sectoral continuity would predict, selected members of the armed forces continued to subvert the emerging consensus in favor of NATO prescriptions. Even after accession in 1999, military leaders were failing to carry out some NATO directives, were reluctant to promote younger, Western-trained officers, and would play different branches of the MoD against one another as a means of shielding the military from civilian oversight. Hazing of conscripts also continued despite NATO prohibitions.[63]

Nevertheless, the dramatic scope of the perceived changes was reflected in the 1998 report submitted by the US Senate Committee on Foreign Relations, recommending that the Senate vote to confirm the accession of Poland, Hungary, and the Czech Republic to the North Atlantic Treaty of 1949. In contrast to the CRS report of 1995 that had called the quality of Polish civilian control into question, the Senate Foreign Relations assessment found that all three countries were "meeting the requirements laid out in the 'Perry Principles.'" Further, the report noted the range of institutional changes that Poland had undertaken to codify democratic civilian control over its armed forces.[64]

## Hungary

The evidence from Hungary confirms the relevance of the uncertainty and credibility hypotheses and provides partial support for the status hypothesis. As in Poland, the hypotheses reveal how powerful the coalition in favor of NATO's democratizing reforms would be, the contours of conflict over policy, and the degree and timing of compliance. Only in the area of political competition in the postcommunist period is the status hypothesis not thoroughly confirmed in Hungary. Whereas the hypothesis predicts that the Hungarian socialists would be sensitive to NATO's assessment of the quality of military reform between 1994 and 1998, the socialists were more concerned with consolidating power over the armed forces. To a certain extent, then, NATO failed to persuade the socialists in Hungary that they should recognize a new source of authority—namely, the alliance's own standards of democratic governance. In sum, Hungary registered weak compliance with NATO prescriptions by the time of accession in 1999, but strengthened compliance thereafter.

In Hungary as elsewhere, military continuity through the transition resulted in a high level of certainty about how civilian-military power relations should be organized, and therefore little regard for NATO's opinion on the issue. The sentiment was essentially that, aside from the General Staff, "nobody should interfere with military matters" (Dunay 2002, 68). The 1989 Miklós Németh defense reforms restructured the military-security apparatus such that the MoD and the General Staff were separated. The MoD was subordinated to the prime minister, and the General Staff and an additional body, the "defense staff," were subordinated to the president. These reforms limited the possibility of civilian oversight of military affairs.

With the president's powers limited, this arrangement not only laid the foundation for military autonomy (as in Poland) but also cut the MoD out of the chain of command. The 1989 reforms constituted a tactical move, taken without reflection on the long-term implications—either for joining NATO or for ensuring democratic civilian oversight (as NATO would have defined it). Rather, the short-term concern of the still-governing communist Hungarian Socialist Workers' Party (MSzMP) was simply to prevent the government from controlling the armed forces and to ensure executive authority instead, assuming the MSzMP would win the presidency (which it did not) (Szenes 2001, 83; Dunay 2002, 70).[65]

The contours of conflict over policy in Hungary, as in Poland, were largely between military officers and their would-be civilian overseers. Through the 1990s, civilians attempted to increase civilian oversight while both retired and active military personnel tried to prevent it. For example, the first civilian defense minister, Lajos Für, claimed as early as 1991 that rather than preserve an Army Command alongside the General Staff, Hungary should look to other European models of civil-military relations in which this redundancy did not exist (Simon 1996, 146). But Hungary's generals resisted. Parliamentarians on the defense committee were similarly stymied in their efforts to exercise authority, at least through the mid-1990s. Lacking military expertise, the defense committee was unable to ask the kinds of questions that would encourage greater transparency on the part of the military. As a consequence, parliamentarians would find themselves in a position of having to go along with whatever the military was proposing or risk their credibility further by raising obstacles without sufficient knowledge to justify their misgivings (Simon 1996, 165). Lack of parliamentary oversight was manifested in two surprising revelations during the mid-1990s: the deployment of eight MiG-29s (combat aircraft) to Poland for a PfP exercise and the purchase of T-72 tanks from Belarus, neither of which had passed through proper legal procedure.

If the contours of conflict in Hungary were the same as in Poland, and if NATO was subjecting both countries to the same kind of accession process, then the question arises of why the civilian coalition in Hungary failed to benefit from NATO's backing and overcome resistance to democratization, as it had in Poland. As one operationalization of the status hypothesis would predict, NATO's power was limited by low public support for membership, which in general reflects a deep ambivalence about the utility of military power in Hungary. In addition, mistrust between civilians and the military hindered cooperation of the kind NATO demanded.

Another condition working against compliance was that political competition did not elicit political party sensitivity to NATO's opinion about defense reform, contradicting what my theoretical framework would predict. When the socialists returned to power in 1994, they appointed a retired colonel, György Keleti, as minister of defense. He reversed earlier civilianization of the MoD by replacing civilians with retired military and by appointing officers to lead nearly all the defense departments (Szenes 2002, 86–87). In a political bid to remove MDF appointees, Keleti was not only putting in military figures but also replacing "their people with ours." Keleti also resisted earlier plans to merge the General Staff with the MoD. Instead, he consolidated the military's power by giving it additional authority over military planning and intelligence (Simon 1996, 159). By contrast, the Fidesz–Hungarian Civic Party (Fidesz-MPP)–led government that came to power in 1998 did show greater sensitivity to NATO prescriptions, but too close to the time of accession to advance compliance before joining the alliance.

Growing civilian competence in parliament (due in part to NATO training), political competition that brought to power parties that were sensitive to NATO's appeals, and NATO's own sustained attention to issues of both mental and technical compatibility elicited moderate levels of compliance with NATO standards of democratic civil-military relations, but not until *after* accession in 1999 (Simon 2003). A strong consensus around the nonparticipation of professional military personnel in political activity was established in both law and practice in the 1990s. The parliamentary defense committee and all its subcommittees turned out to be among the most active and effective in the postcommunist region. By 2001, the formal integration of the General Staff with the MoD that had been debated throughout the 1990s was finally underway. This integration and other reforms were a consequence of the thorough review and prioritization of Hungary's defense reform goals set out in the Strategic Defense Review of 1999, initiated by the Fidesz-MPP government in 1998.

The most significant area of Hungary's noncompliance with NATO's preference for democratic civil-military relations at the time of accession was in the structure and functioning of the MoD and its relationship to the General Staff. Because the MoD and General Staff were separated from 1989 until late 2001, the MoD was unable to exercise effective military oversight. Protracted force reviews, repeated renegotiation with NATO over Hungary's Target Force Goals, and even the lengthy Strategic Defense Review are all evidence that the MoD did not have the channels of authority needed to ensure the armed forces' compliance with its directives. In addition, even by the early 2000s, the MoD was still mostly staffed with either military or retired military personnel. The martial character of the ministry meant that very little civilian expertise had developed there and a fortress mentality prevailed. Links to the media, NGOs, parliament, and public therefore remained weak (Simon 2003, 95–98).

Despite Hungary's failure to fully comply, NATO admitted the country in March 1999, in part because Western advisors did not perceive the lack of readiness until after an invitation was issued. In addition, Hungary had actively contrib-

uted to PfP exercises and had provided useful staging areas in the IFOR (Implementation Force, in Kosovo) and SFOR (Stabilization Force, in Bosnia) missions
in the former Yugoslavia (Szenes 2001, 87), all of which contributed to a favorable
assessment of readiness to join the alliance. The Hungarian case is not an explicit
test of conditionality, because conditionality was not strictly applied. However,
Hungary's willingness to increase compliance in some critical areas even after
accession supports the argument that a social context, rather than incentives
independent of a social context, facilitates compliance.

## Romania

Evidence from Romania confirms the relevance of the three hypotheses tested
here—uncertainty, status, and credibility. The Romanian military remained intact through the transition and, as elsewhere, military personnel were anything
but uncertain about what defense reform should entail—and they were clearly not
concerned with building democratic oversight. Political leaders who emerged in
the transition were also not in any sense uncertain, given their long experience in
governing, albeit under a different regime. In other words, they did not seek out
NATO's counsel in order to gain confidence in their own policies. NATO's status
in Romania was also compromised in the first seven years of transition because of
the lack of political competition. After the first competitive elections in late 1996,
however, efforts to comply strengthened noticeably. And finally, NATO's credibility in demanding democratic civil-military relations during the course of Romania's bid to join the alliance eroded. The erosion occurred not because democratic standards in the alliance had broken down, but rather because, after 9/11,
NATO shifted its priorities away from democratic accountability in favor of foreign policy solidarity and military readiness.

　　Consistent with what the uncertainty and status hypotheses would predict,
Romania undertook virtually no reform that could be construed as consonant
with NATO's policy prescriptions in the early 1990s. Military continuity was a
powerful force for stasis, because the armed forces' role in securing Romanian
independence from the Soviet Union left their legitimacy largely intact (Watts
2003). Moreover, Romanian officers were "capable military professionals comfort-
able with planning, decision-making, and implementation" and "could undertake reform without civilian involvement" (Watts 2002, 15). Military expertise
contrasted with civilian inexperience in the defense sphere. Although the alliance might have wielded influence through civilians, regime continuity limited

NATO's power in the first half of the 1990s. In the absence of organized opposition to the communist regime and political competition in the transition, international legitimacy was not a source of power for the communist successor FSN or the FDSN (later the PDSR), among the major winners in the 1990 and 1992 elections. In addition, the West was generally wary of President Ion Iliescu and his regime and failed to provide even modest military assistance to Romania until late 1993. Given the low levels of compliance through the first seven years of transition, NATO did not issue an invitation for the country to join at the Madrid Summit in 1997.

Both democratization of civil-military relations and efforts to improve technical interoperability with NATO accelerated in 1996, as a consequence of the electoral change that finally gave NATO greater access to Romania's defense reforms. To the surprise of many, an agglomeration of opposition parties, including greens, liberals, and Christian democrats, prevailed in the national elections of November 1996, after also doing well in some local elections five months earlier. The opposition's victory over its postcommunist counterpart essentially amounted to a change in the measure on status. For not only had CDR members campaigned on a platform in part dedicated to improving Romania's international standing, but the new competitive dynamic meant that the socialists would ultimately also become more attentive to the country's status vis-à-vis a range of international institutions when they took power again in 2000.

The CDR-led government initiated several changes aimed at improving democratic oversight and Romanian interoperability with the alliance, starting with the appointment of Western advisors to the MoD (Watts 2001a, 2001b; Gheciu 2005a). NATO's central areas of concern were civilianization of the MoD, apportioning power between government bodies in their oversight of the military, ensuring media and civil-society access to information about the military-security apparatus, and recasting the power and functions of a still heavily militarized and opaque interior ministry. By 1999, the CDR had, with NATO assistance, approached NATO's criteria on all of these issues. Through a government decree in August 1999, Romania improved cooperation and communication between the MoD, NGOs, the media, and parliament. The decree also directed the MoD to equalize the professional status of civilians and military personnel, implement a merit-based promotions system, and increase the civilian presence to 40 percent by 2004. A separate government decree in 1999 also set out rules on the imposition of a national state of emergency, institutionalizing checks, balances, and limits designed to protect a democratic, constitutional order. The 1999 Annual National

Plan, one of several planning reform documents that Romania used in its preparation for NATO membership, outlined a process in which the interior ministry
would be restructured and civilianized (Gheciu 2005a, chap. 5).

These democratizing initiatives notwithstanding, the CDR was in many respects unwilling or unable to follow through on some of the reforms. The CDR's
reign was marked by as much fragmentation, corruption, and mismanagement as
the preceding period (Watts 2001b; 2003, 146; 2005; Barany 2003). Indeed, the
manifest lack of commitment to the logic underpinning NATO norms was the
CDR's method of implementing NATO prescriptions. In anticipation that the
parliament might reject many of the reforms the alliance was suggesting, CDR
leaders skirted democratic procedure by resorting to government decree—a practice that members of the CDR had sharply criticized in their socialist predecessors.
In addition, perhaps out of fear that the military's loyalty more naturally rested with
the socialists than with the liberal coalition, CDR leaders tended to politicize the
armed forces through appointments and promotions (Paşcu 2000, 2).[66]

By the time the PDSR (socialists) returned to power in 2000—and renamed
themselves the Social Democratic Party (PSD) in 2001—it had also become susceptible to the approbation and condemnation of international organizations.
During its first term in power, the PDSR had been content to limit compliance
with NATO's democratizing norms to the appointment of Romania's first civilian
minister of defense in 1994. But after 2000, the center-left coalition arguably
advanced democratization of the defense sphere even further than the CDR. In
particular, the newly appointed minister of defense, Ioan Mircea Paşcu, took steps
to empower parliamentary defense committees in both houses, civilianize the
MoD, and smooth relations between the ministry and the General Staff, which
had broken down under the CDR. An increased role for civilians in military
oversight coupled with a program of reversing politicization paved the way for
civilian-led joint planning and budgeting, as well as the implementation of a
merit-based human resources management system that contributed to professionalization and downsizing in the armed forces (Watts 2001a, 2001b). Strong public support for NATO membership also exerted pressure for compliance (Watts
2001b, 39; 2003).

Romania's admission to NATO depended as much on the changing international strategic context as it did on democratization, however, as the 9/11 attacks
led the alliance to undermine the credibility of its own commitment to democratic civil-military relations. Despite serious lapses in interior ministry and security service reform, Romania secured its membership (Barany 2003, chap. 4;
Gheciu 2005a, chap. 5). Even as NATO was inviting Romania to join the alliance

at the Prague Summit in November 2002, and perhaps even after accession in March 2004, Romania had failed to curb the activities of the secret police in compliance with democratic standards. Moreover, successive governments had contributed to the creation of new secret services in several of the ministries since the communist regime collapsed.[67] Carrying out surveillance in the absence of any public scrutiny, these secret services were, according to Romanian human rights activists, acting with impunity against the population in clear contravention of democratic norms.[68] And, although NATO had demanded that personnel with ties to the Securitate (the communist-era security services) be dismissed from government, the PSD leadership assured its NATO allies that even individuals with one-time dubious connections were nevertheless of the highest integrity.

Although the alliance redoubled its efforts after 1999 to enhance mental inter-operability with candidate states, the substance of mental interoperability shifted toward foreign policy solidarity and a demonstrated ability to contribute militarily, particularly after 9/11. Despite Romania's fully compatible rhetoric on democratic civil-military relations, US and NATO assessments of Romanian reform in the run-up to the 2004 enlargement were decidedly ambivalent.[69] Both the NATO Parliamentary Assembly and the CRS reports were generally up-beat. But the positive assessments focused more on what Romania had achieved in technical capability than in a thorough embrace of democratic values.[70]

## Ukraine

In Ukraine, negative measures on nearly all conditions that facilitate compliance with an international institution's policy prescriptions severely limited the democratization of civil-military relations according to NATO standards, even though NATO was clearly interested in bringing Ukraine into its sphere of influence. A lack of uncertainty among most of the major Ukrainian actors, NATO's low status because of muted political competition and public distrust, and NATO's shifting standards after 9/11 boded poorly for the democratization of Ukrainian civil-military relations. And levels of democratization were low despite a plethora of formal links between Ukraine and NATO. Ukraine was the first Commonwealth of Independent States member to join the PfP in 1994, and signed the Charter on a Distinctive Partnership between the North Atlantic Treaty Organization and Ukraine at the Madrid Summit in 1997. In theory, Ukraine could have used potential alliance membership as a way of securing greater independence from Russia. But the incentive of possible membership did little to motivate the democratization of civil-military relations.

By 2004, Ukraine had developed a model of civilian control in which authority was concentrated in the executive, the MoD had no real oversight capacity beyond what a guarded General Staff would allow, and parliament exercised very little power with respect to budgeting or planning. Executive control stemmed from the 1991 presidential decree according to which the president of Ukraine should coordinate security and defense policy and chair the seventeen-minister National Security and Defense Council. The president appointed the minister of defense and the chief of the General Staff, both of whom were subordinated exclusively to the executive.

Ukraine, like Romania in the early 1990s, made some perfunctory reforms in response to NATO's counsel. But although the formal legal structures would qualify Ukraine as having a decentralized civilian model of military oversight, checks and balances, accountability, and civilian participation were still missing in the early 2000s. For example, by NATO standards, the MoD's role in planning and oversight was under-realized by the early 2000s. The General Staff, although formally an integral part of the MoD in 1997 by presidential decree, nevertheless acted largely of its own accord, making defense policy and relegating the MoD to mostly administrative capacities (Mychajlyszyn 2002, 462). Even by early 2005, the NATO Liaison Office in Ukraine was consulting with the MoD on how to assist the ministry in asserting its authority over military leaders.[71] In addition, although civilianization of the MoD had ostensibly been the aim of successive governments, the transition was more one of form than of fact. All but one minister of defense between independence and 2002 had been a retired officer. And to the extent that the percentage of civilians in the MoD increased, this was mostly due to the presence of retired officers who held generally negative views of civilian competence. Moreover, former military officers took up civilian posts of low policy impact (Grytsenko 1997, 30–31; Mychajlyszyn 2002, 463).

The authority of the Verkhovna Rada (parliament) was also minimal. Although it had been active in the early 1990s in legislating into existence a range of national security institutions, the 1996 Ukrainian Constitution reestablished executive authority. As commander-in-chief, the Ukrainian president oversaw the armed forces in addition to other military formations, had the power to declare states of emergency and war, managed foreign, security, and defense policy, and was responsible for all senior military appointments (Sherr 2005, 159). Because the range of tasks was too unwieldy for an executive to manage effectively day to day, Ukraine had a "President's Administration" of a thousand employees that served the president directly, without accountability to any other government institution.

Moreover, within this model the military acquired significant autonomy, which officers have welcomed (Sherr 2005, 160). In many respects, the system of civilian oversight in Ukraine is what President Lech Wałęsa and Chief of Staff Tadeusz Wilecki had sought to establish in Poland.

The Parliamentary Committee on Defense and National Security was supposed to approve the defense budget, confirm appointments to the MoD and General Staff, and ensure that Ukraine's military planning and missions were consistent with the Constitution. By the late 1990s, however, the Verkhovna Rada was exercising less authority over defense issues than it had in the early 1990s around the time of independence, when it had been a key player in implementing the legislation that created many of Ukraine's national security structures (Mychajlyszyn 2002, 461). In addition, the defense budget remained largely nontransparent. While in a NATO member state literally thousands of articles attached to the defense budget would be public information, in Ukraine the military kept the number of articles to a minimum.[72] In short, there was no civilian consensus on the desirability of democratic control and, in that connection, still very little civilian defense expertise more than a decade after the declaration of independence (Grytsenko 1997).

Finally, there is the issue of "multidimensionality" in Ukraine. Ukraine's post-independence period, like Romania's, has been marked by the proliferation of various security services. The number of people under arms in Ukraine who work in security services other than the armed forces reached the hundreds of thousands by 1997, outnumbering by far the armed forces themselves. Although Ukraine had internal security forces under the Soviet Union, new security services emerged after 1991, including the Border Troops, the Interior Troops, the Ministry of Internal Affairs Troops, the Tax Police, and so on (for a complete list, see Grytsenko 1997, 7). Although in theory such forces were subordinated to the executive, control was in reality fragmented—often among ministries to which the forces were assigned. There was no democratically accountable civilian control over these newly formed security services, any more than over the normal armed forces.

In a clear signal that Ukraine still had significant changes to make in the eyes of Western civil-military relations experts, one observer noted that if Ukraine was going to join NATO, it would have to "implement parliamentary control of the Armed Forces and the security sector, as [civilian control] is understood everywhere in Europe," referring to practices and competencies in personnel oversight, financing oversight, and coordination of ministries. As was clear to this observer, at least, despite all the soothing language in NATO documents about shared values, no meeting of minds had yet occurred between the alliance and Ukraine on basic issues of democracy, human rights, and the rule of law (Fluri 2004, 138–39).

Ukraine's longer-term strategic orientation, given the perception in the eastern and southern parts of the country that NATO is a hostile and aggressive organization, puts the country's membership in doubt. In addition, Russia's sensitivities could prove more salient to NATO policy on Ukraine because of the two countries' historical ties. Nevertheless, NATO officials in early 2005 viewed the possibility of Ukrainian reform as a particularly potent testament to the power of the alliance and the appeal of its values. As an unmistakably eastern, Slavic country with close ties to Russia, Ukraine's conversion to mental interoperability with NATO, including the institutionalization of democratic civil-military relations, would suggest that the alliance could break through the cultural and historical barriers that had long constituted Europe's East-West divide.[73]

## CONCLUSION

Three alternative explanations might account for variation in the democratization of civil-military relations according to NATO prescriptions. Domestic politics, competition among interest groups, and external incentives provide competing hypotheses against which to compare my argument for the social context, as defined by uncertainty, status, and credibility. While each alternative on its own can explain part of the story, attention to the social context reveals more about why we observe particular outcomes and the causal mechanisms at work.

Domestic political explanations, particularly those focused on the importance of democratic opposition under communism, electoral dynamics, or reforming communist parties (Vachudova and Snyder 1997; Fish 1998; Grzymała-Busse 2002; Vachudova 2005), would predict the highest levels of compliance from Poland and Hungary. Democratic opposition movements should have been interested in developing democratic accountability in the armed forces and in subduing the former guardians of hated regimes. Similarly, at least one scholar concluded that NATO did not contribute to democratization anywhere in postcommunist Europe and that outcomes were exclusively domestically driven (Reiter 2001).

It is unlikely, however, that CEE states would have settled on a model of diffuse democratic accountability, shared between government, executive, parliament, and the media, if NATO had not actively intervened. Even in Hungary and Poland, the consensus emerging from state socialism was that political and military guidance should be separate, that the military should retain control of planning, budgeting, and procurement, and that civilian control should be concentrated in the executive. These sentiments were manifest in both the Żabiński and Németh reforms early in the transition, before the alliance presented its own preferred version of power relations between the military and society. Domestic explanations also fail to explain why there was so much variation between Poland, a strong complier, and Hungary, a weak complier, at the time of accession in 1999. Domestic explanations, particularly those predicated on the power of democratic opposition legacies, also have a hard time explaining why Romania, which had no democratic opposition under communism, ultimately rivaled Hungary's moderate compliance by 2001.

Two kinds of interest group explanations suggest alternatives based on competition. First, there was a consistent battle between the military, which sought greater autonomy, and civilians, who sought to maximize their power. The general conflict between officers and politicians was not inevitable, however, insofar as NATO's interventions provoked the conflict by informing civilians that they were not exercising enough control over the armed forces. Again, the Żabiński and Németh reforms illustrated the prior broadly held assumptions about the appropriateness of military autonomy in which civilians and officers alike believed the armed forces should exercise autonomous authority.

Alternatively, it could be that where public support for NATO membership was strong, compliance was higher. Variation in public opinion does not consistently correspond to democratization of civil-military relations, however, except in Ukraine, where public support for membership has been low, along with compliance. Romanian support for membership was consistently high through the 1990s, and yet compliance did not really begin until 1997. Poland follows a similar pattern, failing to comply until NATO had had enough time and contact with Polish officials to exploit their uncertainty and the alliance's own status, thereby marginalizing Polish military tradition and diminishing the army's political power. Hungarian public opinion ultimately warmed to NATO membership in 1997 (and only after a government campaign) but not enough to put pressure on the General Staff to submit to government authority. What these outcomes reveal is that the important underlying variable is the public's belief that military power is an effective means to achieving national goals. Respect for military power and political competition together elevated NATO's status and thus its power. But strong public support for NATO in the absence of political competition or before the alliance had had sufficient time to exploit a favorable social context led to little initial compliance, as shown by Romania and Poland, respectively.

The final group of explanations centers on external incentives. Neoliberal institutionalism and realism would expect vulnerable states to comply with NATO's accession criteria because of the security incentive (Wallander 2000). Extrapolating from arguments about EU leverage, the threat of exclusion should have motivated compliance (Vachudova 2005). Security guarantees are no doubt important in states' calculations, but wide variation in the democratization of civil-military relations signals an uneven interest in winning the security guarantee, even among similarly vulnerable states.

There are several examples of variation that neoliberal institutionalism cannot account for. Poland, a state apparently very motivated to join, nevertheless tested the limits of NATO's patience on centralized civil-military relations right up until the Madrid Summit in 1997, when invitations were issued. Hungary, meanwhile, failed to subordinate its General Staff to civilian oversight until after it was admitted to the alliance. And Romania, another professedly keen candidate, did virtually nothing to get in until 1997.

I do not dispute that resistance to the terms of NATO membership was natural, given that it required changes in basic assumptions about the appropriate balance of power among groups in society. But shifting CEE assumptions about the correct balance of power between the military and civilians required more than the promise of a security guarantee from the world's most successful alliance. It also required that domestic actors believe that the promised security guarantee was worth the costs of meeting NATO standards. In the civil-military relations case, the judgment of worth depended on the alliance's status, which in turn depended on domestic actors' certainty about the proper course of reform, society's convictions about the utility of military power, and the credibility of NATO prescriptions. Whereas neoliberal institutionalism would conceivably predict that similarly vulnerable states would comply with NATO prescriptions in order to win admission, in reality there was significant variation in the timing and thoroughness of reform. That incentives did not vary but states' interpretations of them did illustrates the importance of other factors that contribute to compliance, including domestic actors' perception of where authority appropriately rests.

# CHAPTER FIVE

# Denationalizing Defense Planning and Foreign Policy

In 2003, Poland was the fourth largest provider of military forces to the US-led invasion and occupation of Iraq, contributing approximately 2,500 soldiers and special forces. Over the following two years, as Poland was administering one of only three "stabilization" zones in Iraq, with 9,500 troops under its command, Romania, Ukraine, and Hungary also sent forces. All four countries had also contributed to the multinational effort to eradicate the Taliban in Afghanistan, in some cases sending forces well in excess of those committed by their western European counterparts. For countries that only a decade before were variously pursuing large-scale civil territorial defense programs, ethno-nationalist mobilization linked to historical rivalries, and admission to NATO based on the perceived danger of Russian revanchism, these sizable contributions to multilateral "out-of-area" military operations represented a sea change in international orientations and military cultures.[1] In this chapter I examine why this change occurred, arguing that from the early 1990s NATO was active in denationalizing the frames through which central and eastern European (CEE) states viewed their foreign and defense policies.

Defense planning and foreign policy are among the most revealing public policy manifestations of a state's international purpose. Absent a total breakdown in channels of government authority, the organization of military forces reveals the notions of at least some state actors of what constitutes a threat, who the relevant enemies and allies are, and what priorities command the greatest urgency. Questions concerning security challenges and how best to meet them are almost never subject to objective assessment that results in a spontaneous consensus.

Rather, competing perceptions of threat among domestic actors stem from political struggles over interpretations of the past and the relevance of those interpretations for the future. Such struggles and their resolution have consequences, in turn, for resource allocation among competing groups in society, rival foreign policy priorities, and military-society relations.

For CEE states, domestic political debates about how to restructure defense planning in the post–Cold War period were altered by yet another layer of interference, in addition to the usual domestic and historical factors: NATO enlargement. On the face of it, NATO and many postcommunist states might have shared the same strategic objective—namely, the consolidation of democracy and capitalism, in part through the repudiation of Soviet, and later Russian, authoritarianism and expansionism. Although NATO had been formed in large measure with Soviet containment in mind, the end of the Cold War, the violent break-up of Yugoslavia, and the growing political salience of international terrorism all served to invalidate the alliance's original mission, at least in the minds of NATO's founding members (NATO 1999, 2005). At the same time, however, if there was any unifying rationale underpinning CEE states' desire to join NATO, it was first and foremost to win protection from the Soviet Union, and later from Russia. Even if CEE leaders could appreciate that medium-term trouble was unlikely, instability in the Caucasus, the war in Chechnya, Russian interference in the domestic politics of the "near abroad," and creeping authoritarianism in the post-Gorbachev and post-Yeltsin periods were more than enough to keep at least one lesson from the past very much alive: prepare for Russian aggression.

It was in the tension between CEE's very recent memories of Soviet domination and the changing international strategic context that the first divisions over NATO's perceived purpose emerged. While many postcommunist states were intent on pursuing territorial defense in connection with NATO membership, leaders within the alliance were instead making the case for smaller, more mobile units that could be used for power projection to locales beyond the Article V security guarantee.[2] Conflicts over defense planning priorities reflected divergent perceptions of threat that later translated into disagreements over resource allocations. No doubt to the surprise of many CEE leaders who had campaigned vigorously for NATO enlargement, participation in the alliance would sooner mean supporting operations in Kosovo, Afghanistan, and Iraq than repositioning troops from West to East.[3] Given the "blatant disregard of the East European states' national interests in decisions regarding military doctrine" and that such disregard had been among the "most important complaints of dissidents and democratizers throughout the region's Communist period," it is little wonder that competing threat perceptions and strategic priorities between the alliance and NATO candidates were sometimes a source of tension (Barany 1995, 111).

This chapter examines the extent to which NATO was able to subdue traditional security concerns in postcommunist Europe, both between newly independent states and Russia and among historical rivals that had long-standing anxieties about borders, minorities, and diasporas. I argue that the alliance did much to denationalize defense planning and foreign policy by delegitimizing arguments for defense self-sufficiency that were based on historical vulnerability. In direct confrontations with their CEE interlocutors, Western officials made the case that NATO enlargement was not directed against Russia, that the alliance's mission was evolving to meet not just European but also global security challenges, and that striving for defense self-sufficiency was neither necessary nor financially feasible (NATO 1999). By 2005, NATO had hardly succeeded in putting all of the historically rooted security concerns to one side. But it had dampened suspicions by marginalizing particular nationalist discourses and sidelining potentially provocative policies.

The defense planning and foreign policy outcomes that NATO helped secure included, depending on the country, the softening of ethno-nationalist rhetoric, abandonment of civil territorial defense or a reduction in resources devoted to such programs, and creation of small, specialized, and highly mobile forces for deployment in multilateral operations abroad—referred to by Jacoby (2005, 234) as "niche forces" or "showcase units" (see table 5.1 for deployments to Iraq, for example).

Preceding these last two developments was the transformation in public discourse on the reasons for seeking NATO membership. Just as they had coached CEE leaders on how to frame the question of NATO enlargement (see chapter 4), alliance officials also privately argued to their CEE interlocutors that the correct rationale for joining was related to internal stabilization, modernization, and democratization, not Russian revanchism. Although initially causing considerable confusion among postcommunist leaders—who might have been forgiven for thinking that NATO was primarily a security guarantee against imperial ambitions in the region—the alliance's urging on this point did change the official discourse over the course of a decade. By 1999, even Wojciech Jaruzelski, retired general and first secretary of the Communist Party in Poland when the regime imposed martial law in December 1981, claimed to have come around to the view that NATO membership would be a boon because of its prospective stabilizing, democratizing, and modernizing influences.[4]

TABLE 5.1
*Troop Deployments for Operation Iraqi Freedom (OIF) and Stabilization*

| Country | Military Personnel in the Gulf to Support OIF, March 2003 | Military Personnel on the Ground for OIF, March 2003 | Post Major Combat (stabilization phase) | Approximate Contribution and Pledges, 2003, million US$ |
|---|---|---|---|---|
| United States[a] | 340,000 | NA | 100,000–160,000 | |
| United Kingdom | 42,000 | 26,000 | 12,000 | 177.1 |
| Australia | 2,000 | 2,000 | 2,000 | 60.5 |
| Italy | | | 3,000 | 22.4 |
| **Poland** | 200 | 200 | 2,300 | 250[b] |
| **Ukraine** | 450 (in Kuwait) | | 1,650 | |
| Spain | | | 1,300 | 32.2 |
| Netherlands | | | 1,100 | |
| Japan | | | 1,000 | 101.8 |
| **Romania** | | | 734 | |
| South Korea | | | 650 | |
| Bulgaria | | | 500 | |
| **Hungary** | | | 300 | |
| Philippines | | | 196 | |

*Sources:* Congressional Research Service Reports, Order Code RL31843, "Iraq: International Attitudes to Operation Iraqi Freedom and Reconstruction," December 18, 2003; Order Code RL31701, "Iraq: U.S. Military Operations," April 14, 2003; Order Code RL31339, "Iraq: U.S. Regime Change Efforts and Post-war Governance," September 22, 2003. Washington, DC.

*Notes:* Countries appearing in boldface are included in this study.

[a]The U.S. government does not provide exact numbers, for security/strategic reasons.

[b]Poland agreed to provide US$4 to $5 million, and the United States the remainder.

## NATO INFLUENCE OVER DEFENSE AND FOREIGN POLICY: UNCERTAINTY, STATUS, AND CREDIBILITY

By exploiting uncertainty (H1), domestic actors' perception of NATO's elevated status (H2), and the credibility of its own policies (H3), NATO promoted collective security and thereby undermined competing claims for either defense self-sufficiency or nationalist recruitment (see chapter 1 on the three study hypotheses). As the social context shifted, so too did states' willingness to comply with the NATO version of strategic concerns. Changing articulations of threats underline the contingency of maximizing security. As such, the denationalization of defense planning should be understood as a process through which states' international purposes and orientations are constructed. Since the measures on uncertainty, status, and credibility varied across countries, NATO encountered uneven resistance and achieved variable outcomes.

With respect to territorial defense, uncertainty was weaker in Romania and Ukraine than in Poland and Hungary, because of historical legacies (H1). While Hungary lacked the ambition to pursue the establishment of independent territorial forces during the Cold War, Poland did try to establish such a system but was frustrated in its efforts by Soviet fears that it would undermine the Warsaw Pact's ability to subdue nationalist resistance to Soviet hegemony (Jones 1981; Sanford 1986). Romania, which began extricating itself from the structures of the Warsaw Pact in the late 1950s, established the "War of the Entire People" doctrine while still a member of the Pact, making this country the strongest case of sectoral continuity and thus the weakest case of uncertainty (Watts 2003, 133–34). Ukraine was similarly wedded to national defense. Based on this measure alone, NATO should have exercised less influence over Romania and Ukraine than over the other two countries in debates on territorial defense, because of the continuity of territorial defense in Romania and Ukraine through the transition.

There was also variation over time and across countries in the degree to which domestic actors perceived NATO as having elevated status (H2). Perceived status and the salience of international opinion correspond in part to the quality of political competition. As in the civil-military relations case, however, public confidence in the utility of military power, measured in terms of public trust in the armed forces and public support for NATO membership, also predicts how powerful NATO's approbation will be. Where publics believed that military power is an effective means of attaining national ends, they tended to support high levels of compliance with alliance prescriptions, even when compliance was demanding of resources. But where publics held military power in low regard (as in Hungary and the Czech Republic), social recognition from NATO was a less powerful influence and participation in NATO out-of-area operations was less motivating (see table 4.1 on public support for NATO). The status variable highlights the fact that threat perceptions and compliance with NATO's denationalizing strategy vary more according to social relations than to geostrategic realities.

The weak credibility of NATO policies, measured in terms of both consensus and normative consistency, compromised the alliance's denationalizing power in foreign policy and defense planning (H3). In Europe, at least, territorial defense had provided the organizational basis for military deployments throughout the Cold War, making it difficult for NATO representatives to argue against territorial defense—especially to CEE leaders who initially believed they were joining an alliance dedicated to containing Russian power. Moreover, even some years after the Cold War had ended, western Europe had failed to shift many of its resources from territorial objectives to power projection. Whereas the United States had an

established record of investing in power projection dating from the Cold War, by
the early 2000s Europe deployed less than 5 percent of its more than 2 million
troops in out-of-area missions (Yost 2000).[5] The lack of consensus on the urgency
to develop power projection at the expense of territorial defense would also undermine NATO arguments in favor of denationalization—in the East as well as in
the West.

NATO also encountered resistance to its denationalizing prescriptions because of claims that the West had traditionally reneged on its security guarantees.
Although the alliance could point to more than four decades of solidarity against
the Soviet Union, CEE leaders were more concerned about earlier events. Just as
victory of the Allied forces in World War II had vastly different meanings for
eastern and western European powers (Davies 2004), so the salience of unfulfilled
alliances varied in the minds of French, Polish, Russian, and British leaders more
than fifty years on.

But when it came to demonstrating good relations with neighbors as a criterion
for membership, NATO's credibility was high.[6] With the partial exception of
Turkey and Greece (Krebs 1999), which suffered conflict both before and after
their admission to NATO, the alliance had a convincing record not only of
"keeping Germany down" but also of maintaining high levels of trust, transparency, and stability among members (Wallander 2000). NATO's credibility in
this domain made ethno-nationalist mobilization in CEE much harder to defend
in the light of both NATO and European practice.

NATO failed to win full compliance with its policy prescriptions from any
state. But the alliance did shift CEE defense and foreign policy away from nationalist and territorial concerns and toward collective security and goals of power
projection. A skeptic would probably wonder whether the subordination of regional threat perceptions concerning the former Soviet Union, or other historical
rivalries, to NATO's more optimistic assessment of dangers in the region would do
anything to alter the material facts underpinning those fears—including a history
of Soviet domination, provocatively drawn borders with the dismantlement of
empires, and repeated mistreatment of minorities.

But while international institutions cannot eradicate such facts from the political landscape, their policies can do much to undermine their salience in political
discourse and policymaking. Thus Polish, Hungarian, or Romanian politicians
may couch their reasons for joining NATO in terms of internal stabilization,
modernization, and democratization, but they may privately privilege the strategic advantages of Western security guarantees. Simply altering what actors say
may seem a superficial outcome if contradictory beliefs endure. But altering what

politicians say produces pressure for consistent actions—especially where international institutions and the international and local media scrutinize official discourse and its policy manifestations. It was precisely such pressure that led to a downplaying of the Russian threat across central Europe, the abandonment of civil territorial defense in Poland, and the moderation in tone among Hungarian and Romanian nationalists in the run-up to NATO's first post–Cold War enlargement in 1999.

## DEFUSING HISTORICAL THREATS:
## THE UNCERTAINTY OF ACTORS (H1)
### *Poland*

The measure on uncertainty in the defense planning sphere was mixed for Poland. Civilians had strong views about Poland's historical experience, Russian intransigence, and what these implied for Polish defense. But most were not seasoned experts in formulating and implementing defense policy, providing NATO with its first point of access to defense planning debates.[7] Much as they had inherited a certain idea about the balance of power between civilians and military personnel that encouraged military autonomy (as manifested in the Żabiński Commission report; see chapter 4), political leaders also carried a particular set of beliefs, stemming from the Cold War and earlier, about where Poland should seek security. But as in civil-military relations, by the late 1990s, most civilians were willing to defer to NATO on the question of how best to advance the alliance's agenda.

Polish certainty about the ongoing threat posed by Russia, even in the post-Soviet period, complicated NATO strategy in CEE. Polish-Russian relations were tense through the turbulence of the early 1990s, which fortified Polish calls for NATO enlargement.[8] Central European fears of Russian instability intensified in 1993 with the unexpectedly strong showing of Vladimir Zhirinovsky's nationalist Liberal Democratic Party, which won 78 of 450 seats in the State Duma, the lower house of parliament.[9] With the alliance still hedging its bets on whether to enlarge, calls multiplied from some of CEE's highest-ranking leaders for a stronger commitment from NATO—much to the consternation of Western leaders. The latter feared that it was precisely the characterization of NATO as the savior of central Europe from Russia that would fan the flames of Russian nationalism and undermine attempts to stabilize Western-Russian relations.[10]

In an effort to win both enlargement on NATO's terms and Russian acceptance of it, NATO initiated a concerted, albeit private, campaign to change the way Polish officials articulated threats to national security and their reasons for wanting to join the alliance. The objective was to cultivate pacific Polish-Russian relations and to persuade Russian politicians that just as NATO had "solved Russia's German problem" by insisting on democratizing civil-military relations and restraining Germany's expansionist impulses, the alliance's mission now was to stabilize CEE, not to isolate Russia.[11] NATO officials counseled Polish politicians and defense officials that it was counterproductive to justify Poland's closer ties to the alliance in terms of the threat that Russia might pose.[12] Understanding that antagonizing Russia was incompatible with NATO's larger strategy, Polish officials began to highlight instead the stabilizing and modernizing benefits that membership might bring. In harmonizing Poland's public threat perceptions with its own, NATO narrowed the terms of debate and minimized the justification of Polish defense and foreign policies by reference to Russian hostility.

According to one NATO representative who worked with the Polish defense establishment in the early 1990s, "We were telling them [the Poles] that they couldn't talk about it this way because collective security is as important to Russia as it is to Poland and we [NATO] are trying to be Russia's partner." He explained the apparent paradox to his Polish interlocutors thus: "You want us to let you into the alliance to put you under the security umbrella safe from Russia. How can we be saying both that NATO is not the enemy of Russia but we admit Poland to protect it from Russia?"[13]

But NATO officials' efforts to align Polish foreign policy with that of the alliance were only partially successful. While some of the country's most prominent foreign policy experts were willing to adopt much of the NATO rhetoric, Polish fears about being subordinated to Russian interests were nevertheless manifest. The *Poland-NATO Report* illustrates both tendencies. Published in 1995 and designed to persuade Western leaders of the pressing need to enlarge the alliance, the report stated that "Poland is not today in danger" (Ananicz et al. 1995, 9) and that democratic consolidation was inextricably linked to transatlantic security (10). The report also pointed out, using NATO's own logic of internal stabilization, that "the lack of basic decisions by the West is having an adverse influence on the internal situations of the Central European countries," not least by allowing communist successor parties to regain power throughout much of the region (31). But the authors also noted that while it is fine to engage Russia, the West should not be seduced into believing that Russian elites wished to create a European order based on integration (27). Rather, Russian skepticism toward NATO should be interpreted as that country's effort to forestall enlargement until Russia was strong enough to have "a real say in decisions affecting European security" (27).[14]

One area in which the uncertainty of domestic actors did provide NATO with access to defense planning processes in Poland was territorial defense. Whereas Romania had succeeded in creating enough distance between itself and the Warsaw Pact to conduct defense planning independently, the Soviet Union had kept Poland firmly within the fold. This meant that although Poland undertook some independent foreign policy initiatives and strove to preserve its own distinctive military tradition, the Soviet Union prevented the country from developing territorial defense in the 1960s as Polish nationalists had hoped to do.[15] Discontinuity in territorial defense between the communist and postcommunist periods made it much more difficult for Polish officials to follow through on 1997 campaign pledges to organize, fund, and deploy the large-scale civil territorial initiative that members of Solidarity Electoral Action (AWS) had proposed.

The uncertainty of actors contributed to a social context in which NATO's interpretations of the past and their relevance for the future would ultimately prevail—but not without friction along the way. By advising CEE elites that a constructive justification for joining NATO was internal stabilization rather than external threats, the alliance limited the basis on which politicians could legitimately mobilize domestic support—fearmongering based on the Russian threat was not acceptable from the alliance's perspective. NATO's private campaign to moderate the tone of Polish politicians also undermined military strategies that were blatantly at odds with the alliance's strategic concepts, most notably civil territorial defense. The pressure for consistency between public declarations and actual public policy contributed to the political infeasibility of civil territorial defense in the late 1990s.

## Hungary

The uncertainty of actors and the discontinuity between modes of defense planning under the Warsaw Pact and in the postcommunist period also gave NATO some access to Hungarian national security rhetoric and policy. Although historically different, the uncertainty variable worked in similar ways in Hungary and Poland. Important differences begin with the fact that Hungary was among the last of Hitler's allies, albeit a very reluctant ally by the end of the war. The Hungarian public's subsequent ambivalence toward the armed forces has in all likelihood been fueled as much by the military's passive and muddled role vis-à-vis the Soviet Union (including during the 1956 revolution) as by its lack of success on the battlefield.[16] As in Poland, but not Romania, the army, however reluctantly, also took part in the suppression of Czechoslovakia's Prague Spring in 1968.

Notwithstanding the introduction of a milder regime in Hungary after 1956, perhaps the only things that dampened Hungarian-Russian alienation in the post–Cold War period were the absence of a common border and the perception of even more pressing threats to Hungarian security (Vachudova 2005). Having lost close to two-thirds of its pre–World War I territory and three-fifths of its population in the Treaty of Trianon in 1920, Hungary had long-standing rivalries with Czechoslovakia and Romania as well as concerns about Hungarian minorities in parts of Yugoslavia, Ukraine, and, to a lesser extent, Austria (Barany 1993, 30; Linden 2000; Williams 2002, 229). Whereas the exigencies of surviving Soviet hegemony had mostly sublimated the desire to act on behalf of Hungarian minorities during the Cold War (Barany 1995, 112; Bunce 1999), the postcommunist period provided a new opportunity to organize foreign policy in part by attending to the grievances of the Hungarian diaspora. Indeed, Hungary's amended 1990 Constitution obliged its leaders to do so.

As in Poland, the government that came to power in the transition in Hungary was comprised of former opponents to the communist regime who had little prior governing experience—and thus some uncertainty when it came to formulating policy. Discontinuity in leadership proved to be as important in foreign policy as in other areas in facilitating international influence. The inexperience of Hungarian civilian leaders and their lack of authority over the armed forces made them susceptible to NATO and other international institutional demands in foreign policy matters. Thus, when the new prime minister, József Antall, proclaimed in 1990 that in spirit he was prime minister of 15 million Hungarians (referring not only to the 10.5 million living in Hungary but the millions more scattered throughout CEE), at least one observer explained the inflammatory remark in terms of inexperience rather than revanchism (Barany 1999, 79; also see Williams 2002, 230).[17] Initially, the Hungarian national security debate was characterized by a lack of clear vision, partly owing to inexperienced leadership (Kiss 2003, 138).

Just as supporters of Polish membership in NATO did not initially understand that they would be joining *not* the "old" NATO organized to contain Russian power but a new one concerned with regional stability and out-of-area missions, Hungarian politicians similarly misconstrued the purposes of a range of Western institutions as their member states had previously defined them. One Hungarian foreign policy official noted that at the outset of transition, his countrymen "had a very romantic idea about how international organizations would view Hungary."[18] As they soon learned, however, international organizations had interests and values of their own. Perhaps taking the righteousness of their aims for granted,

Hungarian leaders sought to use the country's frontrunner status with Western institutions to pressure Hungary's neighbors into adopting more democratic measures sooner, in an effort to ensure the minority rights of Hungarian-speakers (Szayna 2001, chap. 2; Williams 2002). Hungarian strategy even went so far as to try to exclude offending nations (Romania and Slovakia) from Western international agreements (Williams 2002, 239).

In the dilemma over whether to prioritize either the welfare of minorities abroad or constructive relations with Western opinion, it was ultimately international organizations, including NATO and the European Union, that imposed a choice. NATO and EU pressure coaxed the political class into formulating and ratifying basic treaties with Slovakia in 1995 and Romania in 1996. These organizations also made it clear that they would not tolerate Hungarian obstruction when it came to judging the viability of any other state for NATO or EU membership.[19] Like the European Union, NATO, with its open-door policy, sought to defuse tensions between states in the region and therefore needed to prevent new members from using their elevated status (and, in NATO's case, security guarantees) to provoke or intimidate states still on the outside (Szayna 2001, 16, 22).

Civilian foreign-policy makers in Hungary also proved susceptible to NATO's influence over managing relations with Russia—again pointing to the power of uncertainty among domestic actors. The withdrawal of 78,000 Soviet troops from Hungary by the end of 1991 was welcomed even if Hungarians had given little consideration to how they would defend themselves thereafter (Barany 1999, 75). But despite the country's geographic vulnerability and historical animosity toward the Soviet Union, by 1995, at NATO's urging, Hungary's foreign policy officials were doing their "best to assuage Moscow's fears about the diminution of Russian security after NATO's expansion" (Barany 1999, 80). An official also argued that "everything must be done . . . to explain to the Russian public . . . that NATO's expansion does not threaten Russia; that on the contrary it also serves the interests of their security." The same official went on to describe Russia as a "great state" that should also "join the community of democratic states."[20]

A final area of sectoral discontinuity and thus uncertainty facilitated NATO influence over Hungarian foreign policy and defense planning. Whereas Poland had tried but failed to develop national territorial defense within the Warsaw Pact and Romania had tried and succeeded, Hungary had never aspired to such levels of military independence from the Soviet Union. More so than Poland and Romania, Hungary remained an obedient if weak contributor to the Warsaw Pact. To be sure, Hungary gained greater maneuverability vis-à-vis the Soviet Union in other areas—especially with economic liberalization and introduction of the New

Economic Mechanism in the late 1960s. But the country never challenged the Soviet Union on military grounds. The largely successful Warsaw Pact domination of Hungarian military affairs meant that in the post–Cold War period, NATO did not have to confront a revival of national mythologies that celebrated defense self-sufficiency, as it did in Poland and, to a certain extent, Romania.

## Romania

Unlike Poland and Hungary, Romania inherited from the communist period a vast professional and civil territorial defense apparatus. This led to a weak measure on uncertainty in the Romanian case. Decades of industrial organization, institutional preparation, and societal mobilization around the idea of defense self-sufficiency proved a formidable barrier to recasting Romanian security goals. The ideational legacy of nationalist military planning limited NATO's access to the country's defense planning reforms into the 1990s.

Although formally a member of the Warsaw Pact until the Pact's demise in 1991, Romania began agitating for national independence in the late 1950s. The head of the Romanian Communist Party, Gheorghe Gheorghiu-Dej, persuaded Nikita Khrushchev to withdraw Soviet troops from Romania in 1958, in part by arguing that the absence of a foreign military presence would bolster domestic support for the communist regime. But by 1964 it was clear that the Romanian leadership had still greater autarkic ambitions. Romania had stopped sending its officers to Soviet military academies, refused to host Warsaw Pact training exercises on Romanian soil, sent few troops to participate in such exercises elsewhere, and replaced the Main Political Administration with party committees styled on the Yugoslav model. Lacking troops on Romanian soil, the Soviets had little means to thwart such initiatives and, particularly given the severing of political ties between the Romanian Main Political Administration and its Soviet counterpart, no remaining channels of political indoctrination (Jones 1981, 36–39, 83–85).

Following the Soviet invasion of Czechoslovakia in 1968, Romania went to some lengths to demonstrate not only its political independence from the Soviet Union (by not participating in the crushing of the Prague Spring) but also its defense self-sufficiency. According to Jones (1981, 83), Ceauşescu mobilized the country's 520,000 regular armed forces as well as 700,000 members of the Patriotic Guard in response to the Soviet Union's actions in Czechoslovakia. The "War of the Entire People" doctrine that provided the rationale for large numbers of regular and reserve military personnel was probably initiated in the late 1950s or early 1960s by Ceauşescu's predecessor, and by the 1970s it included an additional 20,000 troops attached to the interior ministry, Youth Defense Training Formations for sixteen- to twenty-four-year-olds, and a separate department and command for the defense industry.

The Soviet failure to penetrate the Romanian armed forces and the decidedly anti-Soviet orientation of Romanian foreign policy and defense planning from the late 1950s might seem to give the country some natural advantages for NATO accession.[21] But anti-Sovietism is not the same as internationalism, just as the desire to join the alliance never translated into a spontaneous alignment of strategic priorities with NATO in any of the candidate states. In Romania, inherited security institutions as well as ideational legacies reduced its defense planning uncertainty and limited its willingness to reconfigure its forces in line with NATO priorities of the 1990s.

NATO also lacked decisive access to Romanian foreign policy because the first post-revolution government consisted mostly of former communists who had been marginalized in Ceauşescu's regime. They created the National Salvation Front (FSN), which won overwhelmingly in the 1990 elections. They also inherited all of the political conflicts implied by the large-scale presence of ethnic minorities, including a sizable population of Hungarian-speakers. The significant continuity in personnel limited the degree of influence that international institutions could exercise, at least until 1996 when opposition parties coalesced within the Democratic Convention of Romania (CDR) and replaced the communist successor–dominated government with a coalition of their own.

The only area of uncertainty and thus access for NATO might have been provided by the inexperience of civilian leaders in directly managing the military and governing its daily operations. The alliance did ultimately encourage Romania to take on a limited role in multilateral operations in the late 1990s and early 2000s. In addition, FSN leaders (by 1993, the Party of Social Democracy of Romania, PDSR) responded to NATO membership criteria by initiating an offer of reconciliation with Hungary that culminated in a basic treaty in 1996 (Linden 2000, 131). However, it is unlikely that the uncertainty of actors early in transition played a role in the bilateral treaty with Hungary, given the continuity in the armed forces and leadership outlined here.

## Ukraine

The inclusion of Ukraine, the only non-NATO country under consideration here, helps us assess the validity of two claims. The first is that defense and foreign policy denationalization is not simply a consequence of the end of the Cold War and shrinking Russian power. At different points and to varying degrees, Poland, Hungary, and Romania all embraced policies symptomatic of defense denationalization during the 1990s—including rejection of territorial defense in favor of power projection, a shift in emphasis from conscription to professionalization, and abandonment of ethno-nationalist mobilization. That Ukraine did not begin to follow these trends until the social context facilitating NATO influence was in place corroborates my claim that defense denationalization is not "best practice" as defined by strategic context. Rather, contrasts among countries in the 1990s show the independent effect of NATO where the alliance had access to domestic reform processes. NATO's independent effect was the shift in favor of its strategic priorities at the expense of national or historical ones.

The second claim is that even in the absence of clear incentives, international institutions can elicit state compliance given a social context informed by uncertainty, hierarchy, and credibility. The relationship between NATO and Ukraine was changing in the early 2000s. The changes were partly linked to the increasing quality of political competition in Ukraine. Because of the increased status of international institutions, although Ukraine failed to comply with many aspects of defense denationalization it did become a contributor to NATO and US-led multinational military operations.

Through the 1990s, NATO had no significant access to Ukrainian defense reform, because of the lack of uncertainty among domestic reformers. Indeed, from 1991 to 1996 NATO was ambivalent about Ukrainian accession, owing to the perceived incompatibility of the country's economy, political situation, and military-security apparatus with the alliance and Russian claims to a certain sphere of influence. Likewise, Ukraine did not initially strive for membership. It did, however, seek integration with Euro-Atlantic structures. Ukraine joined the Partnership for Peace (PfP) in February 1994 and signed the Charter on a Distinctive Partnership between the North Atlantic Treaty Organization and Ukraine in July 1997. In more radical moves that ended the country's official status as a nonaligned country, Ukraine joined NATO's Planning and Review Process in 2001 and, on May 23, 2002, declared NATO membership as its ultimate goal. Despite the leadership's apparent desire to join, however, NATO has had only a muted impact in key areas such as the democratization of civilian control (see chapter 4) and defense planning. NATO's access to Ukrainian domestic debates has been limited in large measure by the social context—starting with the strong continuity in the military-security apparatus and its commitment to national territorial defense.

Ukraine inherited a substantial defense establishment from the Soviet Union when it declared its independence in 1991. A multinational force of more than 800,000 Soviet military personnel was stationed on what became Ukrainian soil (Grytsenko 1997, 5). Twelve thousand officers and warrant officers who were unwilling to pledge their allegiance to Ukraine were eventually repatriated; 33,000 more servicemen from abroad were then reabsorbed (Sherr 2005, 163). Because the force had been wholly integrated into the Soviet military command, Ukraine lacked some obvious features of an autonomous national defense apparatus, including a Ministry of Defense (MoD; or parallel governing institutions) and an independent weapons production capacity (Grytsenko 1997, 6). Nongovernmental oversight, in the form of free media or independent research institutions, did not exist.

Equally important legacies of the Warsaw Pact and Soviet military control in Ukraine, however, were the attitudes and skills they left behind—both within the officer class and, to a certain extent, within the ranks. The "general war ethos" had not primarily been organized around Ukrainian territorial defense: as an integral part of the Soviet bloc, forces in Ukraine in the Cold War were positioned to launch an offensive on Western territory. And although central, eastern, and even western European states have increasingly moved from conscript to professional armies (Epstein and Gheciu 2006), the idea was anathema to many in both the Russian and Ukrainian military establishments throughout the 1990s. Because conceptions of military service and citizenship were inextricably linked, paying people to undertake military service was traditionally considered "immoral" (Sherr 2005, 166). Finally, in sharp distinction to either Poland or Hungary (but similar to Romania), high-ranking Ukrainian officers benefited from significant command experience. For whereas the Warsaw Pact had been designed to keep the national militaries of the Soviet satellites (such as Poland and Hungary) weak, Ukrainian officers had been an integral part of Soviet command (Jones 1981).

The idea of territorial defense in Ukraine, which dates back to the 1920s, also weakened the measure on uncertainty. For most of the Ukrainian people's history independent statehood had not been a core political objective, but a kind of ethno-political nationalism did finally emerge at the beginning of the twentieth century. Before that time, Ukrainian populations had been integrated mostly into Polish and Russian empires and few had ever imagined or aspired to independence. In the country's western regions, the Ukrainian elite did not conceive of political status independent of Poland (Prizel 1998, 314). In the east, they identified strongly with their Russian counterparts and at most aimed for greater autonomy, but within a larger Russian federation (306). The growing brutality of both the Polish and Russian regimes in the second half of the nineteenth century fomented a new kind of Ukrainian nationalism, however, such that even after the Ukrainian national project failed in 1920, the Ukrainian elite, particularly within the Soviet empire, sought the trappings of statehood—including a territorial army "with Ukrainian as its language of command" (329).[22]

Strong sectoral continuity in the military-security apparatus from the communist period through Ukraine's independence limited the uncertainty of actors in defense planning. NATO therefore had less access to defense planning debates and less power over foreign policy orientation in Ukraine than in Poland or Hungary, because in no sense were Ukrainian commanders novices. Civilians, however, were—as elsewhere in the region. It is notable that Ukraine's growing integration with the alliance in the 1990s and its commitment to join NATO, announced in 2002, were led by civilians. Uncertainty was muted in Ukraine as in Romania, however, because of the continuity in personnel between the communist and postcommunist periods, at least until the quality of political competition improved in the early 2000s.

## NATO'S STATUS AND DEFENSE DENATIONALIZATION (H2)
### Poland

Domestic political conditions supported NATO's strong status in Poland. Political competition effectively dated back through the communist period, for even without a competitive party system, the Solidarity trade union movement served as an alternative source of legitimacy and power to the state-socialist regime. It also provided the wedge that NATO would use in the 1990s to access debates on defense planning. As in Hungary, but not Romania or Ukraine, political competition from the outset of transition ensured that winning international credibility was a major mobilizing force for political parties in Poland. It was not just the fact of political competition that affected reform trajectories, but also the nature of opposition movements in Poland and Hungary, which were democratic and ideologically Western in orientation. Opposition under communism ensured in both countries that the political leaders who took control in the transition aspired to Western practice as the "civilizational standard."[23]

As noted in the civil-military relations case, the Polish public also had high regard for military power, which stemmed from Polish military history. The public's traditional support of the armed forces' mission, coupled with a strong desire for social recognition from international institutions, resulted in a willingness to abide by NATO policy prescriptions, even if in some cases this was against the

TABLE 5.2
*Military Expenditure as Percentage of GDP*

| | Post-1989 NATO Members | | | | Pre-1989 NATO Members | | | | | |
|---|---|---|---|---|---|---|---|---|---|---|
| Year | **Hungary** | **Poland** | **Romania** | **Ukraine** | Italy | France | Netherlands | Germany[a] | United Kingdom | Spain |
| 1988 | 3.5 | 3.0 | [4.3] | NA | 2.5 | 3.8 | 3.0 | 2.9 | 4.3 | 2.1 |
| 1989 | 2.5 | 1.9 | [4.2] | NA | 2.3 | 3.7 | 2.8 | 2.8 | 4.0 | 2.1 |
| 1990 | 2.5 | 2.5 | 3.9 | NA | 2.1 | 3.6 | 2.6 | 2.8 | 4.1 | 1.8 |
| 1991 | 2.3 | 2.2 | 1.5 | NA | 2.1 | 3.6 | 2.5 | 2.2 | 4.3 | 1.7 |
| 1992 | 2.2 | 2.1 | 2.6 | NA | 2.0 | 3.4 | 2.5 | 2.0 | 4.0 | 1.6 |
| 1993 | 1.9 | 2.5 | 1.4 | .5 | 2.0 | 3.4 | 2.3 | 2.0 | 3.8 | 1.5 |
| 1994 | 1.6 | 2.3 | 2.4 | 2.8 | 2.0 | 3.3 | 2.1 | 1.8 | 3.4 | 1.5 |
| 1995 | 1.4 | 2.2 | 2.1 | 3.1 | 1.8 | 3.1 | 2.0 | 1.7 | 3.0 | 1.5 |
| 1996 | 1.5 | [2.1] | [2.5] | 3.3 | 1.9 | 2.9 | 1.9 | 1.6 | 2.9 | 1.4 |
| 1997 | 1.7 | [2.1] | [3.0] | 4.1 | 1.9 | 2.9 | 1.8 | 1.5 | 2.7 | 1.4 |
| 1998 | 1.5 | 2.1 | [3.0] | 3.4 | 2.0 | 2.7 | 1.7 | 1.5 | 2.6 | 1.3 |
| 1999 | 1.7 | 2.0 | 2.7 | 3.0 | 2.0 | 2.7 | 1.8 | 1.5 | 2.5 | 1.3 |
| 2000 | 1.7 | 1.9 | 2.5 | 3.6 | 2.1 | 2.5 | 1.6 | 1.5 | 2.4 | 1.2 |
| 2001 | 1.8 | 2.0 | 2.5 | 2.9 | 2.0 | 2.5 | 1.6 | 1.5 | 2.4 | 1.2 |
| 2002 | 1.7 | 2.0 | 2.3 | 2.8 | 2.1 | 2.5 | 1.6 | 1.5 | 2.5 | 1.2 |
| 2003 | 1.7 | 2.1 | 2.2 | 2.9 | 2.1 | 2.6 | 1.6 | 1.4 | 2.7 | 1.1 |
| 2004 | 1.5 | 2.0 | 2.1 | 2.6 | 2.0 | 2.6 | 1.7 | 1.4 | 2.8 | 1.1 |

*Source:* Stockholm International Peace Research Institute, various years.

*Note:* Countries appearing in boldface are included in this study. Numbers in brackets are SIPRI estimates. Data are not available for Ukraine before 1993.

[a]Through 1991, data are for the Federal Republic of Germany, before unification. For 1991 and later, data are for the united Germany.

better judgment of politicians. Poland has been willing to maintain NATO-set target levels of defense spending—unlike Hungary, with its weaker public support for military power and its own armed forces. Higher levels of military spending in Poland in turn have allowed greater scope for compliance with NATO policy goals, especially regarding operational forces for NATO missions (see table 5.2 on military spending).

The relation between NATO and Polish officials was a hierarchical one, partly because political competition in Poland forced parties to submit to the scrutiny and judgment of international opinion. The perceived subordinate status of Polish actors in relation to their authoritative NATO advisors was also the result of historical factors that are not easily captured by the political competition variable. Polish admiration for military power is a better approximation: NATO commanded respect in Poland for having won the Cold War. Polish outcomes, and the paths by which they were secured, demonstrate the centrality of the status variable.

## Hungary

One would expect Hungary, like Poland, to comply with NATO's denationalizing policies because of its desire for social recognition from Western institutions. Hungary proved more susceptible to NATO's demand that it denationalize its foreign policy than to the alliance's preference that it also internationalize its defense planning. Thus while Hungary stepped away from ethno-nationalist rhetoric in response to NATO pressure it was a poor contributor to multilateral military missions, and thus a weaker complier than Poland overall on the denationalization outcome.

Variation in Hungary's receptivity to the NATO version of denationalization stemmed from contradictory measures on the status hypothesis. Hungary had strong political competition, which explains the movement away from ethnonationalist mobilization. But it had weak public support for military power, which explains why Hungary did not become a powerful player in NATO's out-of-area operations. Political competition ensured that international opinion figured prominently in how political parties competed and how they adjusted over time to international institutional approbation and condemnation. But in Hungary there was a counterintuitive twist on which political groups would be most susceptible to Western institutions' appraisal. For it was not the opposition leaders who replaced the communists in the transition that had the greatest sympathy with NATO's denationalizing worldview: indeed, members of the Hungarian Democratic Forum (MDF) assumed office believing—wrongly—that international institutions would accommodate their nationalist goals.

Just as the communist successors in Hungary proved ultimately more open to Western demands for economic liberalization (Hanley, King, and Tóth János 2002; also see chapters 2 and 3), it was Prime Minister Gyula Horn and his Hungarian Socialist Party (MSzP) that reversed the country's foreign policy course after 1994. Horn cited NATO membership as a key reason for abandoning a nationalist discourse, arguing that failure to reach agreement with Romania and Slovakia on minority rights was among the biggest foreign policy failures of the previous government (Nelson and Szayna 1998; Williams 2002, 234–35). Due to Hungary's strong opposition to communism and support for Western integration, its communist successor party could legitimize itself by out-Westernizing its anticommunist counterparts—a pattern found across CEE.[24]

Although Polish membership in NATO was never threatened by the proclivities of conservative politicians for defense self-sufficiency, Hungary's status with respect to NATO in the early and mid-1990s was uncertain—and the country's politicians knew it.[25] Hungary was not geographically contiguous with NATO's Article V territory, and its military was of questionable use to the alliance. One might therefore conclude that social recognition was a less powerful force for foreign policy change than simply the threat of exclusion from the alliance. But as I argue elsewhere in this volume, an either/or approach to understanding compliance is the wrong way to conceptualize the problem: social forces and incentives must be considered together because it is the social context that constitutes the power of incentives.

Thus, the incentive of membership alone does not explain Hungary's, and especially the MSzP's, attentiveness to the concerns of international institutions with the country's foreign policy toward its neighbors. This is borne out by the fact that in the mid-1990s, Hungarian public support for NATO membership was only 32 percent.[26] It was only through a media campaign, supported by NATO, that the socialists secured the minimum support required for membership by referendum.[27] Tepid public interest in joining NATO probably stemmed in large measure from low levels of support for military power, as reflected in Hungary's poor military-society relations.

Despite low levels of public support for joining NATO, Hungarian politicians staked their reputations on Western institutions' assessments, because Western institutions, including NATO, had defined over decades what it meant to be "European." Thus NATO's conditionality, to the extent that it was used against Hungary, was not meaningful because the impetus to join was so self-evident—as underwhelming levels of support for membership attest, joining was *not* self-evident. Rather, conditionality was powerful because NATO membership, and the implicit social recognition that went with it, was elemental in showing that Hungary was becoming a normal Western democracy. It was especially critical that communist successor parties were seen to be actively engaged in the normalization process. Thus the incentive of membership was crucial, but only because of what membership had come to mean: the achievement of Western, liberal democracy and capitalism, with historical disputes relegated to the past.

## Romania

The status variable receives only partial confirmation in the case of foreign policy and defense denationalization in Romania, because this country registered somewhat stronger compliance than the social context would predict. Poland had strong political competition and high regard for military power, making NATO's status a force for embracing its strategic vision. Hungary had strong political competition but weak regard for military power, resulting in an uneven desire for NATO recognition—while that desire was powerful for politicians, it was not for the Hungarian public. Romania, like Hungary, had mixed measures on the status variable, but in reverse: little political competition until 1996, but strong public confidence in the armed forces (see table 4.2).

The continuity in personnel between the communist regime and the FSN, led by Ion Iliescu, that came to power in December 1989 limited the influence of international institutions on Romania's political discourse and policy. Although there were competitive elections in 1990 and 1992, the opponents of the FSN (which ultimately coalesced in the CDR under Emil Constantinescu) did not pose a serious threat to Iliescu until 1996, when they won both a parliamentary plurality and the presidency. Given the absence of a Western-oriented democratic opposition under communism (unlike in Poland, Hungary, or even Czechoslovakia), Romanian emulation of Western norms was a much less salient part of policymaking in the early 1990s, even if public support for membership of Western institutions was very high.[28]

The continuity in Romanian territorial defense (and thus the lack of uncertainty) and the absence of political competition (and thus the irrelevance of international opinion) boded poorly for institutional influence. It is perhaps surprising, therefore, that Iliescu's PDSR made as many concessions to NATO as it did by 1996. Linden points out, for example (2000, 130–31), that the Romanian-Hungarian basic treaty on Hungarian-speakers' rights in Transylvania was a Romanian initiative in response to the forthcoming *Study on NATO Enlargement* (NATO 1995b), which the elite knew would make peaceful relations among neighbors a prerequisite for NATO membership.[29] Bacon also notes that even in the early 1990s, at least one Romanian lieutenant general (Nicolae Spiroiu) was overseeing the writing of new "laws which redefined the [Defense] Ministry's organization and its relationship with state authority in ways consistent with Western standards and Romania's aspirations of integration into Euro-Atlantic security structures" (1999, 191).

Romanian compliance with NATO norms in the absence of the social context that, I have argued, makes conditionality meaningful and powerful suggests that the social context specified here may not always be essential for winning compliance. The Romanian basic treaty initiative could simply have been a result of Iliescu wanting to defuse tensions with Hungary for domestic political reasons, although this is unlikely given that the treaty alienated the PDSR's coalition partners (the Romanian National Unity Party, PUNR; the Socialist Party of Labor, PSM; and the Greater Romania Party, PRM).[30] An explanation closer to my theory would argue that by August 1995 political competition was taking shape in Romania and that the opinions of international institutions had begun to matter. Given that the elections were still more than a year away, however, this explanation is also not compelling. The most likely explanation for Iliescu's treaty initiative with Hungary is simply that NATO criteria figured prominently in Romanian foreign policy even in the absence of a conducive social context.

But Romanian compliance on the bilateral treaty issue does not seriously undermine my central claim: a particular social context, informed by the uncertainty of target actors, their desire for social affirmation from international institutions, and the credibility of policies, is key to understanding a target state's embrace of Western ideas. Both the Romanian treaty initiative and the authoring of laws are empirically significant pieces of compliance. It is also important to note, however, that the same lieutenant general who began reforming Romania's military-security apparatus was summarily fired from the MoD for doing so (Bacon 1999, 191). The point is that while NATO was able to win a broad consensus for its strategic vision in Poland, due to a generally propitious social context, NATO cultivated no such consensus in Romania. It would be years before the expectations and behaviors of both civilians and officers would catch up with Lieutenant General Spiroiu's legislative efforts. Ratification of the basic treaty with Hungary similarly had little bearing on how Romanians would ultimately choose to allocate their defense resources, although it does show that the social context specified here is not the only possible condition that elicits compliance.

## Ukraine

Through the 1990s and early 2000s, NATO exercised relatively little influence over Ukraine's foreign policy and defense planning agenda because the alliance's status was compromised by weak political competition. Unlike Poland and Hungary, Ukraine did not have a democratic opposition movement under communism that sought close association with the values of Western international institutions. Before Yalta, US and British governments concluded that Ukrainian national aspirations were too weak to champion, and thereafter Ukraine had little in the way of intellectual, economic, or cultural exchange with Western states (Prizel 1998, 342). To the extent that Ukraine developed dissident movements during the Cold War, they tended to be weak and fragmented. Moreover, there was little connection between the aspirations of nationalists in the west or east of the country and a larger population that was mostly cowed and apathetic.

By the mid-1980s, Ukrainian opposition to the communist regime did take on a mass character. The 1986 nuclear disaster at Chernobyl, as well as revelations of Soviet atrocities against Ukrainians during World War II, underlined the injurious consequences of Soviet rule (Prizel 1998, 358–59). By 1990, mass protests, although comprised of groups almost exclusively west of the Dnieper, signified a new Ukrainian national consciousness. The failed coup against Gorbachev in 1991, in addition to Yeltsin's declaration of Russian sovereignty, finally pushed leaders in the Communist Party of Ukraine to move toward Ukrainian independence—even if leader Leonid Kravchuk would have preferred a successful anti-Gorbachev coup to put an end to Gorbachev's liberalizing policies (Prizel 1998, 361–62). Ukraine then voted overwhelmingly in favor of independence from the Soviet Union in December 1991.

But more like Romania than Poland or Hungary, Ukraine also experienced strong continuity between its communist-era leadership and post-independence governments. Low-quality political competition translated into narrow access for international institutions to the country's policy debates. By the early 2000s, however, large-scale demonstrations (with crowds reaching into the tens of thousands) did begin to agitate against the government. And by 2004, political competition was sufficiently powerful in Ukraine to prevent Leonid Kuchma and Moscow's preferred presidential candidate, Viktor Yanukovich, from taking office. With increasing political competition in Ukraine, the country's standing in relation to international institutions became more salient and NATO's access to foreign policy and defense planning increased.

The status of NATO in Ukraine was simultaneously undermined, however, because Russia provided an alternative point of reference for many Ukrainians. For Poland, Hungary, and Romania, escaping Russia's sphere of influence was viewed as essential to national survival. For at least some Ukrainians, however, Russia's own worldview—centered on strong executive leadership and state control of the economy and the distribution of wealth—was a viable alternative to Western norms.[31] Whereas political battles had been fought in Poland, Hungary, and Romania between honoring national traditions and historical experience or adopting Western practices, Ukraine's historical experience had been bound to Russia.

In sum, one could not expect Ukraine to internationalize defense planning or denationalize foreign policy on the basis of its perception of NATO's elevated status in the 1990s. In the absence of democratic opposition under communism and without meaningful political competition until the early 2000s, even if NATO had conferred elevated status on Ukraine, it was unlikely to have carried much weight in domestic politics. Given the Russian or Slavic orientation of large swathes of the population, building a too close relationship with NATO too early might well have jeopardized the political fortunes of Ukrainian leaders.

## NATO'S COMPROMISED CREDIBILITY AND PROBLEMS WITH COMPLIANCE (H3)

The credibility of a policy is measured first in terms of whether institutions or their founding members carry out the policies they urge upon others, and second in terms of whether there is an international, or at least Western, consensus underpinning prescribed practice. CEE perceptions of NATO's compromised credibility in defense planning denationalization complicated the alliance's efforts to denationalize defense policy in the region. NATO's consistency was undermined in the minds of nationalists by inadequate security guarantees from the West in the run-up to World War II. Moreover, there was no obvious consensus among existing alliance members on the shift from territorial to power projection capabilities. On a third measure, however—namely, the rejection of ethno-nationalist mobilization—NATO was credible, given that relations among NATO members (with the exception of Greece and Turkey) were cooperative.

The first weakness in NATO's credibility sprang from history. Poland and Czechoslovakia had staked their hopes on Western security guarantees before World War II, only to be abandoned to Nazi Germany and the Soviet Union. The deal agreed to at Yalta among Allied leaders, in which the region was essentially traded away to the Soviet sphere of influence, was regarded as a second betrayal— particularly by those CEE states that had contributed troops to the Allied war effort. Although these events took place well before NATO was formed, they nevertheless undermined the perceived credibility of Western security guarantees, given NATO's close association with many of the states that had been such disappointing allies in the past.

Of the four countries under consideration here, Poland's defense planning debates were most affected by these historical factors. By contrast, Hungary and Romania had aligned with Nazi Germany, however reluctantly, with Romania only switching sides in 1944—albeit with an enormous contribution of personnel to the Allied effort thereafter (Watts 2003, 132).[32] Ukraine, as part of the Soviet Union, had neither relied on Western security guarantees nor suffered unexpectedly under Yalta. But for Poland, the country that proportionately suffered the greatest loss of life in World War II, themes of vulnerability, betrayal, and self-reliance remained potentially resonant even after the Cold War.

## *Poland*

It was precisely by building on themes of vulnerability, betrayal, and self-reliance that conservative members of Poland's Solidarity Electoral Action mobilized support for a large-scale civil territorial defense program. Deputy Minister of Defense Romuald Szeremietiew placed civil territorial defense (Obrona Terytorialna, OT) at the center of his AWS campaign and made a more formal proposal in late 1997 with the assistance of Radek Sikorski, a former deputy minister of defense under Jan Parys.[33] Szeremietiew's program would have preserved universal conscription and eliminated service deferrals, which were routine in Poland by the late 1990s and had reduced the proportion of those who served to just 15 percent. While maintaining an operational force of both professional and conscript soldiers, Szeremietiew also proposed training a 1.5 million troop territorial force that would be armed with small arms, mines, mobile grenade launchers, and anti-tank and anti-aircraft rockets.[34]

The perceived lack of credibility of NATO and some of its members provided the AWS with justification for OT. In one of his early articles as deputy minister of defense, Szeremietiew wrote that although Poland's prospective membership in NATO was preferable to the kind of alliances made with Britain and France before World War II, he believed that an unhealthy mentality of dependence persisted in Poland. Critiquing the SLD-PSL (Democratic Left Alliance–Polish Peasant Party) coalition that had governed from 1993 until 1997, Szeremietiew argued that Poland had shown excessive compliance with NATO pressure as though "we cannot manage without the West."[35] The emphasis placed by Szeremietiew and others on self-sufficiency had additional policy implications. Reversing the dependence mentality would also mean patriotic awareness education and military training in high schools.[36] Calls for reintegration of the military into society and societal responsibility for national defense reflected Szeremietiew's view that the military could and should be used as a tool to shape the Polish state. Another OT supporter remarked that the consigning of national defense solely to the state and its military was "absolute nonsense" and argued instead for embedding vigilance against the country's enemies in society as a whole and all its institutions.[37] Szeremietiew and other OT advocates shared this view.[38]

Conservative members of the AWS also argued that greater self-reliance required domestic production of arms to equip territorial defense units—an idea popular with workers in the failing defense manufacturing sector. Among the threats to Poland's security listed by Szeremietiew was political pressure to purchase foreign-made weapons that, as he argued, were neither as militarily effective nor as economically efficient as locally produced small arms.[39] Another risk, according to OT supporters, stemmed from the idea, perpetuated by NATO, that Poland faced no immediate threat. For a country sandwiched between Russia and Germany, one high-level defense official argued that historical experience would suggest otherwise.[40] At least two defense officials linked what they saw as dangerous passivity toward NATO to past socialization within the Warsaw Pact.[41]

Territorial defense also had supporters in the military because of doubts about Western security guarantees. Contrary to conventional wisdom of the 1990s that a small, vulnerable, and recently liberated state had little choice but to seek powerful allies, some military personnel argued that mounting a defense was relatively easy and low-cost, given a strong public commitment to take responsibility for national security. One general argued that while it was typical of powerful, wealthy states to impose a high-tech vision of military organization on weaker powers, more important was an "inner resolve not to give in to invasion." Citing World War II, he noted that Poland had invested in expensive, heavy equipment at the time, but, after being abandoned by its allies, ended up sending its prized submarines and destroyers into service for other states.[42] OT would also ensure that not all of Poland's troops were subordinated to NATO command.[43] From the point of view of protecting territorial integrity and national autonomy, then, the bulk of NATO training, which in the 1990s was already geared toward offensive missions, made little sense to either civilian or military OT advocates.[44]

Another reason that NATO's credibility was undermined in the eyes of OT advocates was the lack of uniform consensus in the West on the appropriate balance between territorial and internationally mobile units. Thus, while NATO compatibility emphasized power projection, the alliance de-emphasized territorial security. Given that many Western countries have something equivalent to a home guard, supporters of Poland's civil territorial defense initiative wondered why the country should not be like "any other normal" or "sovereign state."[45]

It is surprising that a territorial defense program at odds with NATO priorities emerged at all in a country facing geostrategic uncertainty and seeking legitimacy through constructive relations with a range of international institutions. In a clear example of how historical experience, social practice, and arguments constitute alliances and enmities, the emergence of OT and the rationale behind it highlight the ways in which the normative inconsistency of the West fueled mistrust among at least some Polish officials. But as discussed in detail below, an equally powerful testament to the role of social relations in structuring interstate affinities and hostilities is the method NATO used to marginalize Polish territorial defense and achieve a greater commitment of resources to its own priorities—namely, collective security.

## Hungary

As noted, there are three areas in which NATO's credibility can be gauged: the consistency of defense planning within the alliance, the credibility of security guarantees, and the ethno-nationalist basis for foreign policy. Although it was primarily the first two that affected Poland's debate on territorial defense, Hungary was more strongly influenced by the third. Because the Soviets exercised almost total control over the Hungarian armed forces under the Warsaw Pact, and because military-society relations deteriorated over the same period, Hungary's defense planning in the early 1990s revealed a general lack of interest rather than a rush to fill a looming security vacuum.

At the outset of transition, and well before NATO membership was on offer, the defense doctrine debate in Hungary veered between two extremes—defense self-sufficiency and abolition of the armed forces. In the end, the country settled on a wholly defensive strategy to forestall military defeat until its allies could assist it, but even this modest plan was under-resourced and poorly implemented (Barany 1999, 80–81). Hence the question of whether Hungary had a defense at odds with or complementary to NATO norms did not surface, except insofar as Hungary had great difficulty delivering the requisite level of defense spending into the 2000s (see table 5.2).

Regarding the credibility of security guarantees, arguments based on Western betrayal did not resonate as in Poland and Czechoslovakia, because Hungary had been a German ally through most of World War II. But the United Nations failed to assist Prime Minister Imre Nagy's neutrality initiative during the 1956 revolution (Barany 1993, 63; Nelson and Szayna 1998), ultimately resulting in the execution of Nagy and two thousand others, and this contributed to public support for neutrality in the 1990s.

However, there was one area in which the alliance's credibility was sound. NATO had been very clear in its expectation that candidates, like members, should "settle any international disputes in which they may be involved by peaceful means in such a manner that international peace and security and justice are not endangered" (NATO 1995b, 3).[46] With the partial exception of Turkey and Greece, members of the alliance have generally sought noncombative ways of settling disputes. As Hungarian Foreign Minister László Kovács observed, "There is nothing that makes the West more nervous than to accept quarrelling Central or East European countries into multilateral structures" (quoted in Williams 2002, 233). Having little discursive space to challenge NATO's stipulation that ongoing interstate disputes be settled peacefully in advance of accession, this is what the MSzP set out to do.

## Romania

Like their Hungarian counterparts, Romanian leaders were susceptible to NATO norms on the incompatibility between bilateral tensions and alliance membership. Although there was not a seamless accommodation by Romania of the whole range of Western policies, NATO's consistency on the importance of minority rights protection and resolving conflicts with neighboring states strongly influenced President Iliescu's decision to launch a basic treaty initiative with Hungary in 1995. As a result, Iliescu's PDSR forfeited the support of three smaller political parties that had been part of the governing coalition, the PRM, PSM, and PUNR (Linden 2000, 134).

The lack of consensus within NATO over force structures contrasted with its consistency on pacific relations among its members. Hungary, because of its low regard for military power and a general lack of interest in defense planning, was less affected by this kind of inconsistency than were Romania and Poland. But in these latter two states, where the military had long been viewed as the appropriate guardian of national independence, the absence of a single model of force projection created considerable discursive space concerning the appropriate balance of territorial and operational forces.

There was very little discussion in Romania about the credibility of NATO security guarantees. That these guarantees were a source of debate in Poland but not in Hungary or Romania reflects diverging experiences during World War II rather than more uniform experiences (at least with the West) during the Cold War. As German allies for much or all of World War II, neither Hungary nor Romania had the same embittering experience of abandonment by the West.[47]

## Ukraine

In Ukraine, as elsewhere in the region, the absence of any single model establishing a balance between territorial and operational forces within NATO put the alliance in a weak position regarding its preference for power projection. The lack of Western consensus on threat perceptions and force structures lay behind

Ukraine's mostly territorial approach to defense planning, which was generally unaffected by NATO's preferences.

The perceived credibility of NATO security guarantees was irrelevant to Ukraine—unlike in Poland, where some, mainly right-wing politicians, played on the country's treatment during World War II and at Yalta. Stalin's promises of semi-autonomy for Ukraine within the Soviet Union after the war proved illusory, with federation quickly giving way to Russification, recollectivization, surveillance, imprisonment, and attacks on Ukrainian nationalism (Prizel 1998, 340–48). Although some western Ukrainians had tried to cultivate Western support for Ukrainian independence at the close of World War II, the real source of disappointment—in both the east and west of the country—was the Soviet Union.

The lack of debate in Ukraine about the viability of NATO security guarantees was not, however, a symptom of Ukraine's indifference to NATO's military power. Ukrainian-Russian tensions emerged at several points over Russia's refusal to acknowledge, even years after Ukraine had formally established its independence, that there was in fact a border between the two countries. Presumably Russia's policy was a symptom of its reluctance to admit that, after three centuries of federation with Russia, Ukraine was finally a separate entity. In the late 1990s Ukrainian-Russian relations were sufficiently tense that Ukraine did seek NATO security guarantees against Russia (Kuzio 2003, 33). Not until April 2004 did both Ukrainian and Russian parliaments finally ratify an initiative on their shared border, concluding an agreement that presidents Kuchma and Putin had signed more than a year earlier.[48] Interest in NATO security guarantees did not elicit strong compliance with NATO policy prescriptions, however—either in defense planning or in civil-military relations.

Western insistence on the inappropriateness of an ethno-nationalist foreign policy might have had some effect on Ukrainian foreign policy. Ukraine was the first country to conclude a bilateral treaty with Hungary (in December 1991) that provided the 150,000- to 200,000-strong Hungarian minority with collective rights to cultural and administrative autonomy (Williams 2002, 234). Hungary agreed in return to renounce any territorial claims—the source of some controversy in the Hungarian parliament. It was reported that Leonid Kravchuk (the first post-Soviet Ukrainian president) pursued the agreement to bolster Western support for Ukrainian independence (Oltay 1992). But given that the agreement was negotiated long before NATO was engaged in the region, there could only have been an indirect link between Western norms and Ukrainian foreign policy.

Whether NATO contributed to Ukraine's foreign policy denationalization later in the decade is open to question. Hungary and Romania were clearly inclined to mobilize domestic political support by making ethno-nationalist claims, and Western international institutions subdued that tendency. Given Ukraine's scant experience with statehood and its people's long-standing participation in multiethnic societies, it is not clear that ethno-nationalist sensitivities would have resonated broadly in Ukraine. To the extent that NATO promoted bilateral accommodation among candidate states, in part by renouncing the exploitation of minority issues for political gain, this was a norm already embedded in Ukrainian society.[49]

## TRANSNATIONAL COALITIONS AND OUTCOMES
### Poland

Uncertainty, a perceived hierarchy between domestic actors and international institutions, and the credibility of international institutions' policy prescriptions all facilitate the compliance of target states. NATO's coalition-building power in Poland was based on the first two conditions. Some uncertainty about how to structure defense policy gave NATO access to defense reform debates at the outset of transition, because a new party came to power and civilians had little defense expertise. Measures on hierarchy were also high, given robust political competition and strong public support for military power. NATO influence in Poland was circumscribed, however, by right-wing politicians' mistrust of Western security guarantees and the lack of Western consensus on the importance of power projection. Thus although Poland did not have a legacy of national territorial defense from the Warsaw Pact, this did not prevent a range of actors, both civilian and military, from mobilizing in support of one in the 1990s. Shifting Poland's strategic orientation away from regional threats to out-of-area missions would first require scuttling Szeremietiew's civil territorial defense plan.[50]

NATO objected to the OT initiative on three grounds. First, given the alliance's insistence that publics support their countries' accession, the fomenting of fear by OT advocates that NATO might or might not provide assistance in an emergency called into question the viability of NATO security guarantees. Second, admitting a member whose political parties insisted on mobilizing public support by demonizing Russia complicated and contradicted one of NATO's most basic messages: that the aim of the alliance was regional stabilization, not Russian isolation. While NATO officials had varying views about the seriousness of these first two issues, there was virtual unanimity on a third: that territorial defense on the scale proposed by Szeremietiew would divert scarce resources from projects that would more clearly advance NATO's mission.

When German officials first became aware of AWS campaign pledges to pursue OT once in office, the German embassy in Warsaw notified other NATO members.[51] NATO officials then began taking steps to curb the program. In delegations to Poland and to Polish delegations in Brussels, NATO representatives repeatedly stressed in closed-door meetings their preference that Poland focus on the basic issues of integration and compatibility with the alliance rather than on territorial defense.[52] They argued that because Poland did not have a single transport vehicle capable of moving troops,[53] the issue of how economical territorial defense would be compared with operational forces was irrelevant: every defense zloty should be allocated to modernizing and equipping NATO-capable forces. NATO communicated this message with such conviction and consistency that Poland's pursuit of OT became an embarrassment around the Polish MoD.[54]

Not only NATO but also some high-level Polish officials objected to the plan. Representing different points on Poland's political spectrum, policymakers explained in private why they hoped Szeremietiew's initiative would fail. Defense Minister Janusz Onyszkiewicz opposed territorial defense because he understood that it was inconsistent with NATO's strategic orientation—he had been among those coached by NATO officials early on about the right and wrong reasons for wanting to join the alliance.[55] As a member of the Freedom Union (Unia Wolności, UW), however, and in coalition with Szeremietiew's party (the AWS), he was politically trapped into not rejecting the plan outright. Two other former officials with contrasting political legacies also wanted to see the territorial defense program fail—and for similar reasons. In addition to challenging NATO's credibility, they argued, OT advocates' views were anachronistic and reminiscent of aspirations to build a self-sufficient, neutral "Great Poland" (Polska Wielka).[56] The debate over territorial defense also divided the military insofar as some viewed territorial forces as second class while others viewed operational units as an extravagance of dubious merit.[57]

One publication, *Nie*—recognized for saying what others were only thinking—articulated what critics of civil territorial defense would reveal in private. Reporting that NATO had recently sent "a document specifying what it expects from the Polish Army," the author observed that the "cost of meeting all of them [NATO's expectations] is much higher than our financial capabilities." As a still prospective member of the alliance, the article concluded, it would be inadvisable for Poland to send signals indicating that its defense officials believed NATO to be "a pro-Russian slacker." "Exotic strategies" (i.e., territorial defense) put Poland in a "bad bargaining position."[58]

To kill the program and limit opportunities to exploit territorial defense for political gain, NATO resolved to confront Szeremietiew directly. The US embassy, in cooperation with Andrzej Karkoszka (former deputy minister of defense), arranged for a meeting in February 1998.[59] A US official briefed Szeremietiew in advance of what promised to be a tense encounter, providing Szeremietiew with an opportunity to save face by preparing an appropriate response ahead of time. In the meeting itself, Western officials first emphasized to Szeremietiew that regardless of historical precedent set by Poland's Western allies, NATO would not abandon a member state under threat. Second, they argued that Russia did not pose either a short- or medium-term threat, but that NATO would nevertheless continue to assess the situation and adapt its strategy accordingly. Finally, given these facts, NATO representatives argued that it was unnecessary for Poland to pursue territorial defense.

In addition to the substantive arguments, the meeting included a forceful message. In what one US official present at the meeting described as a "harsh" encounter, NATO bluntly told Szeremietiew that he should not pursue the plan, because it was incompatible with alliance priorities. Without threatening to exclude Poland from the alliance, NATO officials impressed upon Szeremietiew that there were many other more constructive projects that he could pursue while in office. They urged him, "don't do this."[60] Shortly thereafter, Szeremietiew stopped pursuing the plan, although there was never a public admission that OT had been inconsistent with NATO objectives.[61] Following the private meeting at the US embassy, Szeremietiew denied that OT had ever been in conflict with NATO. Altering the original intent of territorial defense, he rearticulated the once-perceived need for OT as consistent with NATO aims, and explained its abandonment exclusively in terms of domestic debates and budgetary constraints.[62]

The AWS abandoned OT not just because of an isolated incident at the US embassy, but rather because the confrontation with Szeremietiew took place against a backdrop of growing conflict and isolation. Over the previous seven years, the alliance had exploited the uncertainty of domestic actors and its own elevated status in Poland to cultivate coalitions that would support its positions. NATO turned to Karkoszka to set up the crucial meeting with Szeremietiew precisely because the former deputy minister of defense had accrued both domestic and international credibility for his role in democratizing Polish civil-military relations (see chapter 4). Karkoszka's involvement signaled Szeremietiew that he had powerful opponents, not only in NATO but in Poland as well.

Furthermore, some of the same officials whom NATO had already persuaded of the necessity for constructive relations with Russia had initially supported territorial defense.[63] They had halted their public pronouncements on the subject, however, once NATO aired its objections in terms of the need to harmonize Polish and NATO strategy, which included building bridges to the east, not burning them. This shrank Szeremietiew's political base still further.

Finally, OT had become an embarrassment among Polish MoD officials, who without NATO discouragement might have been perfectly amenable to it—it was, after all, consistent with Polish military tradition and had been discontinued in the 1960s only on account of hated Soviet domination. But the incompatibility of OT with NATO's preferences as recognized by MoD officials and critics in the media would have made it difficult for Szeremietiew to sustain support among his colleagues in government had he continued to criticize NATO for insufficient security guarantees. NATO, through its long-term cultivation of sympathetic coalitions, thereby orchestrated Szeremietiew's political isolation, undermining the credibility of his original claims. The abandonment of OT shows the extent to which international institutions, with the help of domestic actors, can delegitimize particular lines of reasoning.[64]

Given that not only NATO but also some Polish officials objected to Szeremietiew's plans, one could argue that OT would have been defeated even without NATO intervention. But two factors suggest otherwise. First, Szeremietiew used OT to galvanize support from the domestic arms–producing constituency and nationalists in his ongoing rivalry with Janusz Onyszkiewicz (a pro-NATO reformer and defense minister on two occasions in the 1990s). As it was a successful element of AWS campaigning, Szeremietiew most likely would not have abandoned his rhetoric on Polish self-sufficiency without external pressure to do so. Second, it was hard for domestic politicians to argue against territorial defense in the light of Poland's very real historical strategic vulnerability and the strength of the domestic arms manufacturers' lobby. NATO's objections to civil territorial defense thus gave its domestic critics a politically convenient means of portraying their own reservations in the most patriotic light possible. Rather than seeming to reject a certain interpretation of the past that celebrated Polish military tradition, OT critics could simply adopt a low profile while NATO pursued its agenda.

## Hungary

Hungary registered strong compliance with NATO demands on bilateral basic treaties with two of the country's historical rivals, Romania and Slovakia. Also, Hungary never posed the kind of problems for NATO that Poland did with its proposals for large-scale territorial defense; it had never aspired to such a system—

not even during the Cold War. But Hungarian compliance was much weaker in making meaningful military contributions to NATO's out-of-area operations. Whereas Poland became a leader in the alliance, Hungary had trouble meeting even the minimum defense spending expectations of 2 percent of GDP.

If uncertainty in Hungary was stronger than in Poland, due to the absence of any historical territorial defense aspirations, Hungary's lower measures on hierarchy and the drive for NATO social recognition translated into weaker compliance elsewhere. Political competition was strong in Hungary and, when combined with NATO's credibility on peaceful bilateral relations, it explains the MSzP's willingness to pursue bilateral treaties. But because regard for military power was weak, as reflected in poor military-society relations, there was little impetus to spend the expected resources on modernization or to make strong contributions to multilateral missions.

Hungary was consistently politically supportive of NATO missions, even if its military contributions were small (see table 5.3 for 2006 military deployments). Hungary assisted NATO in its missions in the former Yugoslavia, relaxed a law that prevented Hungarian troops being deployed outside the country without parliamentary approval, and designated some units for NATO use (Barany 1999, 86; Jacoby 2004, 172).[65] In the Kosovo crisis, Hungary was generally politically supportive but militarily inconsequential. The Fidesz–Hungarian Civic Party (Fidesz-MPP) government, in power from 1998, pledged support for NATO bombing and gave the alliance unlimited access to Hungarian facilities and airspace (over the objections of the socialist opposition), but declined to participate directly. The inadequacy of the Hungarian Defense Force was revealed by Hungary's capacity to patrol its own airspace for only two hours a day and with MiG-29s that lacked NATO-compatible "friend or foe" communications equipment (Jacoby 2005, 240–42).

The Hungarian case raises the question of how enduring the denationalization of its foreign and defense policy is likely to be. For even before Hungary's accession to NATO in March 1999, there was evidence of backsliding. In September 1997, for example, the MSzP foreign minister admitted to officials in Washington, DC, that Hungary's defense expenditure would fall short of its commitments. Such shortfalls have generally been the norm for Hungary (Jacoby 2004, 138). By 2006, Hungarian projections for defense spending in 2007 had fallen to the lowest in the alliance, at 1.1 percent of GDP. After accession, Hungary could not support NATO's out-of-area power projection capability in any significant way, while the country's politicians still seemed intent on acting on behalf of aggrieved minorities abroad (Wallander 2002, 5–6).

TABLE 5.3
*Troop Deployments by Selected Postcommunist States, 2006*

| Area of Operation | Hungary | Poland | Romania | Ukraine |
|---|---|---|---|---|
| Afghanistan | NATO, ISAF: 187 | Army: 87[a]<br>NATO, ISAF: 3<br>UN, UNAMA: 1<br>obs | Army: 400[a]<br>NATO, ISAF: 550<br>UN, UNAMA: 1<br>obs | — |
| Bosnia-<br> Herzegovina | EU, EUFOR II:<br> 117 engineers; 4<br> obs | EU, EUFOR II:<br> 236 (Op Althea)<br>UN, UNMIBH: 1<br> obs | EU, EUFOR II:<br> 120 (Op Althea) | — |
| Burundi | — | — | UN, UNONUB: 2<br> obs | — |
| Côte d'Ivoire | — | UN, UNOCI: 2<br> obs | UN, UNOCI: 5<br> obs | — |
| Cyprus | UN, UNFICYP: 83 | — | — | — |
| Democratic<br> Republic of<br> Congo | — | UN, UNMONUC:<br> 3 obs | UN, UNMONUC:<br> 22 obs | UN, UNMONUC:<br> 13 obs |
| Egypt | MFO: 41 MPs | — | — | — |
| Ethiopia-Eritrea | — | UN, UNMEE: 4 | UN, UNMEE: 7<br> obs | UN, UNMEE: 5<br> obs |
| Georgia | UN, UNOMIG: 7<br> obs | UN, UNOMIG: 5<br> obs | UN, UNOMIG: 5<br> obs<br>EU, EU-OSCE: 5<br> obs | UN, UNOMIG: 3<br> obs |
| Iraq | Army: 393 (peace<br> support) | Army and Air<br> Force: 900 | Army: 860 | Army: 1,621 (peace<br> support) |
| Lebanon | — | 1 military hospital<br>UN, UNIFIL: 210 | — | UN, UNIFIL: 196 |

Since the noncompliance described above occurred after Hungary's invitation to join NATO in July 1997 or after its accession in March 1999, one could conclude that the incentive of membership was the only impetus for even limited compliance. I would argue, however, that mixed measures on the variables under consideration do in fact explain Hungary's uneven compliance. As already noted, military-society relations in Hungary remained weak through the period examined here. That Hungary had only a "small and obsolete force that still [carried] most of the characteristics but not the size of a mass army" by the early 2000s stemmed from a lack of interest in military-security issues (Martinusz 2002, 12). Because the public did not have confidence in military power, it did not favor devoting resources to national security. A key source of NATO's power was therefore

TABLE 5.3 *continued*

| Area of Operation | Hungary | Poland | Romania | Ukraine |
|---|---|---|---|---|
| Liberia | — | UN, UNMIL: 2 obs | UN, UNMIL: 3 obs | UN, UNMIL: 300; 3 obs |
| Moldova | — | — | — | Joint peacekeeping force: 10 |
| Serbia-Montenegro | NATO, KFOR I: 484<br>UN, UNMIK: 1 obs | NATO, KFOR I: 312<br>UN, UNMIK: 1 | NATO, KFOR I: 150<br>UN, UNMIK: 2 obs | NATO, KFOR I: 248<br>UN, UNMIK: 2 obs |
| Sudan | — | UN, UNMIS: 2 | UN, UNMIS: 12 obs | UN, UNMIS: 10 obs |
| Syria-Israel | — | UN, UNDOF: 343 | — | — |
| Western Sahara | UN, MINURSO: 7 obs | UN, MINURSO: 1 obs | — | — |

*Source:* International Institute for Strategic Studies, *The Military Balance*, 1991, 1994, 1995, 1999, 2005–2006.
*Note:* Op, operation; obs, observer; MP, military police.
*Acronyms:* Althea, Military Operation in Bosnia and Herzegovina (EUFOR-Althea); EUFOR, EU Force in Bosnia and Herzegovina; EU-OSCE, European Union–Organization for Security and Co-operation in Europe; ISAF, International Security Assistance Force; KFOR I, the Kosovo Force, a NATO-led international force responsible for establishing and maintaining security in Kosovo; MFO, Multinational Force and Observers (from 1981 Middle East Peace Treaty); MINURSO, UN Mission for the Referendum in Western Sahara; UNAMA, UN Assistance Mission in Afghanistan; UNDOF, UN Disengagement Observer Force; UNFICYP, UN Peacekeeping Force in Cyprus; UNIFIL, UN Interim Force in Lebanon; UNMEE, UN Mission in Ethiopia and Eritrea; UNMIBH, UN Mission in Bosnia-Herzegovina; UNMIK, UN Mission in Kosovo; UNMIL, UN Mission in Liberia; UNMIS, UN Mission in Sudan; UNMONUC, UN Mission in the Democratic Republic of Congo; UNOCI, UN Operation in Côte d'Ivoire; UNOMIG, UN Observer Mission in Georgia; UNONUB, UN Operation in Burundi.
[a]Operation Enduring Freedom.

absent—that is, the public's ability to pressure politicians into maintaining constructive relations with the alliance.

Further to the question of whether compliance stops at the date of entry, not until after NATO accession did some of Hungary's most important defense reviews begin (Simon 2003). Given the problems encountered during the Kosovo campaign and the recommendations of multiple external reviews, at least one of which was so critical as to be devastating, the Hungarian elite became concerned with their country's standing in the alliance.[66] With respect to democratizing civil-military relations and internationalizing defense planning and foreign policy, it was the embarrassment of noncompliance, mostly experienced by Hungary's elites, that spurred the country to action in the early 2000s.

## Romania

Romania differs from Poland and Hungary in having lower levels of uncertainty, a lack of party turnover in transition, and the subsequent absence of party competition. NATO's status was thus compromised in Romania for much of the 1990s. The continuity in personnel from the communist to the first postcommunist governments limited NATO influence with respect to uncertainty. Romania also had extensive territorial defense during the Cold War, potentially complicating NATO's drive for new power projection capabilities. The lack of political competition until the mid-1990s also delayed the exertion of NATO influence based on Romania's desire for social recognition. Given these starting conditions, I would expect NATO to exercise little control over Romanian foreign and defense planning until at least after the CDR took power in late 1996. Further, because of the existence of territorial defense during the Cold War, I would expect considerable friction over NATO demands that Romania develop power projection capabilities at the expense of territorial defense.

But, in fact, Romanian compliance with NATO foreign and defense policy denationalization exceeded the predictions of my theoretical framework. Even in advance of high-quality political competition, the communist successor PDSR in 1995, under the leadership of President Iliescu, had initiated the basic treaty with Hungary—in all likelihood to conform with NATO's expectations of candidate states and at considerable domestic cost. The loss of support from three, smaller nationalist parties on the left and right weakened the PDSR's power base. Only one variable from the social context—the credibility of NATO on the importance of settling disputes—can help explain Romania's willingness to adopt the alliance's priorities.

The denationalization of Romanian defense planning is more consistent with the predictions of the uncertainty, status, and credibility hypotheses, although even here one finds less emphasis on territorial defense than expected given the country's history of territorial forces and geostrategic vulnerability. The continuity in territorial defense does explain why NATO's strategic priorities were the source of conflict (Watts 2005, 103). An advisor to the Romanian presidency, Marian Zulean, noted that the effort since 1999 to move from a "neutralist type of Territorial Defence model and then to strongly emphasise power projection capabilities" had generated significant tension by the early 2000s (2002, 129–30). The result, however, as in Poland, was ultimate deferral to NATO's strategic goals and the redirection of resources toward operational forces to bring them up to NATO standards, with territorial forces getting fewer funds and dependent on "trickle down" (130).

TABLE 5.4
*Troop Levels: Selected Postcommunist States, 1989–1990 to 2004–2005*

| Country | Armed Forces | 1989–1990 | 1990–1991 | 1993–1994 | 2004–2005 |
|---------|--------------|-----------|-----------|-----------|-----------|
| Hungary | Active | 91,000 | 94,000 | 78,000 | 32,300 |
|         | Reserves | 168,000 | 134,400 | 195,000 | 44,000 |
| Poland | Active | 412,000 | 312,800 | 287,500 | 141,500 |
|        | Reserves | 505,000 | 505,000 | 465,500 | 234,000 |
| Romania | Active | 171,000 | 163,000 | 203,100 | 97,200 |
|         | Reserves | 203,000 | 203,000 | 427,000 | 104,000 |
| Ukraine | Active | NA | NA | 438,000 | 272,500 |
|         | Reserves | NA | NA | 1,000,000 | 1,000,000 |

*Source:* International Institute for Strategic Studies, *The Military Balance,* 1989–1990, 1990–1991, 1993–1994, 2004–2005.
*Note:* NA, data not available.

By 2003, Romania's defense strategy reflected alliance concerns more than Romanian military or political tradition. The country had reduced its active-duty military personnel to 97,200 from 171,000 in 1989 (see table 5.4), in keeping with Membership Action Plan suggestions that "countries develop smaller, more capable forces" that "could be used for NATO operations" (NATO Parliamentary Assembly 2002, 7). Fifty thousand troops were dedicated to high states of readiness, while 25,000 territorial force personnel were deployable in 90 to 360 days (Watts 2005, 102). Romania's former reserve forces were dismantled (see table 5.4 for troop reductions).[67]

Between 1989 and 2005, Romania deployed more than 14,000 military personnel to myriad operations around the world. Following 9/11, Romania replaced US forces in the Balkans in an effort to free US troops for the Bush administration's "war on terror." In addition to serving in Bosnia and Kosovo, Romanian forces have also taken part in military actions in Afghanistan and Iraq. Unlike Hungary or the Czech Republic, both wealthier states, Romania has increased defense spending to support such operations even in times of relative austerity—and with substantial public support (Watts 2005, 107–8).

Poland and Hungary are typically grouped together as similar cases that, because of their histories of democratic opposition to communism, enjoyed "front-runner" status vis-à-vis Western institutions from the early 1990s. Such shared legacies did not translate into equal degrees of military reform, however. Poland and Romania have embraced NATO's geostrategic vision to a greater extent than Hungary. The central difference is in public regard for military power, as reflected in military-society relations. Although Romania initially undertook fewer reforms in anticipation of NATO accession than either Poland or Hungary, because of the continuity in its governing personnel from the communist era, by the late 1990s and early 2000s political competition in Romania and strong public support for military power provided NATO with far-reaching access to the country's defense planning review processes. Tension around the forsaking of territorial defense in favor of NATO's operational goals is attributable to the prominent historical role of territorial forces in Romania and the lack of consensus in NATO on power projection capabilities.

## Ukraine

NATO has exercised only limited influence over Ukrainian defense planning. While Ukraine remains primarily committed to territorial defense and has maintained a proportionately larger force than Poland, Hungary, or Romania, it has also participated in multilateral missions led by the United States and NATO, including in Iraq and Afghanistan (Sherr 2005, 171). Ukrainian outcomes suggest there is no "best practice" in defense planning in that the country has sustained large land forces, even if some downsizing and professionalization conform with post–Cold War trends. Ukrainian multilateralism also suggests, however, that NATO can influence policies even in the absence of a clear commitment to expanding its membership.

The social context in Ukraine remained unfavorable from NATO's perspective through the 1990s. There was strong continuity through the transition, both in the regime and in the military-security apparatus, which limited uncertainty. Political competition was also weak, undermining the salience of international opinion and, with it, NATO's status. Finally, although Ukrainians did not question the credibility of Western security guarantees in the way nationalistic Poles did, the Ukrainian population in the east mistrusted NATO and questioned its credibility because of the country's traditional ties with Russia. With public protest against Kuchma's reign beginning in 2000 and increased political competition with Yushchenko's presidential victory in 2004, NATO influence over Ukrainian defense planning seemed to increase in the 2000s.

Given that Ukraine had as much (or more) to fear from Russia as a newly independent state in the post-Soviet period as did Poland, Hungary, or Romania, it might have tried to fulfill NATO membership criteria, even if it was not on explicit offer, in a bid to win over the alliance. Although much of Ukraine's population still favored strong ties to Russia into the twenty-first century, and public support for NATO membership remained low, the population—whether

Russian- or Ukrainian-speaking—was overwhelmingly in favor of Ukrainian independence (see Kuzio 2003, 31–32). Moreover, Russia acted on several occasions to
diminish that independence—by refusing to recognize the international border,
by provoking a crisis to ensure Russian access to the Sea of Azov, or by inter-
fering in Ukrainian elections. Indeed, in response to Russian policy, Ukraine
has at specific points enlisted NATO assistance. But despite the evident incentives of membership, there was no clear hierarchical relation between Ukraine
and NATO through the 1990s and thus only limited compliance on the Ukrainian side.

Ukrainian military reform has been influenced both by national constraints
and, to a lesser extent, by NATO advising. The country had downsized its active
forces to between 200,000 and 300,000 by 2004 (see table 5.4), partly a result of
resource constraints, although this figure excludes the hundreds of thousands
more in other security services, some of which have been created since 1991
(Grytsenko 1997).

More directly linked to NATO urging, Ukraine is also moving from a conscript
to a more extensively professional force, despite serious misgivings among many
senior officers. The country has also taken part in several UN and NATO missions
since 1991. Finally, Ukrainian participation in multinational missions could be
seen as an aligning of Ukrainian and Western security concerns. But Ukraine's
participation in Iraq has also been interpreted as a gesture of contrition for having
sold radar systems to Iraq in 2000 in violation of UN sanctions rather than as an
expression of common strategic interest (Kuzio 2003, 25).[68]

In fact, a range of Ukrainian reforms reveals that in terms of strategic priorities,
Ukraine and NATO still had little in common even as the country was becoming
more serious about its intentions to join the alliance. Despite the move to professionalization and away from conscription, by the early 2000s senior military officers still regarded the armed forces' principal duty as the defense of Ukrainian
territory from external enemies. NATO's view that war-fighting strategies should
focus less on interstate war and more on transnational, terrorist, or criminal
threats "would be disputed with conviction even by many of the most reformist
Ukrainian military officers" (Sherr 2005, 162). In addition, although the "general
war ethos" that implied an East-West conflagration no longer formed the basis of
defense planning in Ukraine, officers still took it for granted that they should plan
for defense self-sufficiency, regardless of the country's evolving ties to NATO.

Another area in which NATO has failed to exercise influence in Ukraine is in
the discourse on why Ukrainian supporters of NATO membership should pursue
that policy. Whereas NATO successfully encouraged Polish and Hungarian offi-

cials to talk about the benefits of membership in terms of internal modernization, democratization, and collective security, Ukrainian supporters of NATO continued to insist that membership was primarily about protecting the country's independence against Russian interference and imperialism. A key goal of the NATO information office in Ukraine is the dissemination of the notion that NATO enlargement should not be construed as a means of containing Russia.[69] But in stark contrast to Poland, Hungary, and Romania, supporters of NATO membership in Ukraine, who mostly reside in the west of the country, argue that strategic balancing against Russia is precisely the reason they want to join, not the democratization or modernization of the security forces. Ukrainian understanding of the image that NATO tries to project, and the centrality of collective security within it, was still very shallow in 2005.[70]

If the social context, rather than incentives alone, facilitates compliance, then more than an invitation to join NATO would be needed to redefine Ukrainian foreign policy toward the Euro-Atlantic community after so many years of unconsolidated national identity. Several processes—a collapse of the Ukrainian military-security apparatus, an increase in the intensity and quality of political competition in the country, and the standardization of a defense planning model within NATO itself—would give the alliance greater access to Ukrainian defense planning and foreign policy. Such changes would likely encourage military reformers to more actively seek NATO expertise at the expense of national tradition and would heighten the salience of international opinion.

The first two of these processes were already underway at the time of writing (late 2007). Ongoing crises of material deterioration and low morale in the armed forces have contributed to downsizing and professionalization, in keeping with NATO preferences but at odds with Ukrainian tradition. Political competition has already encouraged the center-right in Ukraine to seek legitimacy through NATO recognition. President Viktor Yushchenko, for example, has had the political mandate to initiate more thorough reforms than were possible under his center-left predecessors. Political competition could also undermine the disproportionate power of oligarchs whose economic ties to Russia have undermined the formulation of a coherent foreign policy (Prizel 1998; Kuzio 2003). Public support for NATO membership remains low in Ukraine. But evidence from Hungary and the Czech Republic, in particular, suggests that cultivating the minimum level of public support necessary for NATO's purposes is not that difficult. Evidence from those two countries also shows, however, that while helpful to compliance, public support is not as crucial to reform as is uncertainty among domestic actors or perceptions of a hierarchy between domestic elites and NATO representatives.

For even after Hungary secured support for NATO membership in a referendum, compliance did not markedly improve.

## CONCLUSION

NATO's engagement of central and eastern Europe, through enlargement, the Partnership for Peace, an open-door policy, and myriad other agreements, has substantially—thought not wholly—denationalized defense planning and foreign policy in the region. The alliance has de-emphasized territorial defense, discouraged rhetoric that derived its credibility from historical rivalries, narrowed the scope for ethno-nationalist mobilization, and supported bilateral peace agreements. Less positively for CEE armed forces' morale, NATO has also presided over the rise of two-tiered armies that undermine national military traditions by allocating disproportionate resources to units dedicated for NATO missions. NATO-capable units have in turn been used in a range of NATO or US-led operations that at times have been deeply unpopular among CEE publics. Although the desire of CEE states to join NATO was linked to their historical vulnerability, their military-security apparatuses have paradoxically been refashioned to pursue missions largely divorced from those domestic concerns.

Poland, Hungary, Romania, and Ukraine have varied in their willingness to embrace NATO's strategic priorities. And, in keeping with my argument, such variation corresponded more faithfully to a social context defined by uncertainty, status, and credibility than to incentives. Poland and Hungary were equally vigorous in their political campaigns to win membership, and Hungary declared its desire to join before Poland. But Poland has made a far stronger military contribution, while Hungary has consistently spent closer to only half of what NATO asks of its members—both before and after being admitted. This degree of variation is more closely associated with each country's relationship to NATO than with incentives as such, which were basically uniform. In Poland and Hungary, that "relationship" is informed by the perceived status of the alliance. Strong regard for military power in Poland accentuated the alliance's power there, while lower regard for the armed forces in Hungary undermined it.

Romania again shows how similar incentive structures can result in different outcomes. Despite strong public support for NATO membership and a viable candidacy in the 1990s, Romania manifested little compliance with the alliance's prescriptions until political competition elevated the status of NATO in late 1996. The single exception was Romania's effort to forge a bilateral treaty with Hungary as early as 1995. By 2001, however, after two episodes of party turnover in which elections were fought in part over the country's status in relation to international institutions, Romania had surpassed Hungary's level of compliance, measured in terms of defense spending and meaningful military contributions to out-of-area missions (see tables 5.2 and 5.3).

Ukraine declared its intention to join NATO in 2002, and the alliance has kept the possibility of membership alive in the hopes of encouraging Ukraine's Western reorientation. Strong continuity in the regime through the transition, an enduring military structure and culture, and the absence of political competition around constructing a Western identity until at least the early 2000s—all prevented NATO's access to reform debates until the competitive elections of 2004. Thus the Ukrainian focus remained more strongly linked to territorial forces than in Poland, Hungary, or Romania. Nevertheless, NATO and the United States did persuade Ukraine to participate in multilateral missions. And evolving political competition and deterioration of the armed forces' material conditions may yet give the alliance more influence over defense restructuring in Ukraine.

Conditionality was not strictly applied in either Poland or Hungary, although the latter was certainly aware of its precarious position with respect to the alliance in the 1990s, given its weak military, tepid public support, and discontiguous geography. Hungarian bilateral agreements with Slovakia and Romania could be interpreted as resulting from Hungary's questionable status. But as the evidence shows, compliance did not materialize until political competition allowed the socialists to compete with the MDF for NATO approbation—a feature of the facilitating social context. The power of conditionality independent of a particular social context is also called into question by Polish compliance with NATO's request that the AWS abandon civil territorial defense in favor of stronger operational forces. Poland's inclusion in the first round of enlargement was never threatened. Deputy Minister of Defense Szeremietiew and his cohort changed course because they eventually understood that they were significantly out of step with alliance expectations and were embarrassed by that fact. By making territorial defense an embarrassment around the MoD, NATO shifted the meaning of territorial defense from patriotic to anachronistic. A hierarchical relationship that is as well defined and as broadly perceived as that between Poland and NATO can obviate the need for conditionality to elicit compliance.

Whatever the current extent of defense planning and foreign policy denationalization in these four states, domestic actors had conflicting preferences. Some wanted to pursue strategies that closely reflected historical concerns, and they yielded to the NATO agenda only reluctantly. Others perceived a modernizing advantage to aligning with NATO's out-of-area emphasis. In both instances the alliance has had significant constitutive effects in the region. For whether actors comply out of conviction or because of social or material pressure, a state's foreign policy goals and military organization signal its international purpose and orientation. Without NATO, CEE concerns would certainly be regional, with resources allocated to address traditional threats. The shift toward an entirely different set of strategic priorities necessitated changes that bear on what kind of states are evolving in central and eastern Europe, with powerful implications for how they behave internationally.

# Conclusion

Liberalism, in both its economic and political forms, was on the rise in the decades following the end of the Cold War. International capital mobility, trade, and investment reached new highs almost yearly (Simmons, Dobbin, and Garrett 2006). The privatization of formerly state-owned assets and the widespread acceptance of politically independent monetary and regulatory institutions were two more examples of the state's retreat from national economies. The number of countries hosting competitive elections and enlisting the oversight of international election monitors increased dramatically in the same period (Kelley 2008). Although some of these trends could be characterized as global, statistical studies tracking liberalism's new reach show that changes stemming from the collapse of communism in central and eastern Europe (CEE) made up a disproportionate share of the world's marketization and democratization.

Postcommunism has been marked by both convergence and divergence. Countries that had the deepest engagement with international institutions and that eventually joined the path to EU and NATO membership exhibited high levels of convergence around liberal political and economic models. Among Commonwealth of Independent States and post-Yugoslav states, there was much greater divergence in the degree to which political pluralism flourished and in the extent to which states used markets as opposed to authoritative means to coordinate their economic activity. Patterns of convergence and divergence raise the question of whether the European Union and NATO admitted as members those postcommunist countries that had preexisting interests in liberal political and economic policies, or whether international institutions cultivated an interest in liberalization in selected CEE states, thereby setting them on a liberal reform trajectory.

This book has argued that international institutions, including the IMF and the World Bank in addition to those (NATO and the European Union) that offered membership, have had an independent effect on many, though not all, postcommunist countries. In assessing outcomes in the institutionalization of central bank independence (CBI), the internationalization of bank ownership, the democratization of civil-military relations, and the denationalization of defense planning, three kinds of comparison provide evidence for the independent effect of international institutions. The first is in-country comparisons, between what actors initially intended, the actual outcomes, and the proximity of international institutional interference to the point of change. The second kind of comparison is cross-national, between states that had "liberal" legacies (such as Poland and Hungary) and those that did not (such as Romania). Their very different starting conditions, but partial convergence around liberal outcomes in the military-security apparatus and finance, also point to the power of external actors. A third kind of comparison is between countries that were credible candidates for membership organizations (including Poland, Hungary, and Romania) and those that were not (for the purposes of this study, Ukraine). Considerable divergence between Ukraine and the other three countries illustrates the difference that membership can make.

Although all three kinds of comparison could be construed as proving the power of incentives, this book has argued instead that where conditionality has produced its intended effect, it is only because a prior social context imbued incentives with meaning that, from the perspective of domestic actors, made these incentives worthy of compliance. When domestic actors lack experience or certainty, when they perceive themselves to be embedded in a hierarchy vis-à-vis external advisors, and when the policies in question are credible by virtue of widespread compliance among industrialized democracies, international institutions have broad access to domestic policy debates. Under these conditions, domestic actors are sufficiently open to external advice that international institutions have the power to assign meanings and values to particular policies. Given opposite measures on the same conditions, however, international institutions will have little influence in defining what constitutes best practice and countries' compliance with conditionality will be correspondingly weak. Variable responses to similar incentives point to the importance of a social context for conditionality —that is, perceptions of hierarchy that make what international institutions offer appear desirable or not.

The theoretical framework used throughout this volume draws attention to the centrality of relations between international institutions and domestic actors. This is not an approach exclusively centered on persuasion or socialization, and actors have not been uniformly convinced by the "wisdom" of particular policies. To secure policy transfer, international institutions do not have to cultivate majority support for their policies: they need only convince target actors of where authority appropriately lies. By doing so, international institutions invest their relationship to domestic players with a salience that makes compliance desirable for reasons of social standing or status, rather than purely on the basis of distributional or functional concerns. Thus, CBI, internationalized bank ownership, or defense denationalization that departs significantly from a country's military tradition become acceptable not simply because domestic actors agree that the principles underpinning such policies are correct. Indeed, they may not. If postcommunist states sign on to such policies, it is also to exploit international institutions' definition of optimal policy in the service of constructing the Western identity that so many CEE citizens seek.

Evidence of the symbolic rather than functional value of policy was on display throughout the transition. Democratic civil-military relations had no precedent in CEE. And NATO's definition of the concept had no support until the alliance made it clear that closer ties would require an acceptance by CEE states of democratic principles in governing their armed forces. Similarly, the subordination of territorial defense and regional rivalries to far-flung military missions contradicted CEE candidates' perception of what NATO was for and necessitated the creation of two-tiered armies that were anathema to military tradition. CBI and foreign domination of banking sectors also prevailed largely because communist successor parties learned that to win legitimacy, they had to embrace rationality as international institutions defined it. Even if "rationality" meant optimizing externally imposed notions of efficiency over national economic power or political control (which postcommunist political parties were apt to favor, given recent curbs on sovereignty), domestic actors were likely to comply when their social standing depended on it.

In a final examination of the argument outlined here, I review the uncertainty, status, and credibility hypotheses in the light of the empirical evidence. I then assess the explanatory power of these three hypotheses relative to competing approaches for understanding conditionality, socialization, and domestic change in transition states. I conclude by reflecting on what this study's findings imply for the power of international institutions in postcommunist Europe's ongoing transformation, as well as their potential influence globally.

REVIEW OF HYPOTHESES: UNCERTAINTY,
STATUS, AND CREDIBILITY
## Uncertainty (H1)

The uncertainty hypothesis captures the extent to which domestic actors seek external advice as a way of gaining confidence in their policy choices. Sectors that had functioned according to a logic peculiar to state socialism's central planning should have been characterized by greater uncertainty in the transition than sectors whose logics remained intact. Thus actors in economic sectors should have experienced more uncertainty than those in security sectors, since transition implied shifting from an economic plan to a decentralized market—completely different logics of organization; militaries, by contrast, did not undergo the same fundamental shift in operation. Indeed, sectors that functioned according to central planning principles (finance, distribution, production) would experience high degrees of interest demobilization in the context of transition. Accordingly, the uncertainty hypothesis predicts that international institutions would have had greater access early on to economic debates about central and commercial banking than, for example, to debates relating to military-security reforms. Along the same logic, international institutions had more access to reform debates in countries that experienced political turnover in the transition than in countries that did not.

Where central banks and commercial banks were operating in a newly liberalized price environment (as in Poland, Hungary, and Romania by 1990 and 1991, and in Ukraine by 1995), bankers were novices in that they had little experience in governing the economy through open market operations, bank regulation, or market-based lending. Evidence largely confirms this operationalization of the uncertainty hypothesis. All countries under consideration adopted two-tier banking systems, with central banks that were statutorily more independent than hitherto. In Poland and Hungary—where not only central bank bureaucrats but also commercial bankers sought out Western expertise and, in some cases, buyers—the effect was particularly pronounced. In Romania and Ukraine, inexperience among central bankers left them open to IMF and World Bank technical advising. And in turn, this set the stage for conflict between central bankers, who adopted the views of the international financial institutions (IFIs), and the full spectrum of domestic politicians, who did not.

By contrast, and once again in line with the hypothesis, NATO enjoyed relatively little ideational access to militaries early in the transition. Initial reforms of the military-security apparatus reflected not NATO norms but rather national tradition. To be sure, national tradition meant dismantling communist party control over the armed forces; but it did not imply the institutionalization of diffuse democratic accountability with oversight shared among executive, government, and parliamentary bodies. Military establishments had remained intact through the transition. And since the military's function was not peculiar to either a state-socialist or a democratic system, military personnel were not beholden to external advisors in the same way as their economic counterparts. Indeed, military personnel would prove harder to mobilize in favor of new, democratic civil-military relations than their relatively inexperienced civilian would-be overseers.

The second operationalization of the uncertainty hypothesis is whether there was party turnover in government during the transition. In both economic and security sectors, international institutions had somewhat more access to reform debates in countries where new political groups came to power. Again, this received confirmation insofar as the first postcommunist Polish and Hungarian administrations were more open to foreign input on all four issue areas in this study than their Romanian and Ukrainian counterparts. The "noviceness" of Polish and Hungarian governments early in the transition explains why civilians in foreign and defense ministries began challenging military officers' autonomy earlier than in Romania and Ukraine; they were simply more susceptible to NATO's notion of what constituted appropriate power relations between the political and military spheres.

Nevertheless, the uncertainty hypothesis does not receive clear support in all areas. Commercial bankers in Romania and Ukraine lacked expertise in the same way that Polish and Hungarian bankers did. Previous economic systems in all four countries relied on administrative lending without consideration to the cost of credit or risk. In Poland especially, and consistent with the hypothesis, uncertainty translated into an eagerness to enlist Western know-how, but there is little evidence that Romanian and Ukrainian commercial bankers similarly perceived a need for outside assistance. They were more likely to engage in network rather than competitive lending, despite the newly deregulated price environment. Disconfirmation of the uncertainty hypothesis in this case could partly be explained by the lack of perception in Romania and Ukraine of a hierarchical relation with Western institutions, which is in turn linked to the lack of party turnover in the transition. But the hypothesis would predict conflict between bankers and politicians, as in the central banking case, rather than across-the-board resistance to external advising on how to manage market-based lending.

## *Status (H2)*

The status hypothesis captures the extent to which domestic actors view international institutions as authoritative sources of information and, as a consequence, seek their approbation. Note that perceptions of subordinate status do *not* consistently correspond to public enthusiasm for joining the European Union and NATO. If that were the case, then Poland and Romania would have registered the earliest and strongest compliance, which they did not. Instead, the status of international institutions is better operationalized in terms of the *quality* of political competition. Political competition allows parties to use international opinion as a reference point for success or failure, particularly where international institutions are engaged in monitoring and judging political parties' performance. The central difference between the presence and absence of high-quality political competition is that in the first instance, with two or more groups competing for office, international institutions have the power to take sides, confer status, or offer criticism at the expense of some factions but not others. In the absence of pluralism, however, the ruling party can choose the basis on which it mobilizes political support, and international institutions have only weak or no domestic conduits of influence.

In the financial sphere, the status hypothesis as it corresponds to political competition receives strong and consistent confirmation. Status, which IFIs can confer or remove, was particularly powerful in shaping the ongoing reform of communist successor parties. In Poland, the Democratic Left Alliance (SLD), in coalition with the Polish Peasant Party (PSL), was poised to shift away from the liberal economic course established by the first post-Solidarity governments in monetary, regulatory, and bank privatization policy. In the end, the fear of rupturing relations with the Bretton Woods institutions prevented them from doing so. In Hungary, it was the socialists who persistently implemented IFI advice and advanced bank privatization more aggressively than had their Hungarian Democratic Forum (MDF) and Fidesz–Hungarian Civic Party (Fidesz-MPP) counterparts.

The status hypothesis also explains the early differences in international institutional influence over economic policy in Poland and Hungary versus Romania and Ukraine. Whereas in Poland and Hungary economic liberalization began early and in connection with IMF and World Bank technical advising and conditionality, Romania and Ukraine flouted Bretton Woods authority and showed no appetite for anticipatory EU harmonization. The status hypothesis also corresponds to later Romanian and Ukrainian efforts to comply with the IFIs as the transition progressed, however. In Romania, compliance began with the ascendancy of the Democratic Convention of Romania (CDR) in late 1996, whose platform was in part guided by the goal of improving Romania's international standing. And, as in Poland and Hungary, when the communist successors again came to power in Romania in 2000, they continued to follow the liberalizing path, including bank privatization and increased CBI, during their tenure. Ukraine registered a similar pattern, albeit later and on a smaller scale. Statutorily the central bank's status did not change, but over time the bank did begin exercising independent authority. And starting in 2001, Ukraine implemented many of the World Bank's prescriptions that would finally allow foreign investment in banking to increase significantly, beginning in 2004.

The status hypothesis also received strong, though not uniform, support in the military-security cases. Efforts to democratize civil-military relations started earlier in Poland and Hungary than in Romania and Ukraine. This outcome is consistent with the prediction that where political competition is more robust, international institutions exercise greater influence earlier. That Romanian democratization of civil-military relations started after the competitive elections of late 1996, in which a new coalition took power, further corroborates the status hypothesis. Regardless of long-standing public support for Romanian membership in NATO, the alliance had little influence and Romania manifested minimal compliance until party elites were forced to compete on NATO's estimation of their performance. As the transition progressed into the early 2000s, public respect for military power also had implications for how NATO wielded its power. For although Hungarian reform started earlier, Romanian compliance was ultimately stronger, especially with respect to defense spending and the willingness to contribute to out-of-area missions. This kind of variation supports the claim that where societal support for military power was high (as in Poland and Romania), NATO would exercise stronger influence because public support for the military made the country's reputable standing in the alliance more meaningful. In Hungary (and the Czech Republic), by contrast, tepid public support for military solutions, stemming from negative historical experience with its own armed forces, translated into weaker demand for NATO approbation.

In selected instances, outcomes are not entirely consistent with the predictions of the status hypothesis. First, Hungarian compliance with both the democratization of civil-military relations and the internationalization of defense planning was weak. This is surprising for a country that had long suffered geostrategic vulnerability, had a Western-oriented opposition to communism, and had strong political competition in the post–Cold War period. Weak compliance is partly explained by poor military-society relations that dampened NATO's power in Hungary. But while public support for the armed forces in Hungary is not strong, it is not exceptionally low. Second, as noted in chapter 5, Romania complied with at least some of NATO's demands even before political competition heightened the status of international institutions—including work on a bilateral treaty with Hungary. Finally, although the level of Ukrainian defense denationalization is consistent with the status hypothesis (by the early 2000s Ukraine had committed forces to a range of US-led and NATO missions), the theory would predict more movement toward democratic civil-military relations by the same date.

## Credibility (H3)

The study assesses the credibility of policies by measuring the consensus or con-sistency underpinning them. "Consistency" refers to the extent to which inter-national institutions practice what they prescribe or whether their member states abide by those policies. "Consensus" refers to whether institutions and inter-national actors agree on a particular reform course. In all issue areas under consideration, there is at least some consistency *and* consensus insofar as each policy—the democratization of civil-military relations, defense denationalization, CBI, and internationalized bank ownership—enjoys enough support internation-ally to have at least one multilateral organization dedicated to its diffusion.

Nevertheless, consistency and therefore credibility are stronger in the democra-tization of civil-military relations and CBI than in the other two policies. Whereas all NATO members except Turkey had democratic civil-military traditions when the Cold War ended, and there has been global convergence on CBI since the 1980s, few industrialized democracies have historically allowed large-scale foreign ownership in banking. And, within NATO, national defense planning had not converged on power projection at the expense of territorial defense. The credi-bility hypothesis would therefore predict stronger compliance in democratic civil-military relations and CBI than in defense and financial denationalization.

Strong convergence on CBI partially confirms the credibility hypothesis. Ukraine is an outlier statutorily, and yet even Ukraine's central bank, while coor-dinating with government policy, had won the de facto authority to resist govern-ment pressure by the early 2000s. Legally, there has also been strong convergence around democratic civil-military relations among NATO's newest members, al-though, behaviorally, Hungary and Romania have lagged well behind the NATO norm. A complex policy issue, change in military governance is a lengthy process and will most likely progress on a democratic path in CEE countries only with ongoing NATO pressure. Finally, while uneven convergence around defense and foreign policy denationalization is what the credibility hypothesis would predict, there has arguably been more convergence in the internationalization of bank ownership than one would expect based on Western practice. Although international institutions were consistent in their message about the advantages of privatization with foreign capital, the tendency of western European states to protect domestic ownership gave CEE states justification to do the same. But CEE states, particularly those that joined the European Union and NATO, rarely managed to resist pressure to privatize banks with foreign capital.

The credibility hypothesis is as useful for understanding the contours of conflict in target states as it is for anticipating outcomes. Predictably, even on issues backed by a strong consensus, such as democratic civil-military relations or CBI, CEE politicians would use whatever holes existed in the consensus to argue against compliance. Turkey's uneven commitment to democratic civil-military relations and variation across Western countries in the relationship between bank regulation and central banks were two such areas of contention. And, of course, with respect to bank ownership, a typical defense of maintaining national control was that industrialized democracies had usually done the same. In all instances, international institutions would try, with uneven success, to undermine claims for increased power, autonomy, or national tradition by pointing out that European states had generally sidelined such concerns in favor of community norms of integration and cooperation.

## ALTERNATIVE APPROACHES

Having presented the evidence and a review of how powerfully each hypothesis is supported by that evidence, I now turn to the strength of my theoretical approach relative to others. Research on international institutions and domestic compliance has focused variously on conditionality, socialization, preexisting domestic interests, political competition, or some combination of these that attempts to bridge traditions. My approach is a constructivist-rationalist synthesis, which argues that there is a social context in conditionality that either succeeds or fails to render incentives powerful and meaningful. Although I contend that actors' preferences are malleable, in the political world there is rarely a clear distinction between cost-benefit calculation and actions undertaken in the spirit of enacting one's identity. Actors are almost always instrumental. But the kind of instrumentality they exhibit is also an expression of identity, because what actors choose to optimize signals their solidarity with particular communities and rejection of others. However, much of the literature on state compliance with the policies of international institutions considers conditionality and socialization as two distinct mechanisms. Through the following comparison with alternative approaches, I justify my reconciliation of the two.

## Conditionality versus Socialization

Conditionality is the mechanism whereby international institutions seek compliance from target states by promising rewards in exchange for specific domestic reforms. NATO, the European Union, and the Bretton Woods institutions usually engage in some version of conditionality, as assistance or membership is linked to the fulfillment of particular criteria. But as the evidence presented in this book makes clear, conditionality on its own has very uneven effects.

Throughout the chapters we have seen that while incentive structures have often been consistent across countries and over time, domestic compliance has varied. This is not to say that incentives *never* corresponded to compliance. I do argue, however, that when they did correspond, it was because a particular social context was *also* in place that rendered those incentives powerful. Moreover, compliance with international institutions' policy prescriptions has often taken place in the absence of conditionality.

I summarize here some examples of uniform incentives eliciting diverse responses. Bretton Woods conditionality failed to encourage Romania or Ukraine to institutionalize CBI through the mid-1990s, whereas Poland and Hungary actually asked for similar levels of Bretton Woods conditionality and institutionalized CBI years before Romania and Ukraine. Similarly, although Poland, Hungary, and Romania were all credible candidates for EU accession, only Poland and Hungary pursued preemptive compliance with respect to monetary policy. The same dynamic was evident between 1990 and 1997 when Poland, Hungary, and Romania were all pursuing NATO membership. While Poland and Hungary made concerted efforts to comply (even if there was plenty of failure, particularly in Hungary), Romania largely resisted democratization in that early period. Uneven responses to similar incentives were also on display in the case of bank privatization. Whereas Poland agreed to dump its bank consolidation plan under IMF and US Treasury pressure, Romania over the same period failed to fulfill Bretton Woods agreements in which bank privatization was also called for.

The chapters have also highlighted several cases in which the success of conditionality was contingent on a social context. Poland and Hungary were already strong compliers with Bretton Woods conditionality in the early 1990s. But at that point, of course, all the features of the social context that (as I have argued) imbue conditionality with power were also in place—in stark contrast to Romania and Ukraine, where a very different social context prevailed and compliance was correspondingly weak. The detailed case of bank privatization in Poland, described in chapter 3, takes the argument further. Conditionality (in the form of $200 million for bank recapitalization) was proximate to the communist successors' abandonment of bank consolidation. But given the other financial resources available to the Polish government at that time, it is unlikely that the money alone was the catalyst. Rather, the moving force was what the money had come to mean—good relations with the IMF and the US Treasury, two organizations that to many Poles epitomized economic competence. The SLD-PSL coalition essentially used that competence by taking the money and adjusting its policies to recast its enduring communist image.

Finally, the book recounts instances in which conditionality was *not* required to elicit compliance. In Poland, the mid-1990s challenge to CBI was ultimately resolved in favor of international institutional preferences in the absence of conditionality, as was rejection by Solidarity Electoral Action (AWS) of civil territorial defense in 1997. Hungary continued to democratize civil-military relations even after the country had been admitted to NATO. Romania has registered higher levels of compliance with NATO's global strategic orientation *after* joining than could reasonably be predicted with a conditionality hypothesis. And Ukraine rationalized its business environment starting in 2001 with only enough World Bank funds to cover the costs of implementing the reforms. While conditionality was not in place to elicit these changes, the social context that I have argued is necessary to elicit compliance was.

Some scholars, including Stone (2002), Kelley (2004a, 2004b), Schimmelfennig (2005), and Vachudova (2005), have found that conditionality can elicit the intended effect provided that it is actually enforced or when domestic opposition is low. But my evidence suggests that the credibility of conditionality and the strength of the opposition are not always reliable guides. Stone, for example, argues that Poland complied more readily with IMF conditionality than Ukraine because the latter was aware of its strategic importance, particularly to the United States, and could therefore count on new IMF agreements even if it abrogated earlier ones. In other words, Stone's argument is that the reason Ukraine did not comply is that conditionality was not credible. My study does not fully corroborate Stone's interpretation, however. For Romanian compliance was as weak to non-

existent as Ukraine's, despite the fact that Bretton Woods conditionality was presumably more credible in Romania given its smaller size and lesser strategic importance. In addition, looking at Polish reform debates, the reasoning of post-
Solidarity governments does not reflect the logic of conditionality, since they
often asked for conditionality. Even Stone's own account emphasizes that the
IMF gave credibility to stabilization policy—a social effect related to status—
particularly in convincing skeptical or uninformed parliamentarians. Finally,
Stone's labeling of Ukraine as large and strategically important but Poland as
small and less important is highly debatable, given evidence early in the transition
that Poland was considered strategically highly important to the West. Large-scale
loan forgiveness and NATO enlargement both attest to that fact.

The orientation and strength of the opposition to policies that meet the criteria
for international institutional assistance or membership are potentially helpful in
predicting when compliance is more or less likely (Kelley 2004a, 2004b; Schimmelfennig 2005). The liberal perspective points out that where the costs of compliance are too high in terms of domestic political support, politicians will defect.
While these insights ring true, a consideration of the presence or absence of
uncertain actors, their perceived subordinate status vis-à-vis international institutions, and the credibility of policies is meant to address a deeper question about
what constitutes cost in any given political setting. I have shown that perceptions
of cost change over time. Such changes do not correspond consistently to electoral outcomes but correspond instead to social contexts in which international
institutions are more or less able to exploit their authority. It was the communist
successor parties in Poland that first initiated attacks on CBI and attempted a state-
led bank consolidation. The same parties retreated, however, regardless of their
majority in parliament, because their reputations as *reformed* communists depended on it. The communist successors in Hungary and Romania behaved
similarly on returning to power after having been ousted.

At the other end of the ontological spectrum are those who argue that socialization is an important dimension of the process for securing domestic compliance
with international institutional policies (Checkel 2001b, 2005; Gheciu 2005a,
2005b). In her study of NATO influence on postcommunist candidates, Gheciu
points out that while Czech and Romanian elites wanted to win admission to the
alliance, the strongest NATO enthusiasts in CEE countries were, paradoxically,
often the least motivated by concerns with traditional security threats (2005a, 17).
Instead, they sought NATO expertise on building a liberal, Western identity based
in part on a democratically governed military-security apparatus (16). Gheciu

argues that socialization was most likely to occur when NATO abided by its own professed democratic principles and when it came up against CEE actors who lacked a counter-indoctrination, such as communism or nationalism (2005a, chap. 5).

My approach draws on insights from studies that document socialization, but my aim is to move beyond them and broaden the scope of constructivist claims. While theories of socialization show how actors' identities and interests are constituted, they say less about the conditions under which socialization will lead to institutional change. In specifying social contexts, I have shown how not just individual actors but whole party systems can become susceptible to international institutional influence, including nationalists and former communists. My case studies do *not* demonstrate that actors' beliefs about policies changed across the political spectrum. Some actors were persuaded on substance; others were clearly not. But where they complied, actors did so because they came to perceive themselves as embedded in a hierarchy in which international institutions wielded authority. Recognizing the authority of international institutions necessarily also meant that actors subordinated their domestic concerns about autonomy and political power based on historical vulnerability, national tradition, or personal networks. In this respect, the introduction of external incentives and rules can alter the justifications underpinning policies and institutions, as well as the balance of power among groups in society. Changing the logic that supports policies, even through the manipulation of incentives, has constitutive effects on actors and institutions, and even on the organization of finance and defense, which, more than in most other sectors, structures states as democratic or authoritarian, internationally open or relatively autarkic.

Studies of socialization often give the misimpression that constructivism should be limited to making claims about outcomes shaped solely by the proven convictions or identities of actors. Their overattention to what actors "believe" perpetuates the dichotomy between incentives and persuasion. Throughout this study I cast doubt on this dichotomy by arguing that incentives have a subjective quality that allows some states to view compliance as compulsory and others to view it opportunistically, or even as damaging. While I agree entirely with Gheciu's insight (2005a, 16) that entities are powerful not by virtue of resources but rather by virtue of perceived competence, in our increasingly materialist, marketized world, the accrual of resources is itself taken to signify competence. Thus, juxtaposing the power of material and ideational forces misses the more important process through which material capabilities are translated into power.

## Domestic Politics and Preexisting Preferences

An alternative to my explanation for the denationalization of finance and defense centered on social context is one based on preexisting interests. Numerous scholars have pointed to the bureaucratic, intellectual, and political legacies that shaped political and economic reform in the postcommunist transition (e.g., Vachudova and Snyder 1997; Kitschelt et al. 1999; Bockman and Eyal 2002; Grzymała-Busse 2002; Shields 2003; Vachudova 2005). A slightly different interpretation is that geographic proximity to western Europe helps explain postcommunist states' willingness to embrace liberalization, the theory being that countries further west have greater exposure to cross-national flows of Western values, ideas, and methods of organization (Kopstein and Reilly 2000). In support of all these explanations, Poland and Hungary, along with Czechoslovakia and later the Czech Republic, did enjoy "frontrunner" status in the estimation of international organizations that were poised to enlarge. Further, these three countries were the most rapid economic liberalizers.

Some scholars in this school have also refuted the notion that "neoliberal" reformers in CEE were novices and therefore experienced uncertainty (Bockman and Eyal 2002; Shields 2003). If Polish, Hungarian, and Czech reformers were neoliberals from the outset, then international institutions—according to this line of reasoning—had relatively little role to play. The "preexisting interests" argument calls into question the utility of the uncertainty hypothesis (H1), which I have used to assess the openness of domestic actors to foreign expertise. Some have suggested that in these three westernmost CEE countries (Poland, Hungary, and the Czech Republic), liberalization was largely predetermined by prior interest formation among dissidents opposed to state socialism.

As I acknowledge in presenting the evidence, part of the impetus for liberalizing reforms, especially in the economy, undoubtedly came from those with technical expertise, such as the economists who had long theorized the transformation of their state-socialist economies—in some instances with Western interlocutors. But I also argue that the existence of concentrated expertise does not explain, for example, the broader acceptance of a policy such as CBI within former monobanks, parliaments, and societies. It was precisely by exploiting their societies' desire to construct Western identities that *narrow groups* of domestic liberal reformers were able to use the policy prescriptions of international institutions to mobilize support for CBI beyond their initial power base. Russia makes my case. It boasted a vanguard of liberal economists to direct reform, but it fell victim to competing and contradictory economic policies—including a central bank that used its newly won independence to dramatically increase the money supply, to great inflationary effect (Anderson, Berglöf, and Mizsei 1996, 73; J. Johnson 2000; 2003, 300). This suggests that more than technical expertise at the top is needed to secure compliance with external liberal policy prescriptions.

Bank privatization with foreign capital is another example of a controversial issue that was usually resolved via one strategy—internationally competitive tenders that led to foreign domination—despite the professed intention of postcommunist governments, of all legacies, to protect domestic ownership. It is therefore not clear, from the perspective of preexisting interests, why financial denationalization ultimately prevailed when most politicians preferred the opposite outcome. Moreover, some of the most nationally oriented reformers could often be found in former opposition movements, including the MDF and Solidarity. Indeed, conflict over economic policy and the degree of liberalization that was desirable was ultimately a reason that the Solidarity movement ended in fragmentation—a testament to the fact that even within democratic opposition blocs, conflicts over economic policy were far from settled early in the transition.

Outcomes in the military-security apparatus also more strongly corroborate the importance of a social context than of preexisting interests. If Poland, Hungary, and Czechoslovakia were the most democratically inclined, they should not have varied significantly in their willingness to democratize civil-military relations—and yet they did. Romania's stronger compliance than Hungary's with some NATO policy prescriptions also demonstrates how outcomes have not only historical but also more immediate causes. This is not to say that legacies are unimportant. My theoretical framework attempts to capture historical differences, including political competition, in a generalized way to account for such variation. Legacies were important for understanding aspects of initial reform trajectories. But those legacies were quickly subverted by equally powerful forces—including the demands of international institutions—that gave legacies new meaning.

## Political Competition

A related alternative explanation is that political competition facilitates liberalization (Fish 1998; Kitschelt et al. 1999; Orenstein 2001; Grzymała-Busse 2002; Vachudova 2005). Analysts have variously argued that de facto political competition under communism, in which opposition movements challenged the regime's power, forced communist parties to reform themselves even before transition accelerated (Grzymała-Busse 2002); or that political competition leads to higher-quality policy because competition allows new coalitions to mitigate the errors of former governments (Orenstein 2001). Vachudova (2005) argues further, from a rational institutional perspective, that robust political competition allows international institutions, the European Union in particular, to gain leverage with CEE countries. This is because the European Union can help foment political opposition if the incumbent coalition is reluctant to comply, and can provide information to the public on whether the government is taking the necessary steps to gain membership. In one sense my study provides further evidence that these arguments are correct: political competition facilitates liberalization. Indeed, I also argue that the status of international institutions in domestic settings hinges in part on political competition (H2). But my causal story is quite different.

The debate over causality revolves around the following issue. Does political competition facilitate liberalization because incentives and information change the behavior of actors, including politicians, parties, states, and institutions? Or does political competition, in connection with the uncertainty of actors and the perceived credibility of liberalizing policies, *change what actors are*? I argue for the latter, based on the observation that politicians, parties, states, and institutions, by virtue of their recognition of new sources of authority, changed their very nature by redefining their interests. Along with redefined interests came shifts in the balance of power among groups in society, the delegitimization of particular political programs, and basic changes in the purpose of key state institutions. Where they complied with NATO's prescriptions, militaries refashioned their traditions and submitted to diffuse democratic oversight, yielding significant autonomy in the process. Civilian leaders went from supporting the armed forces as a means of preserving territorial integrity to embracing a multilateralism that would be so demanding of resources that defense planning for solely regional concerns became politically untenable.

In the economy, where international institutional authority was accepted, the nature of political entities also changed. Central banks and those staffing them went from being quasi-fiscal instruments of the state to performing politically independent regulatory functions. States pulled back from the economy further by allowing foreign investors to control domestic credit allocation at the expense of their own power. And all the while, it was the nationalists' and communist successor parties' rejection of their pasts—in some instances after significant hesitation— in favor of the economic expertise of international institutions that made such policies seem "normal" and removed them from protracted political struggle.

The difference between approaches that emphasize the power of incentives and information in eliciting compliance and those that place relationships at the center of the analysis is an ontological one. Rationalists assume autonomous actors with fixed interests whose cost calculations and policies change with shifting incentive structures. By contrast, I assume socially constituted actors who will change their policies not solely because new incentive structures or information present themselves, but because heeding the new information or exploiting available incentives reinforces relationships that bolster their status. A formulation that takes relationships and status into account is possible only if one acknowledges that concepts normally taken to be objective—including incentives and information—are actually subject to actors' interpretation. And the advantage of such a formulation is that it leads one to a more accurate assessment of international institutions' potential power than does an analysis based on incentives and information alone.

In some instances, theories based on political competition, incentives, and information overestimate the power of international institutions, because they do not assess perceptions of hierarchy among actors. Perceptions of hierarchy are more difficult for international institutions to orchestrate than the provision of incentives. For example, Hungary had strong measures on all the rationalist variables that would lead one to expect strong compliance with NATO's prescriptions for democratization of civil-military relations, as in Poland. Hungary had a democratic opposition movement under communism that took power in the transition, and robust political competition in the decades that followed. It faced the incentives of NATO membership and was the first CEE country to express its desire to join. But as shown in chapter 4, Hungary registered much weaker compliance than Poland because the same incentives had different power in these two countries, largely owing to lower societal support for military power in Hungary than in Poland.

Political competition, in the abstract, also says little about whether domestic actors perceive themselves to be embedded in a hierarchy in relation to international actors. One has to know what the political competition is about and whether there are alternative sources of external authority. For example, in Ukraine, political competition was increasingly organized around Western integration in the early 2000s because of Yushchenko's presidential victory; but Russia had continually represented an additional source of authority—not only in terms of economic power but also in terms of expertise. Although increasing political competition in Ukraine did correspond to higher levels of compliance with international institutions over time, overtures by NATO and the European Union to encourage Western integration also helped link political competition to an increased salience of international opinion. By operationalizing three aspects of a social context—uncertainty, status, and credibility—the process through which actors come to see themselves embedded in a hierarchy becomes clearer.

## Constructivist-Rationalist Synthesis

Other scholars have made explicit attempts to combine constructivist and rationalist approaches with concepts such as "rhetorical action" (Schimmelfennig 2003) or "embedded rationality" (Jacoby 2004). They also acknowledge that instrumentality among actors is not necessarily at odds with basic constructivist nsights about how social interaction or institutions can affect actors' underlying preferences (Johnston 2001, 2003). In all instances, these authors question the extent to which rule-based behavior is distinct from cost-benefit calculation or, put differently, whether the political world is really defined by two separate spheres of action: the logic of appropriateness and the logic of consequences (March and Olsen 1989, 1998). I have challenged those distinctions here, arguing that for postcommunist states certain kinds of optimization signal solidarity with some communities and the exclusion of others. Thus particular forms of instrumentality are simultaneously expressions of identity.

Among the scholars using different traditions eclectically, Jacoby (2004) sets out to explain a series of outcomes most similar to those I consider here. He argues that the kind of policy transfer that is likely to take place from West to East is based on two variables: the density of actors in the sector in question and the density of rules in the policy area. Depending on rule and actor density, different kinds of emulation are likely to occur, from more to less faithful versions of the rules being transferred. Varying levels of political conflict are also likely to ensue. Where both actor and rule density are high, as in civil-military relations, open struggle is likely to result. Where both are low, policy transfer is expected to be more voluntary, with relatively little political conflict. Actors in Jacoby's account are rational, but CEE elites constantly have to navigate between international institutional demands and the historical context (Jacoby 2004, 30).

The social context approach that I use throughout this study both builds on and departs from "embedded rationality." Both a social context approach and "embedded rationality" reject an objective definition of rationality and, relatedly, see actors as "maximizing" in reference to various, sometimes mutually exclusive, normative contexts. Those normative contexts are informed both by history and by international institutional prescriptions. But I depart from the "embedded rationality" approach by paying greater attention to the variation in social context over time and across countries, and I apply a more systematic method for understanding the circumstances in which international institutions' use of conditionality will elicit the desired effect.

Jacoby's use of the "density of actors" variable overlaps with the uncertainty hypothesis (H1) that asserts that where sectors remain intact through the transition, it will be more difficult, at least initially, for international institutions to exert influence. The logic behind both variables is the same: that invested interests are already certain about how reform should proceed and do not seek the counsel of external advisors. Although Jacoby correctly predicts open struggle in the civil-military relations case, other outcomes are not easily explained by the density of actors and rules alone. Thus, while both Hungary and the Czech Republic were relatively weak compliers with NATO norms of democratic civil-military relations, Poland, which had an equally problematic set of legacies with respect to NATO compliance, nevertheless emerged as a quite strong complier—an outcome Jacoby's "density of actors" hypothesis would not predict. Romania has also been a better performer for NATO in terms of defense spending and military contributions than either Hungary or the Czech Republic. The central difference between these two pairs of states is the level of public support for the idea of a powerful military. As Jacoby also notes, where support was low, NATO exercised less influence (2004, 30, 126). But this insight, which is essential to understanding perceptions of hierarchical relations between candidate states and NATO and thus compliance with the alliance's prescriptions, is not at all captured by the density of rules or actors. By contrast, the perceived status of international institutions (H2), which can change over time, explains more systematically what kinds of variation are to be expected.

It is also not clear that the density of actors is necessarily a barrier to compliance with international institutional policy prescriptions if the actors in a sector, no matter how numerous, have undergone interest demobilization in the transition and are therefore uncertain about how to conduct reform (H1). Central banking bureaucrats across the CEE, for example, were open to external advising (see chapter 2) (J. Johnson 2002, 2006). Although in some cases there was indeed "open struggle" over CBI, it was not between central bankers and international institutions, as Jacoby would predict, but between central bankers and politicians. In the military sphere, as well, Jacoby, Simon, and others have pointed repeatedly to the lack of civilian expertise and conclude that this was detrimental to military reform. Where the lack of civilian expertise translated into neglect, such as in Hungary and the Czech Republic, this was partly true. But it was civilians who proved to be the most accepting of NATO's democratizing norms, providing the alliance with its first point of access to reform processes. Winning over and empowering civilians with military expertise, as NATO defined it, was essential to ultimately securing democratic control.

The social context approach offers a number of advantages to the alternatives. Understanding the social context allows one to assess the relative weight of domestic and international factors in propelling reform. It also demonstrates the subjective quality of incentives and information. At the same time, uncertainty, status, and credibility can be mapped onto the political world in ways that are readily recognizable, enabling us to anticipate outcomes. Finally, with a clear operationalization, the social context is suggestive of the kinds of variation that are likely over time and across sectors and countries. Having examined the social context in European settings, this study also has implications for how international institutions and states interact globally.

## IMPLICATIONS OF THE STUDY

This book has traced significant changes in the way key sectors and state institutions in central and eastern Europe are governed. To varying degrees, Poland, Hungary, Romania, and Ukraine democratized civil-military relations, diffusing civilian control among multiple branches of government and also encouraging societal oversight through media and NGO scrutiny. Where the shift occurred, domestic actors went from supporting narrowly held authority over the armed forces, and by extension military autonomy, to embracing foreign principles of democratic accountability. Central banks also, without exception, became more independent in the transition. Where full independence was achieved, this required a complete reordering of relations among politicians, industry, agriculture, banks, and central bank officials. The international orientation of the four countries also changed, as their foreign policies downplayed long-standing national anxieties about regional threats and as they supported missions or deployed troops in the Balkans, Afghanistan, Iraq, and elsewhere. The internationalization of bank ownership signaled a second kind of reorientation—away from concerns about foreign economic domination and politically or developmentally motivated credit allocation toward an acceptance of international economic integration that would necessarily limit the state's role in the economy.

The study concludes that in finance and defense, international institutions played a critical role in pushing liberalization, along the lines outlined above, because of the fairly consistent correlation between a particular social context and compliance with international institutional policy prescriptions. Compliance is more consistent with the existence or emergence of certain social contexts between international institutions and domestic actors than it is with national legacies, electoral turnover, or the provision of new information or incentives on their own. Rather, interest demobilization among domestic actors, their desire for social recognition from international institutions, and the credibility of the policies in question imbue incentives and information with meaning that makes them worth heeding.

Although the evidence supports the claim that international institutions had a substantial impact on CEE countries, paradoxically, the same evidence should give purveyors of liberalism pause. Because although international institutions heavily influenced the transition, they faced unusually favorable conditions in CEE and nevertheless encountered resistance to their policies in every country and in every policy area. Thus the likelihood that international institutions can exercise commensurate power elsewhere is slim. The social context that prevailed in the fifteen years after transition began was, after all, historically rare and long in the making. Moreover, the circumstances that gave rise to the perceptions of appropriate hierarchy in CEE that in many cases rendered compliance desirable would be difficult to replicate elsewhere.

From the perspective of international institutions, ensuring influence globally depends on factors often beyond their control. The interest demobilization among actors in finance that accompanied the collapse of communism and an abandonment of central planning was on a scale that is unlikely to be repeated (H1). The desire for social recognition from international institutions was operationalized in this study as public esteem for the institutions undergoing reform and as political competition organized at least in part around a modernizing project (H2). While international institutions can do little about the first of these two conditions, they have proved able to cultivate opposition coalitions and provide the principles around which communist successor and nationalist parties can refashion their political programs. This changed the nature of political competition and increased the salience of international opinion. But international institutions could affect party dynamics only by virtue of a power bestowed on them by history—namely, the accrual of perceived legitimacy over decades that was then cemented by defeat of the Soviet Union in the Cold War. International institutions have somewhat more control over the credibility of the policies they pursue (H3). I say "somewhat" because although they can control whether they are consistent in what they ask of target states and in the policies they carry out themselves, they have less jurisdiction over whether their member states abide by the same rules.

But if an elaborate set of conditions must obtain for international institutions to win compliance, then why, according to these findings, are they ever able to exercise influence in the absence of those conditions? And further, states would seem to be responding to incentives all the time—with respect to regional or bilateral trade agreements, to win admission to the World Trade Organization, to receive World Bank or IMF assistance, or to escape international opprobrium. Does this not suggest that states often respond to incentives or information regardless of the social context? Even within the narrow confines of my study, the theory was disconfirmed at points, such as Romania's compliance with NATO demands that candidates reach bilateral peace accords *before* the specified social context was in place. So I would not claim that the social context, as defined here, is universally necessary to elicit compliance.

But I would contend that in nearly every instance of compliance, social forces are in play. In NATO enlargement, for example, similarly positioned and historically vulnerable states responded differently to the possibility of getting security guarantees from the world's most successful military alliance. If the costs and benefits of even NATO's Article V collective defense commitment can be variously construed—as worth pursuing or as meriting ambivalence—then one can safely conclude that very few political choices exclusively reflect the material base, but rather depend on states' and societies' often idiosyncratic understandings of what is optimal.

In no postcommunist country was there an unproblematic adoption of liberal ideals in critical sectors such as finance and defense. After all, free markets impose social costs and perceived vulnerability, and multilateral defense arrangements impinge on military tradition and national autonomy. Nevertheless, policy convergence on liberalization is among the most distinctive trends across a range of states and issue areas in the EU and NATO accession states of central and eastern Europe. The rush to liberalize even affected some countries that were not yet members of the international institutions and whose populations remained, through the early 2000s, deeply divided over where their allegiances lay. That international institutions have weighed in on the side of financial and defense interdependence is clearly the critical explanatory factor. But although by 2007 liberalization outcomes seemed to be the direct result of international institutions' conditionality requirements, this study strongly argues that conditionality alone was not the main source of their influence. Those institutions do apply conditionality and they do engage in the socialization of target actors. But the power of international institutions is at its greatest when a social context allows them to present themselves as the ultimate authority on an issue. Their policies do not become desirable within nations on "objective merits" alone. Rather, only through a social process of attaching elevated status to particular policies have international institutions been able to advance liberalism.

APPENDIX

# · Interviews

Bednarski, Piotr. Bank regulator at General Inspectorate of Banking Supervision, National Bank of Poland (written correspondence). Warsaw, May 18, 2001.

Bielecki, Jan Krzysztof. Prime Minister of Poland, 1990–1991. London, May 26, 1999.

Black, Rebecca. Official of United States Agency for International Development, Warsaw office. Warsaw, April 7, 1999.

Bobinski, Krzysztof. Warsaw correspondent, *Financial Times*. Warsaw, multiple conversations, 1999–2000.

Boyce, Matt. Political Affairs Officer, United States Embassy in Poland, 1994–1998. Berlin, April 21, 1999.

Clarke, Robert L. American advisor to National Bank of Poland, 1992–1996 (telephone). Houston, May 16, 2001.

Dale, Charles. Director, Defense Partnership and Co-operation, NATO Headquarters. Brussels, December 2, 1999.

Doran, Anthony. Official of International Finance Corporation, 1987–1992. Warsaw, October 8, 1999.

Dragsdahl, Jorgen. Warsaw, multiple conversations, 1999.

Fried, Daniel. United States Ambassador to Poland. Warsaw, July 23, 1999.

Goławski, Artur. Journalist, *Polska Zbrojna*. Warsaw, August 4, 1999.

Grudziński, Przemysław. Official of Ministry of Defense; Deputy Minister of Foreign Affairs, Poland. Warsaw, August 11, 1999.

Heimsöth, Hans Jürgen. Political-Military Affairs Officer, German Embassy in Poland. Warsaw, November 17, 1999.

Horner, James E. Employee of Barents Group, LLC, and Managing Director of United States Agency for International Development project "Strengthening Bank Supervision." Warsaw, June 15, 2000.

Hume, Ian M. Resident Representative, World Bank, Poland, 1990–1994. Warsaw, November 11, 1999, and June 5, 2000.

Hundt, Ulrich. Secretary General, European Organisation of Military Associations (EUROMIL). Brussels, December 6, 1999.

Jacobson, Colonel Søren Lyder. Danish Military Attaché, Danish Embassy in Poland, 1994–1998 (telephone). Copenhagen, August 9, 1999.

Jaruzelski, General Wojciech. Warsaw, August 26, 1999.

Jastrzebski, Lieutenant Colonel Mat. United States Embassy in Poland. Warsaw, April 26, 1999.

Kamiński, Antoni. Foreign Policy Advisor to President Lech Wałęsa, 1990–1993. Warsaw, April 29, 1999.

Kaminski, Barbara. Consultant to World Bank in Poland, 1994–1996; consultant to United States Agency for International Development in Poland, 1996–1999 (telephone). Jerusalem, April 28, 2001.

Karkoszka, Andrzej. Deputy Minister of Defense, Poland, 1996–1997. Garmisch-Partenkirchen, Germany, July 6, 1999.

Katsirdakis, George. Senior Officer, NATO International Staff, NATO Headquarters. Bratislava, August 24, 1999, and Brussels, December 7, 1999.

Kawalec, Stefan. General Director, Ministry of Finance, and Chief of Economic Advisors to Deputy Prime Minister and Minister of Finance Leszek Balcerowicz, 1989–1991; Vice Minister of Finance in Poland, 1991–1994. Warsaw, November 2, 1999, and June 15, 2000.

Każimierski, Marcin. Action Head of Section, Ministry of Defense, Poland. Warsaw, August 13, 1999.

Kołodko, Grzegorz. Minister of Finance, Poland, 1994–1997. Washington, DC, February 18, 2000.

Kołodziejczyk, Vice Admiral Piotr (retired). Minister of Defense, Poland, 1990–1991 and 1993–1994. Gydinia, August 23, 1999.

Komański, Brigadier General January. Head, Territorial Defense Directorate, Polish General Staff. Warsaw, August 27, 1999.

Komorowski, Bronisław. Former official of Ministry of Defense; Chairman, Sejm Commission on National Defense, Poland. Warsaw, August 16, 1999.

Koński, Robert. Assistant to Stefan Kawalec, Ministry of Finance, Poland, 1990–1994. Warsaw, June 9, 1999.

Kostrzewa-Zorbas, Grzegorz. Founding member, Atlantic Club, Poland. Warsaw, September 1, 1999.

Łepkowski, Mikolaj. United States Agency for International Development. Warsaw, April 15, 1999.

Michaels, Dan. Warsaw correspondent, *Wall Street Journal Europe*. Warsaw, May 7, 1999.

Milewska, Kristina. Assistant to Regional Resident of the World Bank, Poland, 1990–1998. Warsaw, November 18, 1999.

Mleczak, Lieutenant Colonel Eugeniusz. Spokesman for Ministry of Defense, Poland. Warsaw, August 13, 1999.

Najder, Zdzisław. Warsaw, November 12, 1999.

Osica, Olaf. Journalist, *Polska Zbrojna*; scholar at Warsaw Center for International Relations. Warsaw, November 26, 1999.

Paga, Lesław. Founder and architect of Warsaw Stock Exchange. Warsaw, November 22, 1999.

Parys, Jan. Minister of Defense, Poland, 1991–1992. Warsaw, August 11, 1999.

Remmert, Rainer. Military Affairs Officer, German Embassy in Poland. Warsaw, November 17, 1999.

Rokita, Jan Maria. Chairman, Sejm Commission on Internal Affairs and Administration, Poland. Warsaw, November 26, 1999.

Rotboll, Jens. President, European Organisation of Military Associations (EUROMIL). Brussels, December 6, 1999.

Rozłucki, Wiesław. Architect and President and CEO of Warsaw Stock Exchange. Warsaw, November 23, 1999.

Rymaszewski, Piotr. Economic Advisor to Ministry of Finance, Poland, under Stefan Kawalec. Warsaw, October 18, 1999.

Schlosser, John. Official of United States Embassy in Poland. Warsaw, July 1, 1999.

Sikorski, Radek. Official of Ministry of Defense; Deputy Minister of Foreign Affairs, Poland. Warsaw, August 4, 1999.

Simon, Jeffrey. National Defense University. Bratislava, August 24, 1999.

Simonyi, András. Hungarian Ambassador to NATO. Brussels, December 1999.

Śleszyńska-Charewicz, Ewa. Chairman, General Inspectorate of Banking Supervision, National Bank of Poland, 1992–2000. Warsaw, June 9, 2000.

Świetlicki, Bogusław. Deputy Director, Department of Strategy and Policy Planning, Ministry of Foreign Affairs, Poland. Warsaw, August 4, 1999.

Szeremietiew, Romuald. Deputy Minister of Defense, Poland. Warsaw, September 13, 1999.

Ugolini, Piero. Official of International Monetary Fund (telephone). Washington, DC, April 27, 2001.

Wągrowska, Maria. Editor, *Polska Zbrojna*. Warsaw, August 4, 1999.

Wyczański, Paweł. Research Department, National Bank of Poland. Warsaw, June 14, 2000.


## ROMANIA, 2004

Cojocaru, Simona. Head of Office, Directorate of Strategic Affairs, Ministry of Defense, Romania. Bucharest, November 12, 2004.

Dăianu, Daniel. Minister of Finance, Romania, 1997–1999. Bucharest, November 9, 2004.

Lazea, Valentin. Chief Economist, National Bank of Romania. Bucharest, November 10, 2004.

Livadariu, Lieutenant Colonel Liviu. Head, Bilateral Military Cooperation Section, Ministry of Defense, Romania. Bucharest, November 12, 2004.

Părvulescu, Sorana. Program Officer, Romanian Academic Society. Bucharest, November 11, 2004.

Pietrăreanu, Colonel Dorel. Directorate of International Military Cooperation. Bucharest, November 12, 2004.

Pleşu, Andrei. Professor and Rector, New Europe College; former Minister of Foreign Affairs, Romania. Bucharest, November 9, 2004.

Rauta, Emanuel. Romanian Academic Society. Bucharest, November 11, 2004.

Ştefănescu, Manuela. Association for the Defense of Human Rights in Romania, Helsinki Committee. Bucharest, November 11, 2004.

Vlădescu, Sebastian. Romanian Soft Company, Romanian Center for Economic Policies, and Minister of Finance, Romania. Bucharest, November 9, 2004.

## UKRAINE, 2005

Bilan, Olena. Institute for Economic Research and Policy Consulting. Kyiv, February 21, 2005.

Bodruk, Oleg. Head, Military Policy and Security Department, National Institute for International Security Problems. Kyiv, February 22, 2005.

Duray, Michel. Director, NATO Information and Documentation Centre in Ukraine. Kyiv, February 23, 2005.

Dzherdzh, Serhiy. Head, Ukraine-NATO Civic League; Head, Democratic Action. Kyiv, February 22, 2005.

Grechaninov, General Vladimir (retired). President, Atlantic Council of Ukraine. Kyiv, February 22, 2005.

Greene, James. Head, NATO Liaison Office, Ukraine. Kyiv, February 25, 2005.

Herasymchuk, Serhiy. Consultant to Temporary Special Commission of Verkhovna Rada of Ukraine on NATO-Ukraine Action Plan Implementation Monitoring, 2003–2006. Kyiv, February 23, 2005.

Karwatsky, John. Program Officer, NATO Information and Documentation Centre in Ukraine. Kyiv, February 23, 2005.

Khomeko, Dr. Hyroriy. Vice Rector for International Relations and Associate Professor, Ministry of Foreign Affairs, Diplomatic Academy of Ukraine. Kyiv, February 22, 2005.

Kirsenko, Dr. Mykhailo. Professor and Founder, Diplomatic Academy of Ukraine. Kyiv, February 22, 2005.

Kryvdyk, Ostap. Member, Black Pora. Kyiv, February 23, 2005.

Poltoratskyy, Oleksandr. Academic Board Secretary, Ministry of Foreign Affairs, Diplomatic Academy of Ukraine. Kyiv, February 22, 2005.

Pyshnyj, Andriy. First Deputy Chairman of the Board, Oschadny Bank (State Savings Bank of Ukraine). Kyiv, February 24, 2005.

Sushko, Oleksandr. Director, Center for Peace, Conversion and Foreign Policy of Ukraine. Kyiv, 23 February 2005.

Yatseniuk, Arseniy. First Deputy Head, Ukrainian Central Bank. Kyiv, February 24, 2005.

Zhalilo, Yaroslav A. President, Center for Anti-Crisis Studies; Head, Economic and Social Strategy Department, National Strategic Studies Institute. Kyiv, February 21, 2005.

# Notes

CHAPTER 1: CULTIVATING CONSENSUS

1. In a similar vein, Frank Schimmelfennig argues that it is through the instrumental application of "rhetorical action," not the "logic of appropriateness," that "community rules" affect the decision to enlarge NATO and the European Union (2003, 3).

2. Becker (1976) and Rosenberg (1979) debate rationality with respect to the degree to which conscious calculation must inform decision-making in order to fall under the definition of "rationality."

3. Other examples of work that generally corroborates the obligatory/consequentialist divide include March and Olsen 1989, 1998; Katzenstein, Keohane, and Krasner 1998; Keck and Sikkink 1998; Risse, Ropp, and Sikkink 1999; Börzel and Risse 2000; Checkel 2001a, 2001b, 2005; Checkel and Moravcsik 2001; and Schimmelfennig 2003.

4. Klotz (1995), Keck and Sikkink (1998), Risse, Ropp, and Sikkink (1999), and Checkel (2001b) have used human rights to illustrate this logic at work. Morgenthau (1960 [1948]) and Waltz (1979) provide the classical and structural realist analyses on what constitutes state interests. Frieden (1999) discusses three methods for inferring preferences.

5. Ruggie's insight is taken from Weber and Durkheim.

6. "An action, to be rational, must be the final result of three optimal decisions. First, it must be the best means of realizing a person's desire, given his beliefs. Next, these beliefs must themselves be optimal, given the evidence available to him. Finally, the person must collect an optimal amount of evidence—neither too much nor too little" (Elster 1989, 30).

7. Wendt also questions the viability of such a claim (1999, 165). Also see Barnett and Finnemore 2004.

8. Similar conditions have been specified, although separately and in different form, by constructivists and liberals. See Kindleberger 1975; Ikenberry and Kupchan 1990; Ikenberry 1992; Finnemore and Sikkink 1998; Risse 2000, Checkel 2001b; and Johnston 2001.

9. Democratic opposition under communism and political competition are Vachudova's central hypotheses in explaining outcomes in economic and democratic transition (2005). Building on Vachudova's argument, I argue that political competition in general affords international institutions access to domestic reform processes.

Also see Vachudova and Snyder 1997; Fish 1998; Orenstein 2001; and Grzymała-Busse 2002.

10. "Pareto optimality" refers to an equilibrium in which no actor can become better off without at least one actor becoming worse off. But note that even efficiency gains, in reality, almost always make some players worse off.

11. On the role of social coalitions in policy diffusion, see Jacoby 2000.

12. Because the existence of social concepts depends on the meanings we attach to them, their position relative to us is not separate in the way causal reasoning demands it should be (Ruggie 1982; Kratochwil and Ruggie 1986). For a discussion on the problems of "eclecticism" in social science theorizing, see Kratochwil 2000a, 79–80.

13. Jacoby (2004) points to a similar variable to explain the resistance of CEE militaries to NATO norms: the density of actors.

14. This happened in Lithuania in 1992.

15. For the EU assessment of Ukraine's reform trajectory on everything from human rights to banking, see European Commission 2004.

16. Vachudova (2005) uses domestic variables to explain outcomes in the early years of transition, but then also examines the leverage of the European Union in eliciting greater liberalization and later conformity with its policy prescriptions. She argues that the European Union was influential because it improved the quality of political competition in illiberal states by providing information and a focal point of cooperation for opposition parties. Grzymała-Busse (2002) analyzes the reform of communist parties in the region.

17. Orenstein (2001) argues that political competition, in combination with government strategies and elite learning, explains democratic and economic policy outcomes. He does take international factors into account as well, but as a constraining condition rather than as a core variable in the analysis.

18. An exception is Stark and Bruszt (1998), who argue that the conventional understandings of reform outcomes are oversimplified and misunderstood.

19. To the extent that scholars do raise this question, it is about economic reform rather than democratic governance (Amsden, Kochanowicz, and Taylor 1994; Szacki 1995). Preoteasa (2002) even notes the lack of debate beyond what she calls "neoliberal discourses" in Romania by the late 1990s.

20. Bunce writes: "Central to the story of regime and state collapse in the eastern half of Europe is what has become a familiar set of developments the world over . . . Indeed what is significant . . . is that [the postcommunist cases] represent a remarkably efficient summary, if you will, of global trends" (1999, 9).

21. "Derived from economic transaction-costs approaches, the argument is dependent on structural incentives and opportunities and how they affect strategic choice. However, the argument does not require—and I am not arguing—that the objectives, beliefs, and roles of individual states are irrelevant to institutional adaptation" (Wallander 2000, 712).

22. For an explanation of why political or economic systems constitute "cultural forms," see Dobbin 1994.

CHAPTER 2: INSTITUTIONALIZING CENTRAL BANK INDEPENDENCE

1. Schoppa (1999) also argues that a particular social context is necessary for coercive bargaining between the United States and Japan to elicit its intended effect.

2. Prizel points out, however, that Ukrainian peoples had traditionally been divided between Russian, Polish, and Austro-Hungarian empires and thus, for political strains that had historically been more likely to favor federation with Russia, the "return to Europe" and "central European identity" rhetoric was far from convincing (1998, 365–66). Also see Abdelal 2001, 103–26.

3. Author's interview with Ian M. Hume. (See Appendix for full information on all interviews.) Also see World Bank 1997b, 9, 26.

4. See the report by Bryan Stirewalt and James Horner of KPMG Peat Marwick, LLP, and Barents Group, LLC, for USAID. The report states that "USAID advisors . . . provided detailed written and oral advice during the drafting of the Banking Act and the Act on the National Bank of Poland" (Stirewalt and Horner 2000, 20). In an interview with this author, Horner confirmed that USAID "provided direct advice to the bylaws and the structure as they [the Poles] were proposing to create these separate bodies."

5. Leszek Balcerowicz (1995) called this the period of "extraordinary politics" in which interest demobilization gave the country's leaders enormous latitude to undertake austerity reforms that under normal conditions would be stymied by interest groups.

6. Details of the Enterprise and Financial Sector Adjustment Loan program are available from the World Bank (1997a). World Bank and IMF officials monitored the supervisory board during the bank recapitalization program. This included training and on-site inspections with Polish and IFI officials.

7. From a report by Michael Borish and Company and Triumph Technologies (1998), prepared for USAID.

8. See especially Myant's quotation (1993) of Jacek Kuroń's *Moja Zupa*.

9. The Balcerowicz plan was otherwise known as "shock therapy." Mark Allen, quoted by Stone; and Stone (2002, 99) describing the relationship between Poland and the IMF around the macroeconomic stabilization plan.

10. Author's interviews with Ewa Śleszyńska-Charewicz and Stefan Kawalec.

11. Author's interview with Śleszyńska-Charewicz.

12. Author's interview with James E. Horner. Also see J. Johnson 2006.

13. Author's interview with Hume. The "soft budget constraint" refers to government guarantees under state socialism that produced moral hazard. It had the perverse effect of encouraging hoarding, liberal lending, and shortages (Kornai 1992).

14. Author's interview with Stefan Kawalec. Kawalec had led the campaign in the Sejm (parliament) to overturn Wałęsa's veto. Advisors to the Ministry of Finance in the early 1990s were from the IFIs, but the World Bank also funded missions from western Europe, including from Portugal, France, Germany, Austria, the Netherlands, Ireland, and Britain, and from the United States. Bundesbank officials assisted with monetary

policy, while French and US officials concentrated on supervision (Ugolini 1996; Loungani and Sheets 1997).

15. Author's interview with Śleszyńska-Charewicz.

16. Colin Jones, "Romania: A Fragile Partnership," *Banker* 146 (850), 1996.

17. On the inexperience of the new government, see "Romania: Bid to Prop up Shaky Economy," *Financial Times* (London), 23 January 1997, 3.

18. By 1994, Ukraine's real GDP was only 55 percent of its 1990 level. See Lorenzo Figliuoli and Bogdan Lissovolik (IMF Resident Representatives in Ukraine), "The IMF and Ukraine: What Really Happened," *Zerkalo Nedeli*, 31 August 2002 (translation of Russian version).

19. See "Hungarian Press on Central Bank President's Relief," *MTI Econews*, 29 November 1991; "Policy: Hungary," *Finance East Europe*, 9 October 1991; "Hungary PM Confirms Dismissal of Bank President Was Political," *Agence France Presse*, 30 November 1991; "Hungary Still Boils over Dismissal of Bank President," *Agence France Presse*, 2 December 1991; and Virginia Marsh, "Hungary Acts to Restore Confidence," *Financial Times* (London), 8 February 1995, 2.

20. See, for example, IMF, "Hungary's Stabilization and Reform Yield Solid Results," *IMF Survey*, 21 July 1997, 230–32, Washington, DC.

21. "IMF Re-starts Talks with the New Government," *Finance East Europe*, 24 January 1997.

22. IMF, "IMF Approves Stand-by Credit for Romania," Press Release No. 97/20, 23 April 1997, Washington, DC.

23. "Romania: Bid to Prop up Shaky Economy," *Financial Times* (London), 23 January 1997, 3.

24. IMF, "IMF Concludes Article IV Consultation with Romania," Public Information Notice (PIN), 6 October 1998, Washington, DC.

25. See "Kuchma Upsets Kravchuk for Ukraine Presidency," *Current Digest of the Post-Soviet Press*, 3 August 1994.

26. Author's interview with Hume.

27. Author's interview with Paweł Wyczański. Also see "Sejm to Look at Central Bank Bill," *Polish News Bulletin*, 7 May 1996.

28. These criticisms come from Grzegorz W. Kołodko, "Central Bank Responsibilities: Not Only to God and History," *Polish News Bulletin*, 6 September 1994. Also see "Between Inflation and Recession: A Dispute over Interest Rates," *Polish Press Agency*, 30 September 1994.

29. Anthony Robinson and Christopher Bobinski, "Poland's Politics Lag behind Recovery," *Financial Times* (London), 3 March 1995, 4.

30. "Policy versus Politics," *Finance East Europe*, 18 August 1995.

31. See "Central Bank Facing Changes," *Polish News Bulletin*, 20 September 1995; and Krzysztof A. Kowalczyk, "The NBP's Fortress," *Polish News Bulletin*, 5 October 1995.

32. "Central Bank Facing Changes," *Polish News Bulletin*, 20 September 1995; and "Sejm to Look at Central Bank Bill," *Polish News Bulletin*, 7 May 1996.

33. "Policy versus Politics," *Finance East Europe*, 18 August 1995.

34. Author's interview with Horner.

35. Anna Slojewska, "Criticism of Deputies' Draft Laws: NBP Defends Its Independence," *Rzeczpospolita*, 22 September 1995, 9 (translated in *FBIS-EEU-95-185*, 25 September 1995, 42).

36. The UW legislation was based on proposals the NBP had drafted years earlier with the assistance of World Bank and USAID representatives, many of whom had been contracted from the US Treasury. Author's interview with Barbara Kaminski. Also see "Sejm to Look at Central Bank Bill," *Polish News Bulletin*, 7 May 1996. The NBP proposals had never been submitted to the Sejm because it was prohibited from proposing legislation on its own behalf.

37. Author's interview with Śleszyńska-Charewicz.

38. Author's interviews with Kaminski, Horner, and Robert L. Clarke.

39. Ugolini (1996, 40); author's interview with Horner. Also see "Professor Comments on Dispute between Ministry and Central Bank," *PAP (Polish Press Agency) News Wire*, 3 August 1995.

40. "EMI President Terms Poland Credible Candidate for Membership," *PAP (Polish Press Agency) News Wire*, 17 September 1996.

41. One SLD deputy argued that UW's legislative proposals might be a threat to EU standards, whereas the SLD's proposed "NBP council" was nominally apolitical and therefore perfectly compatible with European standards. See "Coalition, Freedom Union Criticize Each Other's Bills on NBP," *Polish Press Agency*, 30 May 1996.

42. Krzysztof Bobinski, "Survey—Poland: The Central Bank," *Financial Times* (London), 26 March 1997, 4.

43. See the amendments to the *Act on the National Bank of Poland* of 29 August 1997, as published in *Dziennik Ustaw (Journal of Laws)* of 1997, no. 140, item 938; and the amendments to the *Banking Act* of 29 August 1997, as published in *Dziennik Ustaw*, of 1997, no. 140, item 939.

44. The Commission on Banking Supervision included the NBP president, the head of supervision, the head of government deposit insurance, the CEO of the Warsaw Stock Exchange, two appointees of the Ministry of Finance, and two presidential appointees.

45. See the *Constitution of the Republic of Poland*, Articles 227 and 220–2, respectively.

46. Author's interviews with Horner, Kaminski, and Piero Ugolini.

47. One journal speculated that members of the SLD knew that "moves against the central bank would be taken as a sign, at home and abroad, that old centralist habits were reasserting themselves and that warnings that Kwaśniewski's election would reverse market reform in Poland were justified." See "Gronkiewicz-Waltz's Position Vulnerable but Not Hopeless," *Finance East Europe*, 1 December 1995. Kwaśniewski also abandoned his SLD affiliation while president.

48. The Treaty of Rome is available at www.hri.org/docs/Rome 57. The Statute of the ESCB is available at www.ecb.int/ecb/legal/1341/1343/html/index.en.html.

49. "Increased Independence of Central Bank under New Act," *MTI Econews*, 21 November 1991.

50. European Commission, Regular Report on Candidates' Progress toward Accession, Brussels (hereafter, EC Regular Report), 1999.

51. EC Regular Report, 2001, 58. Also see ACT LVIII of 2001 on the Magyar Nemzeti Bank, http://english.mnb.hu/Resource.aspx?ResourceID=mnbfile&resourcename =jegybanktorv—en.

52. Between 1991 and 1997, the level of central bank financing was subject to negotiation between the MoF and the central bank—and thus the commitment to price stability depended very much on the NBP president's attitude. Hanna Gronkiewicz-Waltz was applauded by a range of Western observers for her continuing prioritization of price stability during this period.

53. In Romania, members of the Board of Directors are appointed by the parliament. See the *National Bank of Romania Act*, Law No. 312/28, June 2004, www .bnro.ro/En/Legi/L—StatBNR/.

54. See EC Regular Report, *1998 Regular Report on Romania's Progress towards Accession*, 29.

55. *National Bank of Romania Act.*

56. EC Regular Report, 2004, 88. Calls for such safeguards were also in European Commission 2005, 51.

57. EC Regular Report, 2004, 88.

58. "Ukrainian Leader Urges Cooperation between Cabinet, Central Bank," *BBC Monitoring*, 4 March 2003.

59. IMF, *IMF Survey*, 20 March 2000, Washington, DC; IMF 2005a, 12. Also see "Viktor Yushchenko, Ukraine's Faint Hope," *Economist* (London), 6 May 2000; Thomas Catan, "Former Premier Alleges Kyiv Misused IMF Loans," *Financial Times* (London), 28 January 2000.

60. Western institutions and actors apparently insisted on Yushchenko's appointment. See "Viktor Yushchenko, Ukraine's Faint Hope," *Economist* (London), 6 May 2000.

61. Rybachuk, quoted by Stone (2002, 180). Also see Stone's quotation of Suslov (191).

62. See the *Law of Ukraine on the National Bank of Ukraine*, available in English at www.bank.gov.ua/Engl/B—legisl/index.htm. For EU concerns about the lack of CBI of Ukraine, see European Commission 2004, 13.

63. For these and additional details, see "Ukraine Does Not Meet Conditions for World Bank Loan," *Interfax*, 16 May 1999; Katya Gorchinskaya and Vitaly Sych, "Parliament Tries to Reel in NBU," *Kyiv Post*, 6 June 1999; Ruslan Karpov, "Central Bank Standoff Lingers," *Kyiv Post*, 19 July 1999; and "Ukraine Not to Have EU Tranche until Relations with IMF are Cleared," *Interfax*, 13 December 1999.

64. Author's interview with Arseniy Yatseniuk.

65. "Ukraine Central Banker Vows to Uphold Currency Stability," *BBC Monitoring*, 27 February 2003.

66. See IMF, "Ukraine—Concluding Statement of the 2003 IMF Article IV Con-

sultation Mission," press release, 27 February 2003; and IMF, Public Information Notice (PIN) No. 03/73, 13 June 2003, Washington, DC.

67. IMF, *IMF Survey*, 16 October 2006, 300–301; quotation from IMF, Public Information Notice (PIN) No. 05/156, 11 November 2005, Washington, DC.

68. Note that in the run-up to the 2004 elections, pensions and wages increased substantially. For the respective positions on Ukrainian economic policy, see IMF 2005b.

### CHAPTER 3: INTERNATIONALIZING BANK OWNERSHIP

1. Among industrialized countries, three are outliers. Approximately 99 percent of New Zealand's banking assets and 95 percent of Luxembourg's are foreign owned (Barth, Caprio, and Levine 2001b, 194–97). As a financial center, the United Kingdom also has a high foreign ownership in banking by European standards, at 46 percent (Barth, Caprio, and Levine 2006). See table 3.1.

2. Liz Salecka, "CEE: A Land of Opportunity," *European Banker*, 18 January 2006, 10.

3. According to Naaborg et al., Latvia had the third highest level of foreign ownership in its banking sector, at 78 percent (2003, 26).

4. Note that in the early 2000s, Slovenia had a very low foreign presence in its banking sector, at 15 percent (Naaborg et al. 2003, 26).

5. The Dutch financial group ABN Amro was attempting to buy Banca Anton-Veneta in Italy. Fazio was recorded talking to the head of a mid-sized Milan bank, Giampiero Fiorani. Together they allegedly orchestrated an Italian counter-offer to the ABN Amro bid as a way of preserving Italian ownership, but in violation of European competition rules.

6. By depressing interest rates through regulation, the state can create an excess demand for credit, thereby becoming the lender of last resort for private enterprise and thus allowing the state to choose which projects will receive financing. The costs of financial repression are spread across depositors, as their returns, in keeping with the overall policy, are suppressed. See Fry 1995, 3–19.

7. "Investing—Money in the Bank," *Warsaw Voice*, 21 November 2004.

8. John Reed, "Poland: Foreign Presence Proves Controversial," *Financial Times* (London), 17 April 2000, 2.

9. Author's interview with Stefan Kawalec.

10. This discussion is based on the author's interview with Anthony Doran.

11. Author's interviews with Doran and Kawalec. The World Bank financed the development of Poland's financial sector, committing $200 million, $50 million of which was dedicated to the "Twinning Arrangements."

12. ING (of the Netherlands) invested both in Bank Śląski SA in Katowice (controlling) and Bank Przemysłowo-Handlowy in Krakow (14% as of 1998). UniCredito (of Italy) eventually bought a controlling share in Pekao SA.

13. Stefan Kawalec, the same Polish MoF official who contacted the IFC to act on Sachs's proposal, was also the chief architect of Poland's bank bailout scheme. One

part of the plan caused some friction between Polish officials and their Western advisors. While the Poles wanted a decentralized system of Work-Out Departments, the IMF and World Bank wanted a clearing-house model based on other countries' experience. Eventually Poland prevailed in this debate—largely on the logic of Polish anti–central planning sentiments. Author's interviews with Piotr Rymaszewski, Kawalec, and Robert Koński. Also see Kawalec, Sikora, and Rymaszewski 1994.

14. The original zloty stabilization fund was $1 billion. It was never used, however, because in the course of macroeconomic stabilization there was never a run on the Polish currency. Six hundred million dollars was set aside for the bank recapitalization fund. According to Jan Krzysztof Bielecki, former prime minister, there was very little political controversy around the plan. Author's interview with Bielecki.

15. The New Economic Mechanism of 1968 left banks remarkably unchanged. Even after the 1987 creation of a two-tiered banking system, its basic operating principles were political-administrative rather than market-based. See Young 1989.

16. Hungary also had conditionality agreements with both the IMF and the World Bank between 1990 and 1994 (the first phase of reform), but those agreements were not explicitly tied to bank privatization as in Poland. But a $394 million IMF loan was predicated on cutting the budget deficit, which could have been linked to increasing privatization receipts—in part by privatizing banks.

17. "Law on Financial Institutions: An Econews Amplifier," *MTI Econews*, 15 November 1991.

18. Both *Financial Times* articles by Nicholas Denton, "The Hole at Hungary's Banking Heart," 20 May 1993, 15; and "Hungary Pledges Help for Troubled Commercial Banks," 21 May 1993, 20.

19. "Preparations for Privatisation at BB and MKB," *MTI News*, 19 November 1993; "MKB Managing Director on Future Structure of Banking Sector," *MTI News*, 23 November 1993.

20. "BLB and EBRD Take MKB," *Finance East Europe*, 5 August 1994.

21. The Romanian Banking Institute was established in 1991 and 1992 to provide technical training to Romanian bankers. In addition, the European Union, through its PHARE program, provided funding for assistance in bank auditing, the establishment of work-out units, and strategic banking development and training. The early "blueprint" for banking reform was provided by the IMF and World Bank (Tsantis 1997, 173).

22. Author's interview with Sebastian Vlădescu.

23. Author's interview with Daniel Dăianu.

24. For more on the IMF's views on the Romanian banking reform, see IMF, "IMF Approves Stand-by Credit for Romania," Press Release No. 97/20, 23 April 1997, and "IMF Concludes Article IV Consultation with Romania," IMF Public Information Notice (PIN) No. 98/79, 6 October 1998, Washington, DC.

25. Manufacturers Hanover Trust Co, Société Général, Frankfurt Bukarest Bank AG, and Misr-Romanian Bank had all established operations in Romania under state socialism.

26. "Romania: New Legislation on Foreign Investment," *BBC Summary of World*

*Broadcasts*, 25 April 1991; "New Act on Foreign Investment," *East European Business Law*, 1 May 1991.

27. "Romania: Isărescu to the Rescue," *Banker* 143 (808), 1 June 1993.

28. Thus the SLD and PSL did not initially embrace the idea of stronger ties to NATO, for example, but once in power they quickly changed their minds. See Grzegorz Kostrzewa-Zorbas, "Kameleony I Niezłomni," *Gazeta Polska*, 3 December 1999. Note also that despite public skepticism toward rapid reform and international institutions, when the World Bank and IMF surveyed the political parties on the eve of the elections, they found the SLD to be the best prepared, technocratically, to develop economic platforms. Author's interview with Ian M. Hume.

29. Nicholas Denton, "Delay for Hungary in IMF Pay-outs," *Financial Times* (London), 11 December 1993, 4.

30. Ten percent of Bancorex was merged with the Romanian Commercial Bank. In addition, Dacia Felix, CreditBank, Bankcoop, Banka Albina, Banca Columna, and Banca Internationala a Religiilor all failed and so exited the market in the late 1990s (Cernat 2006).

31. "EU/Romania: Reluctant Reformers Chase Accession Carrot," *European Report*, 22 May 2002.

32. "Romania: Foreign Banks' Invasion Pays," *Banker*, 1 April 2004.

33. Bancorex was at one time Romania's biggest bank. For much of the 1990s, the bank's management engaged in political and self-lending, without quality control. Although Bancorex repeatedly reported healthy returns, the institution was in fact operating at losses amounting to tens of millions of dollars a year. See Cernat 2006.

34. "Romania: Make-or-Break Time," *Banker*, 1 March 2002.

35. Sean Bobbitt, "Ministry Could Sell Foreigners Majority Stakes in Banks," *Warsaw Business Journal*, 24 November 1995, 1.

36. Krzysztof Fronczak, "Banking Sector Privatisation," *Polish News Bulletin*, 27 September 1991; Abarbanell and Bonin 1997.

37. See Stefan Wagstyl, "Polish Concern over Foreign Capital Levels: Stock Exchange Chief Urges Change," *Financial Times* (London), 20 July 1999, 2.

38. The following discussion is based on the author's interview with Grzegorz Kołodko.

39. Kołodko compared Hungary to Slovenia in making this point. Also see Kołodko 2000a.

40. "Strategie Bankowych fuzji," *Życie Warszawy*, 29 November 1995, 8.

41. The 1999 Accession Partnership with Romania states that from 1998 the European Commission had worked closely with the IFIs and the EBRD to facilitate compliance with preaccession priorities. The EC also used data from a range of sources in its annual Regular Reports, including from the Bretton Woods institutions (Sasse 2005). Finally, the World Bank and IMF included in their own publications assessments of how well Romania was doing with its EU accession commitments. See, for example, IMF, Public Information Notice (PIN) No. 06/49, 4 May 2006, Washington, DC.

42. See Sean Bobbitt, "BPH Consolidation Stuns Investors, Analysts, State Officials," *Warsaw Business Journal*, 8 December 1995, 3.

43. Regional banks tended to support the consolidation initiative and government intervention (*East European Banker*, November 1995, 6), as did some high-profile Polish economic-policy makers, including the head of the central bank, Hanna Gronkiewicz-Waltz ("Konsolidacja banków—tak, ale z głową," *Życie Warszawy*, 14 March 1996, 9). The BPH management, already partly privatized, was less enthusiastic, however (Konrad Sadurski, "Rządowy niewypał," *Gazeta Wyborcza*, 30 November 1995, 28).

44. The foreign business press quoted critics who called the plan a "collectivization move" and further compared it to 1945, "when the communists gave peasants small pieces of land, only to take them back again." Bobbitt, "BPH Consolidation Stuns Investors." Also see "Plan Spatski," *Economist* (London), 9 December 1995, 75. A journalist from Poland's leading newspaper, *Gazeta Wyborcza*, asked Kołodko at a press conference in Washington, DC, why he was "re-communizing" Poland's banks. Author's interview with Kołodko.

45. See Konrad Sadurski, "Przymknięta furtka," *Gazeta Wyborcza*, 30 January 1996, 20, for comments by US Treasury and specifically by David Lipton about Poland's proposed bank consolidation. The following discussion is based on the author's interview with Kołodko.

46. The United States had contributed $200 million of the $600 million bank bailout fund administered by the IMF, formerly the zloty stabilization fund. The agreement with the post-Solidarity reformers on privatization by 1996 had been nonbinding. Author's interview with Bielecki.

47. *European Banker*, June 1996, 11; Konrad Sadurski, "Wielka wyprzedaż," *Gazeta Wyborcza*, 10 October 1996, 24. Although some bank consolidation around Pekao SA did take place, the government failed to administer it (E. Balcerowicz and Bartkowski 2001, 18–19, 29). Consolidation was market-driven, and the banking group was subsequently sold in 1999 to UniCredito of Italy and the German insurer Allianz.

48. Author's interview with Kołodko.

49. Konrad Sadurski, "Bankowy zakręt," *Gazeta Wyborcza*, 12 April 1996, 18.

50. Author's interview with Kołodko.

51. "CEE: Expanding across CEE," *European Banker*, 8 November 2006, 9.

52. "Turning Inwards," *East European Banker*, November 1997.

53. "Postabank Reveals Losses of Ft 12 Billion," *East European Banker*, May 1998, 2.

54. "Bank Privatisation to Bring in at Least HUF 50bn," *MTI Econews*, 24 July 2002.

55. "Hungary Takes the Hard Road," *Banker* 144 (815), 1 January 1994; "Hungary Did Not Draw Upon IMF Stand-by Loan in 1993, Bod Says," *MTI Econews*, 9 March 1994; "IMF Loans Talks Set for Next Week," *MTI Econews*, 19 July 1994.

56. BRD became BRD–Group Société Générale after privatization.

57. Liz Salecka, "CEE: A Land of Opportunity," *European Banker*, 18 January 2006, 10. Also see Tsantis 1997, 200–205.

58. See the following EC documents: *1998/261/EC: Council Decision of 30 March 1998 on the Principles, Priorities, Intermediate Objectives and Conditions Contained in*

*the Accession Partnership with Romania*; and *1999/852/EC: Council Decision of 6 December 1999 on the Principles, Priorities, Intermediate Objectives and Conditions Contained in the Accession Partnership with Romania*, Brussels.

59. Secretary Mihai Ionescu and Minister Sebastian Vlădescu. See "Romania Sells Largest Commercial Bank," *Xinhua General News Service*, 21 December 2005; and Nick Spiro, "Romania—Moment of Truth," *Banker*, 1 May 2006.

60. Even with the violations, Romania was not in danger of facing the EU's "safe-guard clause" that would postpone EU accession by a year. See Commission of the European Communities, *Commission Staff Working Document: Romania*, May 2006 Monitoring Report, 16 May 2006, Brussels; "President Believes Romania Ready to Join EU," *BBC Monitoring*, 4 July 2006; "Romanian President Welcomes EU Resolution on Accession," *BBC Monitoring*, 4 July 2006. On the lowering of EU standards, see Tom Gallagher, "Romania Has Not Earned EU Accession," *Financial Times* (London), 26 November 2004, 13; and "How Europe Has Failed the Romanian People," *Independent* (London), 14 December 2004, 33.

61. On the performance of BCR and Eximbank, see "Romania: Make-or-Break Time," *Banker*, 1 March 2002; and on the performance of the state-owned National Savings Bank, see "Romania—Foreign Banks' Invasion Pays," *Banker*, 1 April 2004.

62. Christopher Condon, "Offers for State-Owned CEC Bank Might Disappoint Romania," *Financial Times* (London), 17 July 2006, 19.

63. *Kyiv Post*, 15 February 2006.

64. Natalya Dushkevych and Valentin Zelenyuk, "Ukrainian Banking Sector: Evolution and Current State," *Ukrainian Observer*, No. 225, November 2006.

65. By early 2006, several other foreign interests had a foothold in Ukraine's banking sector—either because they had purchased Ukrainian interests or because they had established their own operations there. Foreign-run enterprises included Citibank Ukraine, Raiffeisen Ukraine, and Calyon Bank Ukraine. Hungary's OTP and France's Crédit Agricole had also established stakes. See "Ukraine: Europe's Banks Vote with their Feet," *Banker*, 1 May 2006.

## CHAPTER 4: DEMOCRATIZING CIVIL-MILITARY RELATIONS

1. The 1981 imposition of martial law under General Wojciech Jaruzelski in Poland is a partial exception to the rule (Sanford 1986; Michta 1990). I say "partial" because Jaruzelski and his regime identified strongly with the Communist Party and acted accordingly, as opposed to acting exclusively with the aim of increasing military prerogatives—even if the latter was the practical effect (Kramer 1998).

2. US Defense Secretary William Perry, quoted in Craig R. Whitney, "Expand NATO? Yes, Say Most Experts, but What Does the Public Think?" *New York Times*, 10 February 1995, A6. Also see Goldgeier 1999, 94–95.

3. The North Atlantic Council had decided to initiate a study on NATO enlargement almost a year earlier. See "Declaration of the Heads of State and Government Participating in the Meeting of the North Atlantic Council," 1 December 1994, para. 6, Brussels, www.nato.int/docu/pr/1994/p94-116e.htm.

4. Author's interview with Jeffrey Simon.

5. Jane Perlez, "Poland's Top Commander Resists Terms for NATO," *New York Times*, 22 January 1997, A3.

6. Jeffrey Simon makes this judgment in all of his studies on civil-military relations in the region.

7. But also note that Romania had cut off military ties to the Warsaw Pact by 1964 and developed a national defense capability. Albania abandoned the Warsaw Pact altogether in 1968.

8. The Rapacki Plan was a 1957 initiative to create a nuclear-free zone in east-central Europe. See Prizel 1998, 87.

9. Although the Polish military was highly reliable in matters of external goals (see R. A. Johnson, Dean, and Alexiev 1980), internal repression was a different matter, due in large measure to public resistance to the communist regime and Soviet hegemony (Kramer 1995).

10. The label "aristocratic" dates from the period of extreme decentralization in Polish political organization, when land-owning nobles had their own militias to protect their property (Michta 1990).

11. These crises included the Parys affair in 1992, the Drawsko affair in 1994, and Komornicki affair in 1995. Parys and Drawsko are thoroughly covered in the literature. For more on Komornicki, see Jerzy Jachowicz and Paweł Wronski, "Barwy wojska," *Gazeta Wyborcza*, 16 April 1995, 3. On all three events, see Simon 1996, chap. 4; Michta 1997; and Kramer 1998, 1999.

12. Kołodziejczyk speculated that the generals wanted his dismissal because he had repeatedly tried to thwart efforts by Wałęsa and Wilecki to create an exclusive and direct line of authority from the president to the military. Author's interview with Vice Admiral (retired) Piotr Kołodziejczyk.

13. The "Komornicki affair" refers to the efforts of military officers to persuade soldiers to favor some candidates over others in the upcoming national elections. See Simon 1996.

14. These twin convictions were reported to the author by Kołodziejczyk, Przemysław Grudziński, and Antoni Kamiński.

15. Author's interview with Grzegorz Kostrzewa-Zorbas.

16. In the Warsaw Pact there was very little attention to an independent Ukrainian military tradition. Author's interview with General (retired) Vladimir Grechaninov.

17. The Russian or Ukrainian word *kontrol* means simply to "check" or "verify," whereas when Westerners talk about civilian control over the armed forces they are referring to a comprehensive system of "direction, management, administration and supervision." Only through direct interaction with their Western counterparts did Ukrainian military personnel began to understand that civilian control was more than simply seeking limited civilian approval (Sherr 2005, 160).

18. Author's interview with James Greene. Grechaninov was one such pro-reform and pro-NATO military figure. Also see "Ukrainian General Describes Army Efforts Aimed at Joining NATO," *BBC Monitoring*, 7 July 2004.

19. Author's interview with Kostrzewa-Zorbas.

20. Author's interview with Kostrzewa-Zorbas.

21. Author's interviews with Radek Sikorski, Jan Parys, Grudziński, and Zdzisław Najder.

22. Janusz Onyszkiewicz and Przemysław Grudziński had been active in the anti-communist Solidarity movement during the Cold War. Both then went on to serve in Solidarity-affiliated governments in the postcommunist period. Onyszkiewicz was among the first civilian deputy defense ministers in Poland. Grudziński served first as an advisor to the government on foreign and defense issues. He later served in a number of foreign policy and diplomatic posts. Michta notes that by 1992–1993, both Onyszkiewicz and Grudziński were very familiar with Western models and NATO standards (1997, 87–88).

23. See Mirosław Cielemecki, "The New Model of Command over the Polish Army Is a Caricature of the U.S. One," *Wprost*, 17 March 1996 (translated in *FBIS-EEU-96-054*, 20 March 1996).

24. *Gazeta Wyborcza* report of 7 February 1996, quoted in "Poland: Holbrooke, Dobrzański Discuss NATO, IFOR," *Warsaw PAP*, 7 February 1996 (translated in *FBIS-EEU-96-026*, 8 February 1996).

25. Karkoszka quoted in Andrzej Mędykowski, "Washington, Brussels, Athens, Warsaw: Horizons of Security," *Polska Zbrojna*, 5 March 1996 (translated in *FBIS-EEU-96-046*, 8 March 1996).

26. Grzegorz Kostrzewa-Zorbas, "Kameleony i niezłomni," *Gazeta Polska*, 3 December 1999.

27. Anna Wiełpolska and Zbigniew Lentowicz, "Muzyka przeszłości," *Rzeczpospolita*, 2–3 October 1993; Longin Pastusiak, "Polska w bezpiecznej Europie," *Rzeczpospolita*, 8 October 1993.

28. Włodzimierz Cimoszewicz quoted in Adam LeBor, "Polish Leaders Cast Doubt on Entry to NATO," *Times* (London), September 21, 1993. Also see Vachudova 1997, chap. 7.

29. The PSL admitted to reversing its position, while Jerzy Wiatr of the SLD denied ever having been against it. See "PSL and SLD for NATO Membership," *Polish News Bulletin*, 12 October 1993.

30. "Onyszkiewicz: Post-Communist Victory Will Hinder NATO Membership," *PAP (Polish Press Agency) News Wire*, 26 August 1993; "Democratic Left Alliance Victory Could Affect Entry to NATO, Rokita Believes," *BBC Summary of World Broadcasts*, 9 September 1993; Hanna Suchocka, "Leftist Election Victory Could Deter NATO," *PAP (Polish Press Agency) News Wire*, 16 September 1993; "Atlantic Club Concerned over Election Results," *Polish Press Agency*, 27 September 1993.

31. Andrzej Karkoszka, who would become a deputy minister of defense in the new administration, was among those who wanted to debate the issue, but recalls that there was intense political pressure not to. Author's interview with Karkoszka.

32. See, for example, "EC and NATO Keep Wary Eye on Poland's 'Communist' Comeback," *Press Association Newsfile*, 20 September 1993.

33. Author's interview with Daniel Fried.

34. Author's interview with András Simonyi.

35. Author's interview with Parys.

36. Author's interviews with Parys and Najder.

37. Author's interview with an anonymous representative from NATO's Public Relations and Press, Bratislava.

38. This conference was "Security in Central Europe," Warsaw, 11–12 March 1992.

39. Janusz Onyszkiewicz argued that Poland should not take this risk without some assurance that NATO would expand its membership.

40. Author's interviews with Parys and Sikorski.

41. Despite the voluminous literature that makes the opposite claim, NATO did not encourage postcommunist states to invest in new weaponry as a way to demonstrate their readiness to join the alliance. In fact, NATO put more basic, less costly reforms first. See Dragsdahl 1998.

42. Author's interviews with Parys, Sikorski, Kołodziejczyk, and Grudziński. In private settings, however, NATO did resort to shaming. Author's interviews with Simon, George Katsirdakis, and Charles Dale.

43. Author's interviews with Sikorski and Parys.

44. Author's interviews with Kołodziejczyk, Kamiński, and Katsirdakis.

45. Author's interview with Greene.

46. Watts offers a different assessment, however: "From the perspective of implementing democratic control, Romania stands well ahead of where the new NATO members were at their invitation [in 1997] and, in several important respects, quite close to where they are now" (2001b, 38).

47. Author's interview with Greene.

48. Author's interview with Michel Duray.

49. See Taras Kuzio, "NATO Summit Commits to 'Big Bang' Enlargement," *Kyiv Post*, 28 November 2002. NATO withdrew its invitation to President Kuchma for the Prague Summit in November 2002 because of allegations of the government's role in the Kolchuga scandal, in which Ukraine was alleged to have sold early-warning radar systems to Iraq (Gallis 2005). Kuchma attended the Prague Summit in any case, only bringing Ukraine's low international standing into sharper relief.

50. One such NGO is the Razumkov Centre, established in 1994, which focuses on a range of economic issues as well as on Ukrainian foreign and security policy. By early 2005, at least 50 NGOs were supporting Ukrainian cooperation with NATO—all of which were in association through the Ukraine-NATO Civic League.

51. For a survey on US-sponsored educational and training programs, see Ulrich 1995, 1999; and Gheciu 2005a.

52. Author's interview with an anonymous Polish official, Department of Strategy and Policy Planning, Polish Ministry of Foreign Affairs, Warsaw.

53. For branches of the US government, PfP served competing objectives—to provide both a road to membership (for the State Department) and a delaying tactic (for the Pentagon). See Goldgeier 1999.

54. Author's interviews with Kostrzewa-Zorbas, Grudziński, and Karkoszka.

55. The questionnaire, dated 4 April 1996, is a memo from the Acting Assistant Secretary General for Political Affairs in NATO to the Members of the Political Committee

at the Senior Level (Reinforced), "Intensified Dialogue with Interested Partners on the Enlargement Study: Questions for Partners," signed by Allen L. Keiswetter. Note that the public record reports that the Defense Planning Questionnaire to Poland, Hungary, and the Czech Republic was released only after these countries had been formally invited to join the alliance at the Madrid Summit in July 1997. See Boland 1998.

56. Author's interview with Karkoszka.

57. On the broad-based nature of this consensus and the people involved, see Simon 2004, 57–67. For additional outcomes that Poland achieved with NATO assistance, see Michta 2002.

58. Author's interview with an anonymous US official, Warsaw.

59. Author's interview with an anonymous US advisor to the Polish government.

60. The article reported that "the Chief of General Staff, Gen. Tadeusz Wilecki, was fighting rules that give civilians in the ministry the final say." "For a variety of reasons," it continues, "Poland, the largest and strategically the most sensitive of the likely new members, has had more difficulty introducing civilian control than the other two." Jane Perlez, "Poland's Top Commander Resists Terms for NATO," *New York Times*, 22 January 1997, A3.

61. Author's interview with Karkoszka.

62. Kwaśniewski portrayed the dismissal as a routine "rotation" in a continuing effort to protect the support of the military constituency. The Polish media reported that it was a thin veil, however.

63. Author's interviews with Matt Boyce, Karkoszka, and A. Kamiński. According to one source, even in 1999, a small group of Polish generals still held exclusive control over the military. Author's interview with Olaf Osica.

64. US Senate Committee on Foreign Relations, *Protocols to the North Atlantic Treaty of 1949 on Accession of Poland, Hungary, and the Czech Republic*, 6 March 1998, 10–11 (on Poland's undertaking sufficient reform) and 16–17 (on all three countries meeting Perry Principles).

65. The MSzMP presided over the defense reforms at a time when it was believed the next president would be popularly elected, in which case it seemed likely that the reform-minded socialist Imre Pozsgay would prevail. Instead, however, parts of the opposition—including the Federation of Young Democrats (FIDESZ) and the Alliance of Free Democrats—succeeded in putting the electoral rules to referendum in November 1989. The opposition succeeded in its aims, securing a system by which the parliament, rather than the population directly, would elect the president. Thus Árpád Göncz of the Free Democrats became the first postcommunist president. See Rothschild and Wingfield 2000, 243–44, 278.

66. But note that Paşcu was a member of the socialist bloc.

67. European Parliament, *Delegation to the EU Romania Joint Parliamentary Committee*, 5 July 2001, 18, Strasbourg.

68. Author's interview with an anonymous NGO representative, Bucharest.

69. For examples of how compatible Romania's drafting of national security strategies had become, see sections of Government of Romania, *White Paper of Security and National Defence*, Bucharest, 2004.

70. See NATO Parliamentary Assembly, "Report of the Sub-Committee on Future Security and Defence Capabilities," Articles 70–75; and Woehrel, Kim, and Erik 2003.

71. Author's interview with Greene.

72. Author's interview with Grechaninov.

73. Author's interview with Greene.

CHAPTER 5: DENATIONALIZING DEFENSE PLANNING AND FOREIGN POLICY

1. "Out-of-area" refers to territory outside the NATO area. NATO 1995a, 232.

2. Article V of the North Atlantic Treaty states: "The Parties agree that an attack against one or more of them in Europe or North America shall be considered an attack against them all."

3. For evidence of such surprise, see the comments of former deputy chief of the Polish mission to NATO, Witold Waszczykowski, who remarked that Poland "would like to enjoy membership in the 'traditional' NATO" (quoted in Szayna 2001, 25).

4. Author's interview with General Wojciech Jaruzelski.

5. Also note that in 1999, US Secretary of Defense William Cohen estimated that while the Europeans collectively spent 60 percent of what the United States spends on defense, they accrued only about 10 percent of the capability. See Elizabeth Becker, "European Allies to Spend More on Weapons," New York Times, 22 September 1999, A13.

6. This does not include minority protection laws, however (Kelley 2004a, 2004b; Grabbe 2005). Western Europe had no single model of minority protection and, of course, some western European states have struggled with minority rights issues, sometimes violently. This lack of consistency in the West complicated EU efforts to forge coherent policies in eastern Europe.

7. Timothy Snyder (2003) argues, however, that Polish Foreign Minister Krzysztof Skubiszewski was a particularly talented and forward thinking foreign-policy maker.

8. For articles that reflect those early tensions, see Jerzy Rajch (in conversation with Grzegorz Kostrzewa-Zorbas), "Zmierzch bloków," *Żolnierz Rzeczypospolitej*, 18 January 1990, 3; and "Nic o Polsce bez Polski: Rozmowa z ministrem spraw zagranicznych prof. Krzysztofem Skubiszewskim," *Gazeta Wyborcza*, 24 January 1991, 1.

9. During his campaign, Zhirinovsky had called for the annexation of Finland, the Baltic States, and Poland.

10. For Polish politicians' fears about Zhirinovsky's strong electoral showing and consequent calls for NATO enlargement: on Polish Foreign Minister Andrzej Olechowski, see Andrew Borowiec, "Russian Victor Alarms Poland," *Washington Times*, 16 December 1993, A12; on defense ministers Janusz Onyszkiewicz and Piotr Kołodziejczyk and Czech President Vaclav Havel, see John Pomfret, "E. Europe Looks West for Security," *Washington Post*, 1 January, 1994, A1. President Lech Wałęsa provided a more muted response in Anthony Robinson and Christopher Bobinski, "Walesa Tells How to Handle Zhirinovsky," *Financial Times* (London), 22 December 1993, 2.

11. US ambassador to Poland, Daniel Fried, in a speech to the US Chamber of Commerce in Poland in defense of NATO enlargement, Warsaw, March 1999.

12. Author's interviews with Vice Admiral (retired) Piotr Kołodziejczyk, Jan Parys, Radek Sikorski, Przemysław Grudziński, and George Katsirdakis.

13. Author's interview with Katsirdakis. Katsirdakis reported having had more success in persuading Onyszkiewicz than Kołodziejczyk.

14. See also the article by Radek Sikorski, who is critical of the report for not recognizing that Western relations with Russia will always come first while Polish interests will always come second. "Odwaga wyciągania wniosków," *Rzeczpospolita*, 20 November 1995, 8.

15. On independent foreign policy initiatives, see Prizel 1998. On military tradition, see Michta 1990. For further details see Epstein 2006b.

16. Barany reports that the Hungarian military's response to the Soviet offensive that began on November 4, 1956, was characterized by confusion more than anything else. Although there was some uncoordinated resistance to Soviet crackdown (mostly from the National Guard), most of the Hungarian Peoples' Army troops stayed in their barracks and, in keeping with orders, did not fire on Soviet troops. Prime Minister Imre Nagy, although declaring Hungarian neutrality on November 1 and wishing to withdraw from the Warsaw Pact, refused to mobilize the army to combat Soviet forces. In late October, some soldiers did abandon their positions, joining the revolution (Barany 1993, 59–65).

17. Barany (1999) notes that before taking office, Antall had been a museum director and his foreign minister, Géza Jeszenszky, a college professor.

18. Author's interview with András Simonyi.

19. Author's interview with Daniel Fried. Also see Williams 2002, 239.

20. The official was Hungarian Prime Minister Gyula Horn, responding to questions from the North Atlantic Assembly meeting in Budapest. See "NATO Parliamentary Meeting in Budapest: Premier Says Russia Must Not Feel Isolated," *BBC Summary of World Broadcasts*, 31 May 1995. Also see the interview in *NATO Review* with András Simonyi (2001), Hungary's first ambassador to NATO, in which he explains that "the Hungarian position has always been that NATO enlargement has nothing to do with fear of Russia."

21. Bacon argues as much in his essay (1999, 193).

22. In response to the disintegration of the Tsarist empire in 1917, Ukraine declared its independence in January 1918. According to Prizel, however, statehood was really an "afterthought," since social grievances of the peasantry had driven the movement. The project fell apart because of the lack of support from urban Russian and Polish populations on Ukrainian territory, from peasants, and from the international community (1998, 323–25).

23. Author's interview with Grzegorz Kostrzewa-Zorbas.

24. The Hungarian Socialist Party did not accept all of NATO's "thresholds," however. Jacoby points out that Horn's government, whether intentionally or not, contributed to the military's autonomy by opposing rapid integration of the General Staff into the MoD and by circumventing parliamentary authority (Jacoby 2004, 139; also see Simon 1996, 60–65; and my discussion in chapter 4).

25. Author's interview with Simonyi.

26. Commission of the European Communities, *Central and Eastern Eurobarometer: Public Opinion and the European Union (19 Countries' Survey)*, March 1996, No. 6, Brussels; see fig. 31. Also see my table 4.1. The 1997 Eurobarometer polling data were collected in November 1996. For Hungarian leaders' concerns about what the polling data might mean, see "Speaker Stresses Need to Inform Public about NATO Membership," *BBC Summary of World Broadcasts*, 30 November 1996. Czech public opinion was even more troubling to the alliance, given both enduring low levels of support for membership and the general lack of concern of the Czech leadership (with the exception of President Vaclav Havel). See Jane Perlez, "New Poll Finds Czechs' Support for NATO Stays Below 50%," *New York Times*, 23 December 1997, A7. After a vigorous government campaign, Hungary conducted a referendum on NATO membership in November 1997. The public voted in favor by a wide margin—85 percent. But with only 49 percent turnout, the depth of public support was still unclear. See Nelson and Szayna 1998; Barany 1999, 87; Jacoby 2004, 144–45.

27. The government's campaign included placing a pro-NATO character in one of the country's most popular sitcoms. See Agnes Csonka, "Government Buys Pro-NATO Sitcom Character," *Budapest Business Journal*, 7 July 1997, 3. The Hungarian referendum revealed strong support for NATO membership among those who voted, but with the minimum turnout necessary for a valid poll. See previous note.

28. Note that Romania was the first postcommunist country to join the Partnership for Peace, in 1994.

29. President Iliescu initiated the basic treaty in August 1995. The *Study on NATO Enlargement* was released a month later. The Perry Principles had made it clear that states hoping for alliance membership should focus on, among other things, forging constructive relations with neighboring states.

30. The PUNR, PSM, and PRM tended to be anti-Hungarian, anti-reform, and anti-Semitic, respectively (Bacon 1999, 186).

31. Prizel argues, for example, that eastern Ukrainians who rejected either Russian hegemony or, later, Soviet rule were primarily concerned with attaining social justice or greater cultural autonomy. Historically, such sentiments were connected to the idea of creating a pan-Slavic federation in which Ukraine would have equal status to Russia (1998, chaps. 8 and 9).

32. Romania fought alongside Hitler, then left the Axis when it tried to quit the war in 1944 and the Nazis tried to prevent it. Romania then joined the allies, with 538,000 troops—and suffered 167,000 casualties—making this the fourth largest military contribution on the allied side. In the nineteenth century the Romanian military had been an instrument of social mobility and nation building (Watts 2003).

33. For the role of territorial defense in the campaign, see "Czy nas obroni armia krajowa," *Rzeczpospolita*, 1 April 1998, 4. For Radek Sikorski's role in promoting territorial defense, see Marek Barański, "Because It Is Not So Bad to Be a Guerilla," *Nie*, 5 March 1998, 5 (translated in *FBIS-EEU-98-070*, 11 March 1998). Szeremietiew narrowly lost out in his bid to become minister of defense to Janusz Onyszkiewicz of the Freedom Union (UW).

34. For details of the plan, see "Strategia obronna AWS: Żołnierz w domu," *Gazeta*

*Wyborcza*, 15 September 1997, 5; and Romuald Szeremietiew, "Siła obronna Polski," *Rzeczpospolita*, 1 September 1997, 7.

35. Romuald Szeremietiew, "Obronność Polski—pytania i wątpliwości," *Rzeczpospolita*, 22 January 1998, 6.

36. On this part of the program, see Paweł Wronski, "Uczeń z kałaszem," *Gazeta Wyborcza*, 21 April 1998, 3.

37. Bronisław Komorowski, "Siła armii and narodu," *Rzeczpospolita*, 14–15 August 1997, 4. Komorowski served as a deputy minister of defense and later as parliamentary Sejm defense committee chairman. He was also as a member of the AWS.

38. See, for example, Szeremietiew, "Siła obronna Polski"; Robert Lipka (another deputy defense minister) in Wronski, "Uczeń z kałaszem"; and Andrzej Walentek, "Levy in Mass," *Polska Zbrojna*, 28 March 1997, 11–12 (translated in *FBIS-EEU-97-064*, 4 April 1997).

39. Szeremietiew, "Siła obronna Polski."

40. Komorowski, "Siła armii and narodu."

41. Szeremietiew, "Obronność Polski"; Komorowski, "Siła armii and narodu."

42. See Paweł Wronski's interview with General Bolesław Balcerowicz, "Nie czołgiem, lecz głową," *Gazeta Wyborcza*, 12 February 1997, 5.

43. Sejm Defense Commission Chairman Bronisław Komorowski, quoted in Zbigniew Lentowicz, "Armia do stu milimetrów," *Rzeczpospolita*, 3 February 1998, 4.

44. Walentek, "Levy in Mass"; Major Ryszard Choroszy, "Analysis: An Uncommon Levee en Masse," *Polska Zbrojna*, 28 November 1997, 20–21 (translated in *FBIS-EEU-97-243*, 20 December 1997); authors' interviews with Parys and Sikorski.

45. Szeremietiew, "Obronność Polski" and "Siła obronna Polski."

46. For additional sources on NATO influence, see Nelson and Szayna 1998; and Barany 1999, 79 (quoting US Ambassador to NATO Robert Hunter).

47. In 1995, however, the "letter of 300," allegedly signed by military officers, including Romanian generals, accused President Iliescu of undermining Romanian independence and sovereignty, of putting the country at the disposal of "traitors and spies," and of "sacking . . . 75,000 military cadres at the request of NATO." Because the letter appeared in *Romania Mare*, the weekly publication of Corneliu Vadim Tudor, chairman of the nationalist Greater Romania Party, it was never clear whether the letter was authentic. Although expressing some sentiments similar to the right wing of the AWS in Poland, it is unlikely such sentiments were very widely held in Romania. The quotations are from "Romanian Military Accuses President of Weakening Defence," *Agence France Presse*, 4 July 1995. Also see Tony Barber, "Romania's Far-Right Flexes Its Muscles," *Independent* (London), 5 July 1995, 11.

48. Askold Krushelnycky, "Russia/Ukraine: Common Ground Reached on Border Agreements," *RFE/RL*, 21 April 2004.

49. This is not to say, however, that other democratic or market-oriented norms were similarly embedded—they were not. Into the early 2000s, Ukraine's leadership, headed by President Leonid Kuchma and Prime Minister Viktor Yanukovich, was accused of curbing press freedoms, ordering the deaths of opposition political leaders and journalists, and economic corruption. See Kuzio 2003.

50. That OT would have been focused on eastern instability was explained to the author in interviews with Artus Goławski, Parys, Sikorski, and Romuald Szeremietiew. On the perceived eastern threat, see Radek Sikorski, "Nie będzie NATO," *Gazeta Polska*, 26 January 1996.

51. Author's interview with Hans Jürgen Heimsöth.

52. Those who knew of such interactions or were there at the meetings included Kostrzewa-Zorbas, Parys, Sikorski, Karkoszka, Marcin Każimierski, John Schlosser, Fried, and Katsirdakis.

53. The Balkans are used as an immediate example here. Polish troops eventually sent on the Kosovo mission in 1999 traveled by train.

54. Author's interviews with Katsirdakis and Każimierski.

55. Author's interview with Katsirdakis.

56. Author's interviews with Kostrzewa-Zorbas and Karkoszka. Kostrzewa-Zorbas doubted there was anything suspect about NATO security guarantees, arguing that if Russia ever advanced on Poland it would be "World War III."

57. Artur Goławski, "Terminator z OT," *Polska Zbrojna*, 6 February 1999, 20; Lentowicz, "Armia do stu milimetrów."

58. Barański, "Because It Is Not So Bad to Be a Guerilla."

59. Author's interviews with an anonymous US Official, Warsaw, and Karkoszka.

60. The substance of the meeting was recounted to the author by an anonymous US official in Warsaw. This official was also responsible for briefing Szeremietiew beforehand about what would be conveyed in the meeting, so that Szeremietiew would be prepared with a response.

61. There was still a territorial defense division within the Polish MoD, but it was dedicated to search and rescue and preparation for and relief of natural disasters. From 1997 on, between 3 and 3.5 percent of the defense budget would be dedicated to OT, a much smaller proportion than its advocates had planned. Author's interviews with Brigadier General January Komański and Bronisław Komorowski, two early and strong supporters of Polish territorial defense.

62. Author's interview with Szeremietiew.

63. This included former minister of defense Jan Parys and his deputy Radek Sikorski.

64. Not everyone was convinced. Parys, the one-time defense minister, remained skeptical of NATO's commitment to defend its eastern flank. Sikorski, by 1999 a deputy minister of foreign affairs, also remained privately supportive of some degree of defense self-sufficiency.

65. Hungary's support of NATO's Implementation Force (IFOR) in Kosovo and Stabilization Force (SFOR) in Bosnia was particularly notable in terms of what it signaled for Hungarian foreign policy denationalization, because of Serbia-Montenegro's recruitment of Hungarians living in the Vojvodina to join the Yugoslav National Army. Thus Hungary's support of NATO was essentially provided against the interests of Hungarian-speakers in the former Yugoslavia.

66. Author's interview with Simonyi; Martinusz 2002; Jacoby 2005, 241–42.

67. For more detail on Romania's defense planning, see Government of Romania,

*White Paper of Security and National Defence*, Bucharest, 2004; and Government of Romania, *Romania's Annual National Plan of Preparation for NATO Membership, 2003–2004*, 4 November 2003, Brussels: NATO, 2003.

68. Sherr also notes that Ukrainian participation in Iraq has been "deeply unpopular" (2005, 170), even among Ukrainian democrats such as Yulia Tymoshenko.

69. Author's interview with Michel Duray.

70. Multiple interviews by the author in Kyiv, Ukraine.

# References

Abarbanell, Jeffrey, and John Bonin. 1997. Bank Privatization in Poland: The Case of Bank Śląski. *Journal of Comparative Economics* 25 (1): 31–61.

Abdelal, Rawi. 2001. *National Purpose in the World Economy: Post-Soviet States in Comparative Perspective.* Ithaca, NY: Cornell University Press.

Ábel, István, Pierre L. Siklos, and István P. Székely. 1998. *Money and Finance in the Transition to a Market Economy.* Cheltenham, UK: Edward Elgar.

Adler, Emanuel, and Michael Barnett, eds. 1998. *Security Communities.* Cambridge: Cambridge University Press.

Albert, Michel. 1993. *Capitalism vs. Capitalism.* New York: Four Walls Eight Windows.

Alesina, Alberto, and Lawrence H. Summers. 1993. Central Bank Independence and Macroeconomic Performance: Some Comparative Evidence. *Journal of Money, Credit, and Banking* 25 (2): 151–62.

Amsden, Alice, Jacek Kochanowicz, and Lance Taylor. 1994. *The Market Meets Its Match: Restructuring the Economies of Eastern Europe.* Cambridge, MA: Harvard University Press.

Ananicz, Andrzej, Przemysław Grudziński, Andrzej Olechowski, Janusz Onyszkiewicz, Krzysztof Skubiszewski, and Henryk Szlajfer. 1995. *Poland-NATO Report.* Warsaw: Center for International Relations, Euro-Atlantic Association.

Anderson, Ronald W., Erik Berglöf, and Kálmán Mizsei. 1996. *Banking Sector Development in Central and Eastern Europe.* London: Centre for Economic Policy Research.

Bacon, Walter M., Jr. 1999. Romanian Civil-Military Relations after 1989. In *The Military and Society in the Former Eastern Bloc*, ed. Constantine P. Danopoulos and Daniel Zirker, 179–200. Boulder, CO: Westview Press.

Balassa, Ákos. 1992. The Transformation and Development of the Hungarian Banking System. In *Monetary and Banking Reform in Postcommunist Economies*, ed. David M. Kemme and Andrzej Rudka, 6–42. New York: Institute for East-West Security Studies and Westview Press.

Balassa, Ákos, Iván Berend, and András Vértes. 1990. The Transformation of the Hungarian Economic System. In *The End of Central Planning? Social Economies in the Transition: The Cases of Czechoslovakia, Hungary, China and the Soviet Union*, ed. David M. Kemme and Claire E. Gordon, 33–55. New York: Institute for East-West Security Studies and Westview Press.

Balcerowicz, Ewa, and Andrzej Bartkowski. 2001. *Restructuring and Development of the Banking Sector in Poland: Lessons to Be Learnt by Less Advanced Transition Countries.* CASE Reports No. 44. Warsaw: Center for Social and Economic Research.

Balcerowicz, Leszek. 1995. *Socialism, Capitalism, Transformation.* Budapest: Central European University Press.

Barany, Zoltán D. 1993. *Soldiers and Politics in Eastern Europe, 1945–1990: The Case of Hungary.* New York: St. Martin's Press.

———. 1995. The Military and Security Legacies of Communism. In *The Legacies of Communism in Eastern Europe,* ed. Zoltán D. Barany and Iván Völgyes, 101–17. Baltimore: Johns Hopkins University Press.

———. 1999. Hungary: An Outpost on the Troubled Periphery. In *America's New Allies: Poland, Hungary and the Czech Republic in NATO,* ed. Andrew A. Michta, 74–111. Seattle: University of Washington Press.

———. 2003. *The Future of NATO Expansion: Four Case Studies.* Cambridge: Cambridge University Press.

Barnett, Michael N., and Martha Finnemore. 2004. *Rules for the World: International Organizations in World Politics.* Ithaca, NY: Cornell University Press.

Barth, James R., Gerard Caprio Jr., and Ross Levine. 2001a. *Bank Supervision and Regulation: What Works Best?* Minneapolis: University of Minnesota, Carlson School of Management.

———. 2001b. The Regulation and Supervision of Banks around the World. In *Integrating Emerging Market Countries into the Global Financial System,* ed. R. E. Litan and R. Herring, 183–240. Washington, DC: Brookings Institution Press.

———. 2006. *Rethinking Bank Regulation: Till Angels Govern.* New York: Cambridge University Press.

Becker, Gary. 1976. *The Economic Approach to Human Behavior.* Chicago: University of Chicago Press.

Berger, Helge, Jakob De Haan, and Sylvester C. W. Eijffinger. 2001. Central Bank Independence: An Update on Theory and Evidence. *Journal of Economic Surveys* 15 (1): 3–40.

Bobrowski, Ryszard, Marcin Kaźmirski, and Witold Waszczykowski. 2006. Chronology of Selected Events in Poland's Political and Military Contacts with NATO. *Central European Review.* www.centraleuropeanreview.pl/numer22/22chrono.htm.

Bockman, Joanna, and Gil Eyal. 2002. Eastern Europe as a Laboratory for Economic Knowledge: The Transnational Roots of Neoliberalism. *American Journal of Sociology* 108 (2): 310–52.

Boland, Frank. 1998. Force Planning in the New NATO. *NATO Review* 46 (3): 32–35. www.nato.int/docu/review/1998/9803-09.htm.

Bonin, John, Kálmán Mizsei, István Szekély, and Paul Watchel. 1998. *Banking in Transition Economies: Developing Market Oriented Banking Sectors in Eastern Europe.* Cheltenham, UK: Edward Elgar.

Boote, Anthony R., and Janos Somogyi. 1991. *Economic Reform in Hungary since 1968.* Washington, DC: International Monetary Fund.

Börzel, Tanja A., and Thomas Risse. 2000. *When Europe Hits Home: Europeanization and Domestic Change.* EUI Working Paper No. 2000/56. Florence: European University Institute.

Brown, Melville. 2004. *Review and Analysis of the Ukrainian Banking Sector.* Washington, DC: US Treasury.

Bryant, Christopher G. A., and Edmund Mokrzycki, eds. 1994. *The New Great Transformation? Change and Continuity in East-Central Europe.* New York: Routledge.

Bunce, Valerie. 1999. *Subversive Institutions: The Design and the Destruction of Socialism and the State.* Cambridge: Cambridge University Press.

———. 2003. Rethinking Recent Democratization: Lessons from the Postcommunist Experience. *World Politics* 55 (2): 167–92.

Bychenko, Andriy, and Leonid Polyakov. 2000. UCEPS Sociological Study: How Much of NATO Do Ukrainians Want? *National Security and Defence* (July 1): 14–22.

Cernat, Lucian. 2006. *Europeanization, Varieties of Capitalism and Economic Performance in Central and Eastern Europe.* London: Palgrave Macmillan.

Chang, Ha-Joon, and Peter Nolan, eds. 1995. *The Transformation of the Communist Economies: Against the Mainstream.* New York: St. Martin's Press.

Checkel, Jeffrey T. 1997. International Norms and Domestic Politics: Bridging the Rationalist-Constructivist Divide. *European Journal of International Relations* 3 (4): 473–95.

———. 2001a. The Europeanization of Citizenship? In *Transforming Europe: Europeanization and Domestic Change,* ed. Maria Green Cowles, James Caporaso, and Thomas Risse, 181–97. Ithaca, NY: Cornell University Press.

———. 2001b. Why Comply? Social Learning and European Identity Change. *International Organization* 55 (3): 553–88.

———. 2005. International Institutions and Socialization in Europe: Introduction and Framework. *International Organization* 59 (4): 801–26.

Checkel, Jeffrey T., and Andrew Moravcsik. 2001. A Constructivist Research Programme in EU Studies. *European Union Politics* 2 (2): 219–49.

Collier, Paul, 1997. The Failure of Conditionality. In *Perspectives on Aid and Development,* ed. Catherine Gwin and Joan Nelson, 51–78. Washington, DC: Overseas Development Council.

Collins, John, and Jason D. Meyer. 1995. *NATO's Military Enlargement: Problems and Prospect.* Washington, DC: Congressional Research Service.

Cottey, Andrew, Timothy Edmunds, and Anthony Forster, eds. 2002. *Democratic Control of the Military in Postcommunist Europe: Guarding the Guardians.* New York: Palgrave.

Cowles, Maria Green, James Caporaso, and Thomas Risse, eds. 2001. *Transforming Europe: Europeanization and Domestic Change.* Ithaca, NY: Cornell University Press.

Cukierman, Alex. 1992. *Central Bank Strategy, Credibility and Independence: Theory and Evidence*. Cambridge, MA: MIT University Press.

Cukierman, Alex, Geoffrey P. Miller, and Bilin Neyapti. 2002. Central Bank Reform, Liberalization and Inflation in Transition Economies: An International Perspective. *Journal of Monetary Economics* 49 (2): 237–64.

Cukierman, Alex, Steven B. Webb, and Bilin Neyapti. 1992. Measuring the Independence of Central Banks and Its Effect on Policy Outcomes. *The World Bank Economic Review* 6 (3): 353–98.

Dąbrowski, Marek, and Rafał Antczak. 1995. *Economic Transition in Russia, the Ukraine and Belarus in Comparative Perspective*. CASE Studies and Analyses No. 50. Warsaw: Center for Social and Economic Research.

Dăianu, Daniel. 1997. Bank Restructuring in Romania: Remarks on Transforming the Banking Sector in Romania. In *The New Banking Landscape in Central and Eastern Europe: Country Experience and Policies for the Future*, 153–66. Paris: OECD.

Davies, Norman. 2004. *Rising 44: The Battle for Warsaw*. New York: Viking.

Dobbin, Frank. 1994. *Forging Industrial Policy: The United States, Britain, and France in the Railway Age*. Cambridge: Cambridge University Press.

Doltu, Claudia. 2002. Banking Reform in Romania. In *Banking Reforms in South-East Europe*, ed. Željko Šević, 285–308. Cheltenham, UK: Edward Elgar.

Dragsdahl, Jorgen. 1998. NATO Resists Pressures to Militarise Central Europe. In *Occasional Papers on International Security Issues*, No. 28. July. Washington, DC: BASIC.

Duenwald, Christoph, Nikolay Gueorguiev, and Andrea Schaechter. 2005. *Too Much of a Good Thing? Credit Booms in Transition Economies: The Cases of Bulgaria, Romania and Ukraine*. Washington, DC: International Monetary Fund.

Dunay, Pál. 2002. Civil-Military Relations in Hungary: No Big Deal. In *Democratic Control of the Military in Postcommunist Europe: Guarding the Guards*, ed. Andrew Cottey, Timothy Edmunds, and Anthony Forster, 64–90. New York: Palgrave.

Dyson, Kenneth, ed. 2006. *Enlarging the Euro Area: External Empowerment and Domestic Transformation in East Central Europe*. Oxford: Oxford University Press.

Eijffinger, Sylvester C. W., and Jakob De Haan. 1996. The Political Economy of Central Bank Independence. In *Princeton Studies in International Economics*, No. 19. Princeton, NJ: International Economics Section, Department of Economics, Princeton University.

Ekiert, Grzegorz, and Jan Kubik. 1999. *Rebellious Civil Society: Popular Protest and Democratic Consolidation in Poland, 1989–1993*. Ann Arbor: University of Michigan Press.

Elborgh-Woytek, Katrin, and Mark Lewis. 2002. *Privatization in Ukraine: Challenges of Assessment and Coverage in Fund Conditionality*. Washington, DC: International Monetary Fund.

Elster, Jon. 1989. *Nuts and Bolts for the Social Sciences*. Cambridge: Cambridge University Press.

Encutescu, Sorin. 2002. Parliamentary Liaison and Public Opinion. In *Romanian*

*Military Reform and NATO Integration*, ed. Larry Watts, 37–52. Iaşi, Oxford, and Portland, OR: Centre for Romanian Studies.

Epstein, Rachel A. 2005a. NATO Enlargement and the Spread of Democracy: Evidence and Expectations. *Security Studies* 14 (1): 59–98.

——. 2005b. The Paradoxes of Enlargement. *European Political Science* 4 (4): 384–94.

——. 2006a. Cultivating Consensus and Creating Conflict: International Institutions and the (De)Politicization of Economic Policy in Postcommunist Europe. *Comparative Political Studies* 40 (8): 1019–42.

——. 2006b. When Legacies Meet Policies: NATO and the Refashioning of Polish Military Tradition. *East European Politics and Societies* 20 (2): 254–85.

——. 2008. The Social Context in Conditionality: Internationalizing Finance in Postcommunist Europe. *Journal of European Public Policy* 15 (6). In press.

Epstein, Rachel A., and Alexandra Gheciu. 2006. Beyond Territoriality: European Security after the Cold War. In *Developments in European Politics*, ed. Paul Haywood, Erik Jones, Martin Rhodes, and Ulrich Sedelmeier, 318–36. London: Palgrave Macmillan.

Epstein, Rachel A., and Juliet Johnson. 2009. The Limits of Europeanization: The Czech Republic, Poland and European Monetary Integration. In *The Changing Power and Politics of European Central Banking: Living with the Euro*, ed. Kenneth Dyson and Martin Marcussen. Oxford: Oxford University Press. In press.

European Central Bank. 2006. Convergence Report December 2006. www.ecb.int/pub/pdf/conrep/cr200612en.pdf.

European Commission. 2004. *European Neighbourhood Policy: Ukraine: Country Report*. Brussels: European Commission.

——. 2005. *Romania: 2005 Comprehensive Monitoring Report, 25 October*. Brussels: European Commission.

——. Various years. *Central and Eastern Eurobarometer*. Brussels: European Commission.

——. Various years. Regular Reports on Candidates' Progress towards Accession. Brussels: European Commission.

Feldmann, Magnus. 2007. The Origins of Varieties of Capitalism: Lessons from Post-Socialist Transition in Estonia and Slovenia. In *Beyond Varieties of Capitalism: Conflict, Contradictions, and Complementarities in the European Economy*, ed. Robert Hanké, Martin Rhodes, and Mark Thatcher, 328–50. Oxford: Oxford University Press.

Finnemore, Martha, and Kathryn Sikkink. 1998. *Activists beyond Borders: Advocacy Networks in International Politics*. Ithaca, NY: Cornell University Press.

Fish, Steven M. 1998. The Determinants of Economic Reform in the Post-Communist World. *East European Politics and Societies* 12 (1): 31–78.

Fluri, Philip. 2004. Parliamentary Oversight over the Defence and Security Sphere. In *Ukraine-NATO: The Future Depends on the Past*, 138–39. Kiev: Razumkov Centre.

Frieden, Jeffry. 1991. Invested Interests: The Politics of National Economic Policies in a World of Global Finance. *International Organization* 45 (4): 425–51.

———. 1999. Actors and Preferences in International Relations. In *Strategic Choice and International Relations*, ed. David Lake and Robert Powell, 39–76. Princeton, NJ: Princeton University Press.

Friedman, Milton. 1953. *Essays in Positive Economics.* Chicago: University of Chicago Press.

Fry, Maxwell J. 1995. *Money, Interest and Banking in Economic Development.* Second Edition. Baltimore: Johns Hopkins University Press.

Galin, Igor. 1999. Mass Public Opinion in Ukraine about NATO and NATO-Ukraine Relationships. NATO. www.nato.int/acad/fellow/96-98/galin.pdf.

Gallis, Paul. 2005. *The NATO Summit at Prague, 2002.* CRS Report for Congress. Washington, DC: Congressional Research Service.

Gamble, Andrew, and Gavin Kelly. 2002. Britain and EMU. In *European States and the Euro*, ed. Kenneth Dyson, 97–119. Oxford: Oxford University Press.

Garton Ash, Timothy. 1993. *In Europe's Name: Germany and the Divided Continent.* London: Cape.

Gerschenkron, Alexander. 1962. *Economic Backwardness in Historical Perspective: A Book of Essays.* Cambridge, MA: Belknap Press of Harvard University Press.

Gheciu, Alexandra. 2005a. *NATO in the "New Europe": International Socialization and the Politics of State-Crafting after the End of the Cold War.* Stanford, CA: Stanford University Press.

———. 2005b. Security Institutions as Agents of Socialization? NATO and the "New Europe." *International Organization* 59 (4): 973–1012.

Ghizari, Emil Iota. 1992. Banking Reform in Romania. In *Monetary and Banking Reform in Postcommunist Economies*, ed. David M. Kemme and Andrzej Rudka, 115–22. New York: Institute for East-West Security Studies and Westview Press.

Goldgeier, James M. 1999. *Not Whether but When: The US Decision to Enlarge NATO.* Washington, DC: Brookings Institution Press.

Goldstein, Judith, and Robert O. Keohane. 1993. *Ideas and Foreign Policy.* Ithaca, NY: Cornell University Press.

Grabbe, Heather. 2002. EU Conditionality and the *acquis communautaire. International Political Science Review* 23 (3): 249–68.

———. 2005. Regulating the Flow of People across Europe. In *The Europeanization of Central and Eastern Europe*, ed. Frank Schimmelfennig and Ulrich Sedelmeier, 112–34. Ithaca, NY: Cornell University Press.

Grabel, Ilene. 2003. Ideology and Power in Monetary Reform: Explaining the Rise of Independent Central Banks and Currency Boards in Emerging Economies. In *Monetary Orders: Ambiguous Economics, Ubiquitous Politics*, ed. Jonathan Kirshner, 25–53. Ithaca, NY: Cornell University Press.

Grilli, Vittiorio, Donato Masciandaro, and Guido Tabellini. 1991. Institutions and Policies: Political Monetary Institutions and Public Financial Policies in Industrial Countries. *Economic Policy* 6 (2): 341–92.

Grytsenko, Anatoly. 1997. *Civil-Military Relations in Ukraine: A System Emerging from Chaos.* Kyiv: Ukraine Centre for European Security Studies.

Grzymała-Busse, Anna. 2002. *Redeeming the Communist Past: The Regeneration of Communist Parties in East Central Europe*. New York: Cambridge University Press.

Haftendorn, Helga, Robert O. Keohane, and Celeste A. Wallander, eds. 1999. *Imperfect Unions: Security Institutions over Time and Space*. New York: Clarendon.

Haggard, Stephen, and Chung H. Lee. 1993. Political Dimensions of Finance. In *The Politics of Finance in Developing Countries*, ed. Stephen Haggard, Chung H. Lee, and Sylvia Maxfield, 3–20. Ithaca, NY: Cornell University Press.

Hall, Peter A., and Robert J. Franzese. 1998. Mixed Signals: Central Bank Independence, Coordinated Wage Bargaining, and European Monetary Union. *International Organization* 52 (3): 505–35.

Hall, Peter A., and David Soskice, eds. 2001. *Varieties of Capitalism: The Institutional Foundations of Comparative Advantage*. New York: Oxford University Press.

Hanké, Bob, Martin Rhodes, and Mark Thatcher, eds. 2007. *Beyond Varieties of Capitalism: Conflict, Contradictions, and Complementarities in the European Economy*. Oxford: Oxford University Press.

Hanley, Eric, Lawrence King, and István Tóth János. 2002. The State, International Agencies, and Property Transformation in Postcommunist Hungary. *American Journal of Sociology* 108 (1): 129–67.

Hjartarson, Joshua. 2004. Foreign Banks, Domestic Networks and the Preservation of State Capacity in Internationalized Financial Sectors. Unpublished manuscript.

Hughes, James, Gwendolyn Sasse, and Clair Gordon. 2004. *Europeanization and Regionalization in the EU's Enlargement to Central and Eastern Europe: The Myth of Conditionality*. Basingstoke, UK: Palgrave Macmillan.

Hunter, Wendy, and David S. Brown. 2000. World Bank Directives, Domestic Interests, and the Politics of Human Capital Investment in Latin America. *Comparative Political Studies* 33 (1): 113–43.

Ikenberry, G. John. 1992. A World Economy Restored: Expert Consensus and the Anglo-American Postwar Settlement. *International Organization* 46 (1): 289–321.

Ikenberry, G. John, and Charles Kupchan. 1990. Socialization and Hegemonic Power. *International Organization* 44 (3): 283–315.

IMF. 2005a. *Staff Report of the 2005 Article IV Consultation: Supplementary Information*. Washington, DC: International Monetary Fund.

——. 2005b. *Ukraine: 2005 Article IV Consultation and Ex Post Assessment of Longer-Term Program Engagement, Number 05/415*. Washington, DC: International Monetary Fund.

——. Various years. *IMF Survey*. Washington, DC: International Monetary Fund.

——. Various years. Press Releases. Washington, DC: International Monetary Fund.

——. Various years. Public Information Notices. Washington, DC: International Monetary Fund.

International Institute for Strategic Studies. Various years. *The Military Balance*. London: International Institute for Strategic Studies.

Jacoby, Wade. 2000. *Imitation and Politics: Redesigning Modern Germany*. Ithaca, NY: Cornell University Press.

———. 2004. *The Enlargement of the EU and NATO: Ordering from the Menu in Central Europe.* Cambridge: Cambridge University Press.

———. 2005. Military Competence or Policy Loyalty: Central Europe and Transatlantic Relations. In *The Atlantic Alliance under Stress: US-European Relations after Iraq,* ed. David Andrews, 232–55. Cambridge: Cambridge University Press.

Johnson, Juliet. 2000. *A Fistful of Rubles: The Rise and Fall of the Russian Banking System.* Ithaca, NY: Cornell University Press.

———. 2002. Financial Globalization and National Sovereignty: Neoliberal Transformations in Post-Communist Central Banks. Unpublished manuscript.

———. 2003. Past Dependence or Path Contingency? Institutional Design in Postcommunist Financial Systems. In *Capitalism and Democracy in Central and Eastern Europe: Assessing the Legacy of Communist Rule,* ed. Grzegorz Ekiert and Stephen E. Hanson, 289–316. New York: Cambridge University Press.

———. 2006. Two-Track Diffusion and Central Bank Embeddedness: The Politics of Euro Adoption in Hungary and the Czech Republic. *Review of International Political Economy* 13 (3): 361–86.

———. 2008. The Remains of Conditionality: The Faltering Enlargement of the Euro Zone. *Journal of European Public Policy* 15 (6). In press.

Johnson, Ross A., Robert Dean, and Alexander Alexiev. 1980. *East European Military Establishments: The Warsaw Pact Northern Tier.* Santa Monica, CA: RAND Corporation.

Johnston, Alastair Iain. 2001. Treating International Institutions as Social Environments. *International Studies Quarterly* 45 (4): 487–515.

———. 2003. The Social Effects of International Institutions on Domestic (Foreign Policy) Actors. In *Locating the Proper Authorities: The Interaction of Domestic and International Institutions,* ed. Daniel W. Drezner, 145–96. Ann Arbor: Michigan University Press.

Jones, Christopher D. 1981. *Soviet Influence in Eastern Europe: Political Autonomy and the Warsaw Pact.* New York: Praeger.

Katzenstein, Peter J., ed. 1996. *The Culture of National Security: Norms and Identity in World Politics.* New York: Columbia University Press.

Katzenstein, Peter J., Robert O. Keohane, and Stephen D. Krasner. 1998. International Organization and the Study of World Politics. *International Organization* 52 (4): 645–85.

Kawalec, Stefan, Sławomir Sikora, and Piotr Rymaszewski. 1994. Polish Program of Bank Enterprise Restructuring: Design and Implementation, 1991–1994. Budapest. Unpublished manuscript.

Keck, Margaret E., and Kathryn Sikkink. 1998. *Activists beyond Borders: Advocacy Networks in International Politics.* Ithaca, NY: Cornell University Press.

Kelley, Judith G. 2004a. *Ethnic Politics in Europe: The Power of Norms and Incentives.* Princeton, NJ: Princeton University Press.

———. 2004b. International Actors on the Domestic Scene: Membership Conditionality and Socialization by International Institutions. *International Organization* 58 (3): 425–58.

——. 2008. Assessing the Complex Evolution of Norms: The Rise of International Election Monitoring. *International Organization* 62 (2): 221–255.

Keohane, Robert O. 1984. *After Hegemony*. Princeton, NJ: Princeton University Press.

Killick, Tony. 1996. Principals, Agents and the Limitations of BWI Conditionality. *The World Economy* 19 (2): 211–29.

Kindleberger, Charles. 1975. The Rise of Free Trade in Western Europe, 1820–1875. *Journal of Economic History* 35 (1): 20–55.

Kirshner, Jonathan D. 2001. The Political Economy of Low Inflation. *Journal of Economic Surveys* 15 (1): 41–70.

Kiss, Zoltan L. 2003. Changes in Hungarian Public Opinion on Security, Defence and the Military. In *The Public Image of Defence and the Military in Central and Eastern Europe*, ed. Marie Vlachova, 123–40. Geneva and Belgrade: Centre for the Democratic Control of Armed Forces.

Kitschelt, Herbert. 2003. Accounting for Postcommunist Regime Diversity: What Counts as a Good Cause? In *Capitalism and Democracy in Central and Eastern Europe: Assessing the Legacies of Communist Rule*, ed. Grzegorz Ekiert and Stephen E. Hanson, 49–86. New York: Cambridge University Press.

Kitschelt, Herbert, Zdenka Mansfeldova, Radosław Markowski, and Gábor Tóka. 1999. *Post-Communist Party Systems: Competition, Representation, and Inter-Party Cooperation*. New York: Cambridge University Press.

Klotz, Audie J. 1995. *Norms in International Relations: The Struggle against Apartheid*. Ithaca, NY: Cornell University Press.

Kołodko, Grzegorz W. 2000a. *From Shock to Therapy: The Political Economy of Postsocialist Transformation*. New York: Oxford University Press.

——. 2000b. *Post-Communist Transition: The Thorny Road*. Rochester, NY: University of Rochester Press.

Kopstein, Jeffrey S., and David A. Reilly. 2000. Geographic Diffusion and the Transformation of the Postcommunist World. *World Politics* 53 (1): 1–37.

Kornai, János. 1992. *The Socialist System: The Political Economy of Communism*. Princeton, NJ: Princeton University Press.

——. 1997. Adjustment without Recession: A Case Study of Hungarian Stabilization. In *Lessons from the Economic Transition: Central and Eastern Europe in the 1990s*, ed. Salvatore Zecchini, 123–51. Dordrecht, Netherlands: Kluwer.

Kramer, Mark. 1995. Cold War Crises: Poland, 1980–81: Soviet Policy during the Polish Crisis. *Cold War International History Project* 5:116–26.

——. 1998. The Restructuring of Civil-Military Relations in Poland since 1989. In *Civil-Military Relations: Building Democracy and Regional Security in Latin America, Southern Asia, and Central Europe*, ed. David Mares, 132–62. Boulder, CO: Westview Press.

——. 1999. Neorealism, Nuclear Proliferation, and East-Central European Strategies. In *Unipolar Politics: Realism and State Strategies after the Cold War*, ed. Ethan B. Kapstein and Michael Mastanduno, 385–463. New York: Columbia University Press.

Kratochwil, Friedrich. 1989. *Rules, Norms, and Decisions.* Cambridge: Cambridge University Press.

——. 2000a. Constructing a New Orthodoxy? Wendt's "Social Theory of International Politics" and the Constructivist Challenge. *Millennium* 29 (1): 73–101.

——. 2000b. How Do Norms Matter? In *The Role of Law in International Politics*, ed. Michael Byers, 35–68. New York: Oxford University Press.

Kratochwil, Friedrich, and John Gerard Ruggie. 1986. International Organization: A State of the Art or an Art of the State. *International Organization* 40 (4): 753–75.

Krebs, Ronald R. 1999. Perverse Institutionalism: NATO and the Greco-Turkish Conflict. *International Organization* 53 (2): 343–77.

Krok-Paszkowska, Anna Van Der Meer. 2000. *Shaping the Democratic Order: The Institutionalisation of Parliament in Poland.* Leiden, Netherlands: Garant Uitgevers N V.

Kuroń, Jacek. 1991. *Moja Zupa.* Warsaw: Polska Oficyna Wydawnicza BGW.

Kuzio, Taras. 2003. Ukraine's Relations with the West: Disinterest, Partnership, Disillusionment. *European Security* 12 (2): 21–44.

Landesmann, Michael A., and István Abel. 1995. The Transition in Eastern Europe: The Case for Industrial Policy. In *The Transformation of the Communist Economies: Against the Mainstream*, ed. Ha-Joon Chang and Peter Nolan, 136–61. New York: St. Martin's Press.

Legro, Jeffrey W. 1996. Culture and Preferences in the International Cooperation Two-Step. *American Political Science Review* 90 (1): 118–37.

Linden, Ronald H. 2000. Putting on Their Sunday Best: Romania, Hungary and the Puzzle of Peace. *International Studies Quarterly* 44 (1): 121–50.

Loungani, Prakash, and Nathan Sheets. 1997. Central Bank Independence, Inflation, and Growth in Transition Economies. *Journal of Money, Credit, and Banking* 29 (3): 381–99.

Maliszewski, Wojciech S. 2000. Central Bank Independence in Transition Economies. www.gdnet.org/pdf/818—Wojciech.pdf.

March, James G., and Johan P. Olson. 1989. *Rediscovering Institutions: The Organizational Basis of Politics.* New York: Free Press.

——. 1998. The Institutional Dynamics of International Political Orders. *International Organization* 52 (4): 943–69.

Martinusz, Zoltán. 2002. *Criteria of Success and Failure in Hungary's Democratisation Process—A Methodological Experiment for Comparable National Case Studies.* Geneva: Geneva Centre for the Democratic Control of Armed Forces.

Maxfield, Sylvia. 1997. *Gatekeepers of Growth: The International Political Economy of Central Banking in Developing Countries.* Princeton, NJ: Princeton University Press.

Michael Borish and Company, Inc., with Triumph Technologies, Inc. 1998. *An Assessment and Rating of the Polish Banking System.* Summer. Washington, DC: USAID.

Michta, Andrew A. 1990. *Red Eagle: The Army in Polish Politics, 1944–1988.* Stanford, CA: Hoover Institute Press.

———. 1997. *The Soldier-Citizen: The Politics of the Polish Army after Communism.* London: Macmillan Press.

———. 2002. NATO Standards and Military Reform in Poland: A Revolution from Without. In *Norms and Nannies: The Impact of International Organizations on the Central and East European States*, ed. Ronald H. Linden, 165–78. New York: Rowman and Littlefield.

Moravcsik, Andrew. 1999. Is Something Rotten in the State of Denmark? Constructivism and European Integration. *Journal of European Public Policy* 6 (4): 669–81.

Moravcsik, Andrew, and Milada Anna Vachudova. 2003. National Interests, State Power, and EU Enlargement. *East European Politics and Societies* 17 (1): 42–57.

Morgenthau, Hans J. 1960 [1948]. *Politics among Nations: The Struggle for Power and Peace.* Third Edition. New York: Alfred A. Knopf.

Myant, Martin R. 1993. *Transforming Socialist Economies: The Case of Poland and Czechoslovakia.* Brookfield, VT: Edward Elgar.

Mychajlyszyn, Natalie. 2002. Civil-Military Relations in Post-Soviet Ukraine: Implications for Domestic and Regional Stability. *Armed Forces and Society* 28 (3): 455–79.

Naaborg, Ilko, Bert Scholtens, Jakob de Haan, Hanneke Bol, and Ralph de Haas. 2003. *How Important Are Foreign Banks in the Financial Development of Eastern Transition Countries?* CESifo Working Paper No. 1100. Munich: Ifo Institute for Economic Research.

Nagy, Pongrác. 2003. *From Command to Market Economy in Hungary under the Guidance of the IMF.* Budapest: Académiai Kiadó.

National Bank of Poland. 2001. Summary Evaluation of the Financial Situation of Polish Banks. www.nbp.pl/en/publikacje/o—nadzorze—bankowym/synteza2001—en.pdf.

NATO. 1995a. *NATO Handbook.* Brussels: NATO Office of Information and Press.

———. 1995b. *Study on NATO Enlargement.* Brussels: NATO.

———. 1999. The Alliance's Strategic Concept. Press Release NAC-S(99)65. www.nato.int/docu/pr/1999/p99-065e.htm.

———. 2005. NATO and the Scourge of Terrorism. *NATO Topics.* www.nato.int/terrorism/five.htm.

NATO Parliamentary Assembly. 2002. *Report of the Sub-Committee on Future Security and Defence Capabilities: Military Preparations of NATO Candidate Countries.* Brussels: NATO.

Nelson, Daniel N., and Thomas S. Szayna. 1998. NATO's Metamorphosis and Its New Members. *Problems of Post-Communism* 45 (4): 32–43.

Notermans, Ton. 1999. Policy Continuity, Policy Change, and the Political Power of Economic Ideas. *Acta Politica* 34 (3): 22–48

Olson, Mancur. 1982. *The Rise and Decline of Nations: Economic Growth, Stagflation, and Social Rigidities.* New Haven, CT: Yale University Press.

Oltay, Edith. 1992. Minorities as Stumbling Block in Relations with Neighbors. *RFE/RL Research Report* (July): 31–32.

Onuf, Nicholas. 1989. *World of Our Making.* Columbia: University of South Carolina Press.

Orenstein, Mitchell A. 2001. *Out of the Red: Building Capitalism and Democracy in Postcommunist Europe*. Ann Arbor: University of Michigan Press.

Organisation for Economic Co-operation and Development. 2001. *Ukraine Investment Policy Review: The Legal and Institutional Regime for Investment: Assessment and Policy Recommendations*. Paris: OECD.

Ost, David. 2005. *The Defeat of Solidarity: Anger and Politics in Postcommunist Europe*. Ithaca, NY: Cornell University Press.

Paşcu, Ioan Mircea. 2000. *Immediate Defense Priorities*. December. Bucharest: Romanian Department of Defense.

Piroska, Dóra. 2005. Small Post-Socialist States and Global Finance: A Comparative Study of the Internationalization of State Roles in Banking in Hungary and Slovenia. Dissertation, Central European University, Budapest.

Polillo, Simon, and Mauro F. Guillén. 2005. Globalization Pressures and the State: The Worldwide Spread of Central Bank Independence. *American Journal of Sociology* 110 (6): 1764–802.

Posen, Adam. 1993. Why Central Bank Independence Does Not Cause Low Inflation: There Is No Institutional Fix for Politics. In *Finance and the International Economy*, ed. Richard O'Brian, 40–65. Oxford: Oxford University Press.

———. 1995a. *Central Bank Independence and Disinflationary Credibility: A Missing Link?* Federal Reserve Bank of New York Staff Reports No. 1. May. New York: Federal Reserve Bank of New York.

———. 1995b. Declarations Are Not Enough: Financial Sector Sources of Central Bank Independence. In *NBER Macroeconomic Annual 1995*, 253–74. Cambridge, MA: MIT Press.

Powers, Denise V., and James H. Cox. 1997. Echoes from the Past: The Relationship between Satisfaction with Economic Reforms and Voting Behavior in Poland. *American Political Science Review* 91 (3): 617–33.

Preoteasa, Isabela. 2002. Intellectuals and the Public Sphere in Post-Communist Romania: A Discourse Analytical Perspective. *Discourse and Society* 13 (2): 269–92.

Prizel, Ilya. 1998. *National Identity and Foreign Policy: Nationalism and Leadership in Poland, Russia and Ukraine*. Cambridge: Cambridge University Press.

Ralston, David B. 1990. *Importing the European Army: The Introduction of European Military Techniques and Institutions into the Extra-European World, 1600–1914*. Chicago: University of Chicago Press.

Razumkov Centre. 2004. *Ukraine-NATO: The Future Depends on the Past*. Kyiv: Razumkov Center.

Reiter, Dan. 2001. Why NATO Enlargement Does Not Spread Democracy. *International Security* 25 (4): 41–67.

Risse, Thomas. 2000. Let's Argue! Communicative Action in World Politics. *International Organization* 54 (2): 1–39.

Risse, Thomas, Stephen C. Ropp, and Kathryn Sikkink, eds. 1999. *The Power of Human Rights: International Norms and Domestic Change*. Cambridge: Cambridge University Press.

Ritson, Marjorie. 1989. Commentary. In *Banking in Comecon: Structures and Sources of Finance*, ed. Anne Hendrie, 98–102. London: Financial Times Business Information.

Roe, Alan, Katalin Forgacs, Andriy Olenchyk, Stephen Peachey, Angela Prigozhina, Yuri Vlasenko, and Ihor Zhyliaev. 2001. *Ukraine: The Financial Sector and the Economy*. Washington, DC: World Bank.

Rosenberg, Alexander. 1979. Can Economic Theory Explain Everything? *Philosophy of the Social Sciences* 9 (4): 509–29.

Rothschild, Joseph, and Nancy M. Wingfield. 2000. *Return to Diversity: A Political History of East Central Europe since World War II*. New York: Oxford University Press.

Ruggie, John Gerard. 1982. International Regimes, Transactions, and Change: Embedded Liberalism in the Postwar Economic Order. *International Organization* 36 (2): 379–415.

———. 1998. What Makes the World Hang Together? Neo-Utilitarianism and the Social Constructivist Challenge. *International Organization* 53 (4): 855–85.

Sanford, George. 1986. *Military Rule in Poland: The Rebuilding of Communist Power, 1981–1983*. New York: St. Martin's Press.

Sasse, Gwendolyn. 2005. *EU Conditionality and Minority Rights: Translating the Copenhagen Criterion into Policy*. EUI Working Paper, European University Institute, Robert Schuman Centre for Advanced Studies, European Forum Series. Florence: European University Institute.

Schimmelfennig, Frank. 2003. *The EU, NATO and the Integration of Europe*. Cambridge: Cambridge University Press.

———. 2005. Strategic Calculation and International Socialization: Membership Incentives, Party Constellation, and Sustained Compliance in Central and Eastern Europe. *International Organization* 59 (4): 827–60.

Schimmelfennig, Frank, and Ulrich Sedelmeier. 2005. *The Europeanization of Central and Eastern Europe*. Ithaca, NY: Cornell University Press.

Schoppa, Leonard. 1999. The Social Context in Coercive International Bargaining. *International Organization* 53 (2): 307–42.

Schweller, Randall L. 1998. *Deadly Imbalances: Tripolarity and Hitler's Strategy of World Conquest*. New York: Columbia University Press.

Schweller, Randall L., and William C. Wohlforth. 2000. Power Test: Evaluating Realism in Response to the End of the Cold War. *Security Studies* 9 (3): 60–107.

Sherr, James. 2005. Ukraine: Reform in the Context of Flawed Democracy and Geopolitical Anxiety. *European Security* 14 (1): 157–73.

Shields, Stuart. 2003. The "Charge of the Right Brigade": Transnational Social Forces and the Neoliberal Configuration of Poland's Transition. *New Political Economy* 8 (2): 225–44.

Simmons, Beth, Frank Dobbin, and Geoffrey Garrett. 2006. Introduction: The International Diffusion of Liberalism. *International Organization* 60 (4): 781–810.

Simon, Jeffrey. 1996. *NATO Enlargement and Central Europe: A Study in Civil-Military Relations*. Washington, DC: Washington National Defense University.

———. 2003. *Hungary and NATO: Problems in Civil-Military Relations*. Lanham, MD: Rowman and Littlefield.

———. 2004. *Poland and NATO: A Study in Civil-Military Relations.* Lanham, MD: Rowman and Littlefield.

Simonyi, András. 2001. Interview: András Simonyi: Hungarian Herald. *NATO Review* 49 (1): 22–23.

Sissenich, Beate. 2007. *Building States without Societies: European Union Enlargement and the Transfer of EU Social Policy to Poland and Hungary* Lanham, MD: Lexington Books.

Snyder, Timothy. 2003. *The Reconstruction of Nations.* New Haven, CT: Yale University Press.

Sochan, Peter. 1996. *The Banking System in Ukraine.* Warsaw: Center for Social and Economic Research.

Stark, David, and Laszlo Bruszt. 1998. *Postsocialist Pathways: Transforming Politics and Property in East Central Europe.* New York: Cambridge University Press.

Stirewalt, Bryan D., and James E. Horner. 2000. *Poland–National Bank of Poland: Final Report.* 1 March. Washington, DC: USAID.

Stockholm International Peace Research Institute. Various years. *SIPRI Yearbook of World Armaments and Disarmament.* Stockholm: Alqvist and Wiksell.

Stone, Randall W. 2002. *Lending Credibility: The International Monetary Fund and the Post-Communist Transition.* Princeton, NJ: Princeton University Press.

Strekal, Oleg. 1994. The Ukrainian Military and Civil-Military Relations in the Post-Cold War Era. In *INSS Occasional Paper*, No. 2. Air Force Academy, CO: US Air Force Institute for National Security Studies.

Szacki, Jerzy. 1995. *Liberalism after Communism.* Budapest: Central European University Press.

Szayna, Thomas S. 2001. *NATO Enlargement, 2000–2015: Determinants and Implications for Defense Planning and Shaping.* Santa Monica, CA: RAND Corporation.

Szenes, Zoltán. 2001. The Implications of NATO Expansion for Civil-Military Relations in Hungary. In *Army and State in Postcommunist Europe*, ed. David Betz and John Löwenhardt, 78–95. Portland, OR: Frank Cass.

Thomas, Daniel. 2001. *The Helsinki Effect: International Norms, Human Rights, and the Demise of Communism.* Princeton, NJ: Princeton University Press.

Tsantis, Andreas. 1997. *Developments in the Romanian Banking Sector*, 167–216. Paris: OECD.

Ugolini, Piero. 1996. *National Bank of Poland: The Road to Indirect Instruments.* Occasional Paper No. 144. Washington, DC: International Monetary Fund.

Ulrich, Marybeth Peterson. 1995. When East Meets West. *Airpower Journal* VIV (SE): 4–16.

———. 1999. *Democratizing Communist Militaries: The Cases of the Czech and Russian Armed Forces.* Ann Arbor: University of Michigan Press.

Vachudova, Milada Anna. 1997. The Systemic and Domestic Determinants of the Foreign Policies of East Central European States. Dissertation, St Antony's College, Oxford University, Oxford.

———. 2005. *Europe Undivided: Democracy, Leverage, and Integration after Communism.* New York: Oxford University Press.

Vachudova, Milada Anna, and Timothy Snyder. 1997. Are Transitions Transitory? Two Types of Political Change in Eastern Europe since 1989. *East European Politics and Societies* 11 (1): 1–35.

van Elkin, Rachel. 1998. Privatization. In *International Monetary Fund Occasional Paper*, No. 159, ed. Carlo Cottarelli, 63–67. Washington, DC: IMF.

Vasquez, John A. 1997. The Realist Paradigm and Degenerative versus Progressive Research Programs: An Appraisal of Neo-traditional Research on Waltz's Balancing Proposition. *American Political Science Review* 91 (4): 899–912.

Verdier, Daniel. 2000. The Rise and Fall of State Banking in OECD Countries. *Comparative Political Studies* 33 (3): 283–318.

Wallace, Helen, and A. Mayhew. 2001. *Poland: A Partnership Profile*. OEOS Policy Paper. Brighton: University of Sussex, Sussex European Institute.

Wallander, Celeste A. 1999. *Mortal Friends, Best Enemies: German-Russian Cooperation after the Cold War*. Ithaca, NY: Cornell University Press.

——. 2000. Institutional Assets and Adaptability: NATO after the Cold War. *International Organization* 54 (4): 705–35.

——. 2002. NATO's Price: Shape up or Ship Out. *Foreign Affairs* 81 (6): 2–8.

Walt, Stephen M. 1987. *The Origin of Alliances*. Ithaca, NY: Cornell University Press.

——. 1996. *Revolution and War*. Ithaca, NY: Cornell University Press.

Waltz, Kenneth N. 1979. *Theory of International Politics*. Reading, UK: Addison-Wesley.

Watts, Larry L. 2001a. The Crisis in Romanian Civil-Military Relations. *Problems of Post-Communism* 48 (4): 14–26.

——. 2001b. Democratic Civil Control of the Military in Romania: An Assessment as of October 2001. In *Civil-Military Relations in Post Cold War Europe*, ed. Graeme P. Herd. Sandhurst, UK: Conflict Studies Research Centre.

——, ed. 2002. *Romanian Military Reform and NATO Integration*. Iaşi, Oxford, and Portland, OR: Centre for Romanian Studies.

——. 2003. Ahead of the Curve: The Military-Society Relationship in Romania. In *Soldiers and Societies in Postcommunist Europe: Legitimacy and Change*, ed. Andrew Cottey, Timothy Edmunds, and Anthony Forster, 131–52. New York: Palgrave.

——. 2005. The Transformation of Romanian Civil-Military Relations: Enabling Force Projection. *European Security* 14 (1): 95–114.

Wendt, Alexander. 1999. *Social Theory of International Politics*. Cambridge: Cambridge University Press.

Weyland, Kurt. 2005. Theories of Policy Diffusion: Lessons from Latin American Pension Reform. *World Politics* 57 (2): 262–85.

Williams, Margit Bessenyey. 2002. European Integration and Minority Rights: The Case of Hungary and Its Neighbors. In *Norms and Nannies: The Impact of International Organizations on the Central and East European States*, ed. Ronald H. Linden, 227–58. Lanham, MD: Rowman and Littlefield.

Woehrel, Steven, Julie Kim, and Carl Erik. 2003. *NATO Applicant States: A Status Report*. CRS Report for Congress. Washington, DC: Congressional Research Service.

World Bank. 1993. *The East Asian Miracle*. New York: Oxford University Press.

——. 1997a. *Implementation Completion Report, Poland: Enterprise and Financial Sector Adjustment Loan*. Report No. 16743. Washington, DC: World Bank.

——. 1997b. *Poland Country Assistance Review*, Vol. I. Report No. 16495. Washington, DC: World Bank.

——. 1999. *Ukraine Country Assistance Strategy: Progress Report*. Report No. 19225. Washington, DC: World Bank.

——. 2000. *Ukraine Country Assistance Evaluation*. Report No. 21358. Washington, DC: World Bank.

World Values Survey. Various years. Public Confidence in the Armed Forces. www.worldvaluessurvey.org.

Yost, David S. 2000. The NATO Capabilities Gap and the European Union. *Survival* 42 (4): 97–128.

Young, David G. 1989. Commentary. In *Banking in Comecon: Structures and Sources of Finance*, ed. Anne Hendrie, 71–73. London: Financial Times Business Information.

Zulean, Marian. 2002. Professionalisation of the Romanian Armed Forces. In *The Challenge of Military Reform in Postcommunist Europe: Building Professional Armed Forces*, ed. Anthony Forster, Timothy Edmunds, and Andrew Cottey, 115–32. New York: Palgrave Macmillan.

Zysman, John. 1983. *Governments, Markets, and Growth: Financial Systems and the Politics of Industrial Change*. Ithaca, NY: Cornell University Press.

# Index

A page number followed by the letter *t* indicates a table.

parliament of, 143–144; price liberalization in, 46; public confidence in military, 120*t*; public opinion on NATO,
127*t*; Russia and, 176; Soviet Union and,
170; status in, 52–53, 126–127; troop
deployments by, 182*t*; troop levels, 185*t*;
uncertainty in, 45–48, 116–117; World
Bank and, 46–47
Ukrainian Popular Rukh, 46, 52
UkrEximBank, 84, 103
UkrSibBank, 103
UkrSotsBank, 84, 103
uncertainty hypothesis: central bank independence and, 33–34, 38–48; civil-
military relations and, 109–111, 111–117;
defense planning and, 155–164; definition of, 14; among domestic actors, 9; in
finance, 14; Hungarian bank privatization and, 80–81; Hungarian central
bank independence and, 42–43; Hungarian civil-military relations and, 115–
116; Hungarian defense planning and,
157–160; hypothesis of institutional
influence, 14–15; NATO and, 152–153;
overview of, 195–196; Polish bank privatization and, 78–80; Polish central
bank independence and, 38–42; Polish
civil-military relations and, 111–114;
Polish defense planning and, 155–157;
Romanian bank privatization and, 81–
83; Romanian central bank independence and, 43–45; Romanian defense
planning and, 160–161; sectors and, 18;
Ukrainian bank privatization and, 83–
84; Ukrainian central bank independence and, 45–48; Ukrainian civil-
military relations and, 116–117; Ukrainian defense planning and, 161–164
United Kingdom, 53; central bank independence in, 36*t*; defense spending in,

165*t*; foreign investment in, 72*t*; Iraq
War deployments, 152*t*
United Nations (UN), troop deployments,
182*t*
United States: central bank independence
in, 36*t*; deployments in Iraq, 152*t*; for-
eign investment in, 72*t*
United States Agency for International
Development (USAID): central bank
independence and, 31, 39; Poland and,
39, 57
USD. *See* Social Democratic Union
(USD)
UW. *See* Freedom Union (UW)

variation, in institutional influence, 14–17
Venezuela, foreign investment in, 100*t*
Verkhovna Rada, 144–145
Vnesheconombank, 84

Wałêsa, Lech, 113–114, 121
Waniek, Danuta, 135
"War of the Entire People" doctrine, 160–
161
Warsaw Pact, 112, 159–160, 173
Wielkopolski Bank Kredytowy, 78
Wilecki, Tadeusz, 113, 136
World Bank: central bank independence
and, 31; Hungary and, 42–43, 98;
Poland and, 39, 40; Romania and, 82;
Ukraine and, 46–47
Wörner, Manfred, 128

Yanukovich, Viktor, 170
Yugoslavia, 116, 181
Yushchenko, Viktor, 64, 188

Żabiński reforms, 121
Zhirinovsky, Vladimir, 155
Zulean, Marian, 184–185